# THE JUSTICE COOPERATIVE

# The Justice Cooperative

JOSEPH P. MARTINO

ELDERBERRY PRESS, LLC
OAKLAND

# ELDERBERRY PRESS, LLC

All Elderberry Press books are available from your favorite bookstore,
amazon.com, or from our 24 hour order line: 1.800.431.1579

Library of Congress Control Number:   2004101719
Publisher's Catalog-in-Publication Data
The Justice Cooperative/Joseph P. Martino
ISBN 1-932762-00-0
1.  Murder——Fiction.
2.  Self-defence——Fiction.
3.  CCP——Fiction.
4.  Civil Rights——Fiction.
5.  Concealed Carry Permit——Fiction.
6.  Justice——Fiction.
I.  Title

This book was written, printed, and bound in the United States of America.

To Nan, who encouraged me to see it through

# ONE

"Oh, my God! No!"

Tom Borden grabbed the remote and thumbed the OFF button. The news anchor's face shrunk to a point and disappeared.

"What's wrong, honey?"

Judith Borden stood up and strode to his chair. Wordlessly, she thrust the newspaper at him. The headline seemed to leap off the page.

JUDGE ORDERS PRISONERS RELEASED

Capitol City, June 2. Federal District Court Judge Oliver Woods today ruled that the state's prisons were overcrowded. "This overcrowding is a violation of the Constitutional protection against cruel and unusual punishment," the judge stated. Under Judge Woods's order, all prisoners who have served more than half their sentences, except those who have records of violence within the prison, are to be released immediately to eliminate overcrowding.

A spokesman for the governor's office later met with reporters. "We disagree with the ruling, but there is no point in appealing", he said. "The State Attorney General has pointed out that all the legal precedents support the judge's ruling. Moreover, it would be nearly impossible to get a stay of the ruling while we appealed. Accordingly, we will begin to release the prisoners tomorrow. It is unfortunate that during the last session the legislature refused to appropriate the additional funds for prison construction that the governor had requested. The governor sees no point in calling the legislature back into emergency session to reconsider the matter, since new prisons could not be constructed in time to satisfy the judge's order. The governor plans to renew his request for additional prison construction early in the next session."

The Majority Leader of the House denied that the problem lay with the legislature. "We tried to accommodate the governor, but he wouldn't budge on an increase in the sales tax to pay for prison construction. He insisted the money come from cuts somewhere else in the budget. We tried to compromise by taking it out of funds for highway construction, but he refused. Maybe next year he'll be more reasonable."

There was more, but Tom paid it no attention. He lowered the paper as his wife began to speak. Her voice was icy and flat, as though she didn't dare trust it to carry any emotion.

"You know what this means, don't you? Harry Grubbs will be turned loose. He's ten days past the midpoint of his sentence."

Both he and Judith had been dreading Grubbs's eventual release. He knew her emotional scars went deep. He should have known that she'd been counting down the days.

The images of that night came flooding back to him, tumbling over one another.

The thunderous pounding at the door.

The door bursting open as he approached it.

The burly man charging at him like a quarterback.

The half-seen blow to his head.

Judith's screams that dragged him back to consciousness.

The pain in his wrists as he strained at the telephone cord that bound his arms tightly behind his back.

The horror he felt as the intruder pinned Judith to the floor, his body rising and falling.

Judith's sobs as the intruder left.

Then the aftermath.

The cold, unfeeling police officers as they asked their probing questions.

Judith's pain as the police doctor scraped samples from her for evidence.

The hatred on Grubbs's face as they identified him in the police lineup.

Then the question of AIDS. Tom had asked that Grubbs be tested. The prosecutor told Tom that under state law it was illegal to provide information about an AIDS test to anyone but the person tested. Telling others was a violation of the individual's privacy. Tom had demanded, hadn't Grubbs violated Judith's privacy? His protests did no good. The law allowed for no exceptions.

Then the trial. Tom cringed once more at the memories.

Judith on the witness stand, being forced to answer the most intimate questions.

Grubbs's sleazy lawyer, who tried to blacken Judith's character and discredit her virtue.

The assistant prosecutor, whose blunder nearly lost the case despite the DNA evidence.

The numbness he felt even when the jury returned a guilty verdict. Somehow it wasn't enough.

His utter incomprehension when the judge decided to impose only the minimum possible sentence.

The discovery that at the time of the attack, Grubbs had been out on parole from another rape conviction.

Grubbs's shouted threat, accompanied by a shaken fist, as he was led out to begin his sentence: "When I get out, I'll get you!"

And ever since then, Tom's humiliation, his deep burning shame that he'd been unable to protect Judith.

Their low-rent apartment suddenly had too many ugly memories in it. They couldn't stay there. They'd bought a house in a more expensive part of town. The mortgage payment was too much for his paycheck; Judith had to take a job as well. That meant postponing a family. Not that it made much difference. The memory of that night haunted their infrequent attempts at lovemaking.

Tom stood up and hugged Judith. The muscles in her back were like taut cords. Her arms were like steel pipes. He touched his cheek to hers, then brushed his lips across her neck. She gave no response.

Defeated, he finally stepped back, holding only her arms in his hands. He looked her over. Externally, she appeared the same as she had on their wedding day. Shoulder-length brown hair. Heart-shaped face. Brown eyes. Upturned nose. A light dusting of freckles across her face. Forehead that came just to his eye level.

But the smile he'd loved was gone. Outside she was the same. Inside she was in deep freeze.

He shook his head and released her. One more time he'd failed to break through what he'd come to think of as the shell she'd crawled into.

"Judy, honey, listen to me", he said. "It won't happen again. I swear it. This time I'll protect you."

But even as he spoke them, the words sounded hollow. What could he do that he hadn't already done? And why should he think he could do any better the next time?

As he lay in bed that night, unable to sleep, he played back the scene yet one more time in his mind. It had all happened so quickly. There had been no time to react. Before he was fully aware he was being attacked, he'd been knocked out of the fight.

Unable to think of anything he could have done differently, he raged at the judge who would grant early release to a wolf in human form, who'd already struck at least twice, and who was clearly a menace to the community. But then, he realized, this really hadn't changed things much. Grubbs's sentence would have been up in little more than a year anyway. He and Judith would have faced this problem sooner or later. The day of reckoning had simply come earlier than they had expected.

# TWO

Guns. Handguns. Shotguns. Long guns. Guns in glass display cases. Guns in wooden wall racks. More guns than Tom had ever seen in his whole life.

He had clocked out at the end of the regular workday, passing up a usually-welcome chance to earn some overtime. He stood just inside the door of the gun shop, uncertain about what to do next. So far as he knew, his father had never owned a gun; had never even touched one since he came back from Korea. His mother had forbidden him and his brothers to play with toy guns. But last night, he'd reluctantly come to the conclusion he needed a gun.

He looked around the shop. In the back wall, behind the display cases, a doorway led into what looked like some kind of workshop. On the display case on the side farthest from the door stood a cash register. In the middle of the floor, between the display cases, stood display racks of things that were totally unfamiliar to him. In the air there was a pungent scent, like some kind of solvent. It reminded him of the smell of the cutting oil his machines used at the plant.

Tom approached the man standing behind the cash register.

Tom thought, *He looks too old to be just a clerk. White hair. Bald spot. Bifocals. He must be the owner.*

"Can I help you?" the proprietor asked.

"Uh, yes. I need a gun. Right away."

The proprietor studied Tom for a moment. "I can sell you a gun. But not right away. There's a seven-day waiting period."

"I guess I remember reading about a waiting period when they were debating it down in Capitol City, but I forgot about it. Besides, I thought it was five days."

"That's five business days. Add in the weekend and it comes to seven days."

"But I need a gun right now. A man who threatened my life got out of jail today."

"Look," the proprietor said. "I don't know you. For all I know, you're one of those BAT-men who's always trying to trap me into an illegal sale, so they can take away my firearms dealer's license or even jail me. If your story is true, you have my sympathy, but I'm not going to break the law for you."

"Batmen?" Tom said, a puzzled look on his face.

"The Bureau of Alcohol, Tobacco, Firearms and Explosives. They have a 'revenooer' mentality. They treat every gun shop like it was a moonshiner's still-house. They're always around here snooping through my paperwork, looking for some kind of violation. If a customer so much as puts his name in the wrong block on the form, and I don't catch it, I can be fined or even lose my dealers' license.

"Now, it sounds to me like you need help, even if you'll have to wait. What kind of a gun do you want?"

Tom gave a sigh of frustration, then held his hands about a foot apart. "I want the biggest, most powerful gun you can sell me. Something like 'Dirty Harry' used in the movies."

The proprietor leaned on the counter, eyed Tom for a moment, then asked in a quiet voice, "Ever fired a gun before?"

"No," came the hesitant admission.

"I don't recommend a .44 Magnum for first-time gun buyers. It kicks like a mule. It'll take you a couple of seconds to get your sights back onto your target after your first shot. If you don't stop your attacker with that first shot, you may not live long enough to aim a second shot. Even if you hit the guy with your first shot, the bullet is likely to go right through him, and hit whoever's on the other side. If you're unfamiliar with guns, a .44 Magnum is likely to scare you even more than it scares the guy you're defending yourself against."

"Okay, what do you recommend?" Tom asked.

The proprietor straightened up. "The usual rule is, the biggest gun you feel comfortable shooting. You ought to test fire several guns to see what suits you. But you've let yourself run out of time for that. Even if you place an order now, it'll take seven days before I can let you walk out of here with it."

"But I never needed a gun before."

The proprietor gave a negative shake of his head. "No, you did need a gun. You just didn't realize it. The time to buy a gun is before the bad guy comes bustin' through your door. Since they passed that waiting period law, that means at least seven days before."

"Well, if you recommend against a 'Dirty Harry' gun, what should I get?"

"Your basic choice is between a revolver and a semi-automatic pistol." The proprietor pointed to some of the guns in a display case. "The revolver has the advantage that it'll put up with a lot of neglect and still work when you need it. The disadvantage is that the trigger pull on a revolver is pretty stiff, which means it's harder to shoot accurately, and it holds only six shots. With an automatic, there's more mechanical stuff to go wrong, which means you can't just let the thing sit around for years. You have to keep it cleaned and oiled. But it holds more cartridges than a revolver, and the trigger is usually easier to pull."

"I'm a machinist. I'm willing to do what has to be done to keep the gun in good shape. I think I'll go for the automatic."

"Okay, then you have to decide what caliber you want. For someone just starting out, I usually recommend a 9-millimeter. A 9-millimeter gun holds more cartridges than one for the .40 or the .45. Even though they've got this ten-round limit on magazines, the most popular .45's hold only seven rounds. Besides, with a 9-millimeter the kick is less. You'll find it easier to learn to shoot.

"Once you get used to shooting, you may want to move up to a bigger caliber. Guns hold their value pretty well, if you take care of them, so you won't lose much money if you decide to trade up later."

The proprietor stopped for breath, then eyed Tom. "Now, are you married?"

"Yes. It's my wife that I'm worried about. I need to protect her."

"You can't be around her all the time. She has to be able to protect herself. If you need a gun, she needs a gun too."

"I'm not sure she'll want a gun."

"If there's really some guy after you, she doesn't have much choice. And the longer she puts off ordering one, the longer it'll be before she has one."

"I guess you're right. What do you recommend?"

"Some dealers will try to sell a woman something small. Something 'ladylike.'" The derision in his voice was palpable. "I don't. She needs something with stopping power. I'd recommend she get a 9-millimeter just like I'd recommend for you. Any woman can learn to shoot a 9-millimeter pistol.

"Something else I'd recommend. If you're at work during the day, it's most likely that the time you'll need to defend yourself inside your house'll be after dark. A gun won't do you any good if you can't see the sights. I recommend you get tritium sights put on your guns. They glow in the dark. I can order them at the same time you order your guns, and they'll already be installed when your waiting period is up.

"I'm open 'til nine tonight." He pointed at the clock above the cash register. "What I recommend is that you get your wife down here so she can try holding several models and see which fits her hand best. Then place your orders. So long as you order before I close tonight, the waiting period is up when I open for business in seven days.

"And another thing," he went on. "Simply buying a gun isn't enough. You have to be able to use it. You need some training." He reached under the counter and came up with a business card. "This is a place I recommend — the Self Defense Academy. They're thorough, and their focus is on self-defense, not on target shooting. After a day there, you'll be able to shoot straighter than most crooks. And more important, you'll be confident you can hit what you're shooting at."

"Okay, I'll get my wife. One other thing. Do I need a permit for the gun?"

"Not to keep it in your house. And in this state you don't need a permit to carry an unloaded gun in the trunk of your car. But if you want to carry a loaded gun around with you, the law says you need a permit."

"How do I get one?"

"In this city, forget it. The law says you can put in an application to the police. If you meet one of the conditions in the law, like you regularly carry money to a bank, or you believe your life is threatened, they're supposed to issue you a permit. However, our chief of police has decided that no citizen is ever justified in carrying a gun. So the cops don't even keep any application blanks down at the station house. You can defend yourself inside your house, but that's about it."

"I guess that's better than nothing." Tom sighed. "Okay, we'll be back soon."

# THREE

Judith's mother thrust a plate at Tom. "Here, have some more cornbread. My land, Tom, you've been eating like a canary."

"Thanks, Mom, but I've had all I want." Despite the mouth-watering aroma of the stack of yellow squares of cornbread, he gently pushed away the plate that she had placed in front of him.

She turned to Judith. "Judy, you're not feeding Tom right. He looks thin as a rail. I taught you to cook better than that."

*That's right*, Judith thought. *You taught me to cook the way you feed dad. You can joke about his "love handles," but when he dies of a heart attack, we'll all be crying. I'm not going to do that to Tom.*

"Please, Mom," Tom spoke. "Judy feeds me fine. I work it off at the plant. And right now I'm saving some room for that cherry pie I saw in the kitchen."

"Well, if everyone's ready for pie, I'll go bring it in." She got up and headed for the kitchen.

Judith's father turned to Tom.

"How long're you kids staying with us? Can you stay over 'til Sunday? We're having the Legion picnic on Sunday. Judy always liked that."

"No, Dad, we have to be back Friday night," Tom explained. "We've got something lined up for Saturday, and we'll have to get up early for that. I figure we'll have to leave here right after lunch on Friday."

"I'm on the committee for the Legion picnic this year. I been watchin' the weather forecast. We're supposed to have good weather this weekend."

"That's good. We'll need it ourselves."

"You goin' to be outside?"

"Yes. Kind of a one-day camping trip. Hiking in the woods."

"Judy used to hike around in the wood-lot at the back end of the farm. I guess you don't do much of that in the big city."

"No, we don't have much chance for hiking. We don't even go to the city parks. It's too late when we get home from work."

Judith's mother returned with a pie and a half-gallon of vanilla ice cream. "Here you are, everyone. Fresh cherries, picked from our own tree." She cut the pie in quarters, then put a huge scoop of ice cream on each piece.

"Please, Mother, cut mine in half," Judith said. "I don't want to get sick."

"Why, child, are you expecting? You didn't say anything about it."

"No, Mother, not yet. It's just that I really can't eat all that much."

"Well, that's a shame. Your sister-in-law Sally's expecting her second. They just told us last week. It'll be due about next March. She and Jim are just tickled pink. And so are we. That'll be our second grand-child."

"That's great news, Mother," Judith replied. "I'm happy for them. And for you."

"Well, don't you tell 'em I told you. They asked me to keep it quiet. They wanted to tell you themselves."

"I won't mention it."

"We'll act surprised when we hear it," Tom added.

With that they dug into the pie. Tom thought, *This is even better than mother used to make.* But he decided that was a compliment he'd better not pay his mother-in-law. No point in seeming disloyal to his own mother. They might start wondering what other disloyalty he was capable of.

When dinner was finished, Judith and her mother gathered the dishes and carried them to the kitchen. Judith's father hitched his chair around to face Tom and spoke.

"Listen, Tom, I can read the papers. Did that guy who hurt my daughter get out of jail?"

"Yes, Dad. He was one of those who got an early release. He got out yesterday."

"What're you doin' to protect her?"

"Please, Dad. You know what we've done. We've moved to a better house, even though it costs a lot more money. It's in a good neighborhood, and there's very little crime. She's as safe as we can manage."

"I know, Tom, but you promised to take care of her, and I want to see that you do it."

*You don't want it any more than I do,* Tom thought to himself, but refrained from saying it. "I think we're safe now. At least as safe as anyone can be, with so many crooks running around. What's it like here? Are you and Mom safe?"

"There's more crime around here in town now than there was when we moved in off the farm. Used to be hardly anybody here in town ever locked their doors. Now everybody does. The city council leaned on old Chief O'Leary and got him to retire. Figured he wasn't up to handling the crime any more."

"They got a younger guy as Chief of Police?"

"Yeah. He's even younger than some of the cops on the force."

"Somebody from around here?"

"Nah!" Came the reply, accompanied by a look of disgust. "They brought in some hotshot from downstate and made him Chief. A college guy with a degree in criminology. The older cops don't like him. Say he ain't got any street experience. His college professors stuffed his head full of nonsense about why folks steal and kill, and how we got to be nice to 'em 'cause it's really our fault."

"Sounds like things're getting worse here," Tom said, a worried frown on his face. "Are you sure you and Mom'll be okay?"

"Yeah. We ain't got that much to steal. Besides, I got out that pistol I brought back from 'Nam. Oiled it up, took it out to the farm, and shot it a few times. I'll use it on anyone who comes in here. How 'bout you? You got a gun?"

"We have some on order. They'll come in next week."

"Can you take a gun to work with you?"

"I can't get a license. Police in the big city don't want people to have guns."

"Yeah. That new Chief has been tryin' to get the city council to pass gun registration. Says it'll cut crime. Baloney! They'll do that over my dead body. The only reason cops ever want to register honest folks' guns is so they can confiscate 'em later. Crooks sure ain't going to register their guns."

Judith's mother returned from the kitchen and said "The dishwasher's running. Now let's watch the videotape of Jim and Sally's little boy."

• • •

Tom pulled his pajama bottoms on, then stopped to look at himself in the mirror over the dresser. Was Judith's mother right? Was he too thin? In high school, he'd been too short for basketball and too scrawny for football. But he'd filled out during his apprenticeship at the mill, when the older heads had assigned him to do a lot of the heavy-lifting work. His stomach was still flat, and his face was still long and thin. At his high school class's ten-year reunion last year, he'd seen that some of his classmates who had been athletes were already getting spare tires and jowly faces. So far he'd avoided that. He brushed his hair back from his face. Still black, like his eyes. No sign of it getting either thin or gray. Time for a haircut, he thought. *I better get one after work next week.* Satisfied that he wasn't as undernourished as his mother-in-law implied, he finished dressing for bed.

Judith climbed into bed and lay on her back, arms under her head, elbows spread out. She stared at the ceiling.

Tom reached for the light, then stopped. "Something wrong, honey?"

"Not really, I guess. Mother's anxious for another grandchild. I can't blame her. I want children too. But I wish she'd let up on me. It doesn't make things any easier, with her always after me about it."

"Is that what she was talking about while you two were in the kitchen?"

"She was hinting at it pretty strongly. What were you and Dad talking about while we were in the kitchen?"

Tom hesitated, then spoke. "He's worried about your safety, now that Grubbs is out of jail. Said he wants to be sure I take care of his daughter."

She turned to look at him. "As if you weren't worried, too. That isn't fair of him."

He decided not to mention how inadequate his father-in-law's words had made him feel. "I don't think he meant anything by it." *He didn't have to mean anything. The words still cut like a knife.* But he didn't say that, either. He reached again for the light and turned it out.

# FOUR

"What a beautiful place." Judith gestured at the scene outside the windshield.

"Yeah, it sure is."

They drove up a long winding lane. The trees were thick on either side, and their branches met overhead. At the end of the lane, they found themselves on a hilltop with the land falling away on three sides. Across the valleys the hills were covered with trees, all lush green.

In front of them stood a cabin built of squared-off logs, with a metal door and barred windows. Tom pulled alongside one of the cars already parked in a graveled area next to the cabin. He got out of the car, walked around, and opened the door for Judith.

Judith stretched her arms over her head, and twisted from side to side. "Ouch! I'm stiff after that long ride."

"Yeah. Me too. My bottom was beginning to feel like part of the upholstery."

A tall, huskily-built man gripping a clipboard in his hand and a cigar in his teeth, and wearing a safety-orange vest, stepped out of the cabin.

"Hello, folks. What're your names?"

"Tom and Judith Borden."

He made a couple of checkmarks on the clipboard. "May I see your drivers licenses?"

He scanned each license, checked the pictures against their faces, and handed the licenses back.

"I'm Pete Baron, head instructor here at the Self Defense Academy." He gestured toward the cabin. "Get your name tags off the table inside the door. There's coffee and some donuts while you're waiting."

"I hope this works," Judith said in a low voice as they entered.

"Yeah. We can't hide out upstate at your folks' place any longer. We've both used up all our vacation time, and have to get back to our jobs."

Inside the cabin, Tom looked around. There were several long, narrow tables set up, school-room style, with folding chairs behind them. At the front of the cabin there was a blackboard and a projection screen.

At the back of the cabin Tom noted two doors, one labeled STORAGE and one labeled RESTROOM. There was a line at the restroom. As one person stepped out, another stepped in and bolted the door with an audible *click*.

Just inside the cabin door, there was a table with a pot of coffee and a box of donuts. The smell of fresh coffee reminded Tom how long it had been since he'd eaten breakfast. However, he felt a more urgent need.

While he waited in line at the restroom, Tom looked around at the other people in the cabin. Not quite two dozen. About two-thirds men, mostly young. Most of the women seemed to be with a man, apparently wives or girlfriends. Everyone was wearing the boots and outdoor clothing the acceptance letter from the Academy had recommended.

As he came out of the restroom, Tom poured himself a cup of coffee, grabbed some cream and sugar, then looked around for Judith. He saw that she had taken a seat at a table halfway back, and had placed her purse on an empty chair next to her. On the other side of her sat a young black man. Next to him sat one of the couples, both appearing middle-aged. As he took the seat next to Judith, he noticed the black man's nametag identified him as "George."

Baron stepped to the front of the room. "Okay, folks, we're ready to start. Here's the program for the day. We'll start with a presentation on the justified use of lethal force. Then we'll talk about defensive tactics inside the home. After that, those of you who have your own guns will bring them in from your cars. Those who asked to use Academy guns will get them at that time. We'll talk a bit about holding your guns and using the sights. By then it'll be time for lunch. After lunch we'll go down to the range, where you'll practice firing for the rest of the day. At the end of the day we'll come back here to the cabin where we'll show you how to clean your guns.

"And now, to talk about justified use of lethal force, here is retired judge Bill Leahy."

A tall, white-haired man strode briskly to the front of the room, placed some papers on a podium, and turned to face the group.

"Good morning, everyone. I'm going to give you a quick summary of gun law, and the justified use of lethal force. I can't turn you into experts, but I'll try to tell you what you need to think about before you pull the trigger.

"To begin with, your right to own a gun is protected by the Second Amendment to the U.S. Constitution, as well as by our own state constitution. Note that word 'protected.' The Constitution doesn't grant us any rights at all. Instead, it forbids the government to interfere with our rights. The so-called Bill of Rights should really be called the Bill of Limitations. That is, limitations on government powers. Every article in it really prohibits the government from doing something."

"You may hear people say the Second Amendment is meant only to allow the National Guard to have guns. That's wrong. The word 'people' in the Second Amendment means the same as it does in the First, Fourth, Fifth, Ninth and Tenth Amendments.

It means everyone."

The judge picked up a paper and read from it.

"That right to own guns goes all the way back to England. Blackstone, in his *Commentaries*, stated that the right to keep and bear arms was one of the 'absolute rights' of an Englishman.

"Incidentally, that's a right that Englishmen have allowed themselves to lose today. They've allowed their government to disarm them. As anyone with any sense would expect, the violent crime rate has gone way up because the average Englishman can no longer defend himself against an armed crook. The same thing happened in Australia. The government confiscated all the honest people's guns. The crooks kept the tools of their trade. Murder, robbery and assault rates shot way up.

"Well, enough of the problems of Englishmen. Back to our own history. George Mason, a delegate to the Constitutional Convention, said that the most effective way to enslave a people was to disarm them. Alexander Hamilton wrote in the *Federalist Papers* that Americans didn't need to worry about the federal government becoming tyrannical because of what he called 'the advantage of being armed which the Americans possess over the people of almost every other nation.' So you see, your right to own a gun is definitive. The people who wrote the Constitution meant it to be an individual right."

"Excuse me, Judge," said a man in the back of the room. "All those quotes you gave are a couple of centuries old. Do they still apply today?"

A smile crossed Leahy's face. "To save time, I was going to leave out some more modern quotes. But since you've asked, I'll give some."

He picked up a paper from the podium. "In 1989, then-senator Hubert H. Humphrey said, 'The right of citizens to bear arms is just one more guarantee against arbitrary government, one more safeguard against a tyranny which now appears remote in America, but which historically has proved to be always possible.' And that, mind you, from a politician with impeccable liberal credentials.

"Senator Humphrey was speaking about a possible threat from the federal government. However, it's not unheard-of in American history for a local government to be bought and owned by local businesses, or by criminal interests such as illegal gambling or drug dealing." He read from another paper. "In 1924, the North Carolina supreme court wrote, about the right to keep and bear arms, 'This is not an idle or an obsolete guarantee, for there are still localities, not necessary to mention, where great corporations, under the guise of detective agents or police forces, terrorized their employees by armed force. If the people are forbidden to carry the only arms within their means, among them pistols, they will be completely at the mercy of these plutocratic organizations.'" He looked up. "That's pretty definite, wouldn't you say?

"There's another thing. The court there was clearly saying that people had the right to buy inexpensive firearms, if they couldn't afford high-quality ones. The gun-grabbers who sneer at what they choose to call 'Saturday Night Specials' and 'junk guns' are really trying to keep the poor from defending themselves."

He put down the paper and continued, "This business of defending yourself against local government is not just a theory. In fact, in 1947, in Athens, Tennessee, there was an armed revolt against a corrupt local government. The government officials had stolen the elections, threatened the lives of opposing poll-watchers, and had their thugs beat up at least one voter. The people's appeals to state and federal government officials did no good. So the citizens of Athens took up arms. They were led by World War II veterans who said they had fought against this kind of government overseas, and they weren't going to put up with it at home. After an all-day siege of the county jail, where the corrupt sheriff had hidden the ballot boxes, the citizens got the resignation of the corrupt officials."

"That's strange," Judith whispered to Tom. "That wasn't in any of my history books."

"Nor mine," he replied. "You'd think something like that would be important enough to write about."

Tom spoke up. "Excuse me, Judge, but neither my wife nor I ever learned about that in school. Was it very widely known?"

Judge Leahy shuffled through the papers on the podium and came up with one. "It was reported in *Time*, *Newsweek*, and *The New York Times*. A local Congressman also gave a favorable speech about it." He waved the paper. "Here's a copy of his speech from the *Congressional Record*. The revolt got national publicity at the time. Hollywood even made a movie about it, although they changed some of the story around. I can't say why it wasn't in your history books."

Tom thought to himself, *Maybe I'm being cynical, but I have an idea why it wasn't.* Aloud, he said, "Thank you, Judge."

Leahy smiled and looked toward the man who had asked about modern quotations. "Satisfied?"

"Yes. Thank you."

Leahy replaced the papers on the podium and continued. "The people who wrote the Constitution had two things in mind. First, you have a right to own a gun to protect yourself against criminals. Second, you and your fellow citizens have a right to own guns to protect yourselves against a tyrannical government. Remember, the Constitution is only a piece of parchment. It doesn't enforce itself. Your gun, and your neighbors guns, are the ultimate defense of the Constitution against a government that usurps unconstitutional powers, just as it was not only for the citizens of Lexington and Concord, but for the citizens of Athens, Tennessee.

"However, the right to own a gun doesn't extend to committing a crime with it. In this state, if you have a firearm in your possession while you're committing a felony, you get a mandatory minimum sentence of three years. Moreover, the three-year sentence for carrying a firearm must be served prior to whatever the sentence is for the felony.

"Unfortunately, that law hasn't worked out very well. Too many prosecutors make their work easier by accepting a plea bargain that reduces a felony to a misdemeanor. That way the mandatory sentence never comes into play. Even worse, judges often reduce the sentence for the crime itself, to balance the extra sentence for using a gun."

Tom heard someone behind him mutter, "Yeah, that's what happened the last time my gas station was held up. The cops caught the crook as he was drivin' away. He got off with six months plus probation. The next robber'll get six feet deep in the cemetery, not six months in the county jail."

Judge Leahy continued. "That law shows that while the Second Amendment protects your right to own a gun, that right can be limited by the several states.

"Another limitation is that convicted felons are prohibited from owning guns. The Supreme Court put a peculiar twist on that. If a state or city passes a gun registration law, it can't be applied to felons. Requiring a convicted felon to register a gun violates his right against self-incrimination. So only honest people can be required to register their guns."

Tom heard the gas station owner mutter, "Sounds like something the politicians would do."

"All right," Leahy continued, "you're allowed to own a gun for self-defense. What can you do with it?

"Under the law in this state, you may use a firearm to prevent what the law calls 'forcible and atrocious crime.'" He picked up the paper and read again. "That includes crimes such as murder, robbery, burglary, rape, and arson. It does not include felonies not accompanied by force, such as theft, picking a pocket, or larceny." He laid the paper down and leaned on the podium.

"Even in crimes accompanied by violence, you are justified in using a gun to defend yourself only in absolute or apparent necessity. The danger must be evident and immediate.

"However, the danger need not be real if you have reasonable grounds to believe that danger exists. For instance, when someone breaks into your house, and you fear for your life, you are justified in using a gun, no matter what the intruder's actual intentions were. You don't have to wait until he shoots at you or stabs you before shooting at him.

"Once the danger is past, though, shooting is no longer justified. If the intruder surrenders to you at the sight of your gun, or turns and runs away, you are no longer justified in shooting him.

"Shooting someone who threatens you must be a last resort. You may not do it if there is some other way of avoiding the problem. Outside your home, you must retreat if you can possibly do so. Otherwise you'll be charged with using excessive force. However, inside your home, you are not required to retreat. You may defend your home as soon as an intruder enters.

"Defending your life with lethal force doesn't extend to defending your property. Only in the face of a threat to your life or safety, or that of someone in your household, are you justified in using lethal force, including a gun.

"Now, do you have any questions?"

Someone in back spoke up. "What if a burglar breaks into my house and starts carrying off my TV set. Can I shoot him?"

"If he's already leaving, he's no longer a threat to your life. You would not be justified in shooting him. You may not use deadly force to defend mere property."

George, the black man next to Judith, spoke up. "Judge, you're talkin' 'bout property like it ain't important. That ain't so. Momma always tol' us to work hard and make somethin' of ourselves. Couple years ago, my older brother got a job after school in a car-wash. End of the first week, he was comin' home with his pay. He got jumped by one of the neighborhood no-goods. Took all his money. Momma say, 'It happen all the time. Don't let it stop you.' So he went back the next week, worked all week, and the same thing happen. Same guy jumped him and took his pay. The cops wouldn't do nothin', even though he told 'em who done it. They say, 'Only fifty bucks. Petty larceny. We got bigger crimes to worry about.' That was it. He tol' me, no point in workin', you only get robbed. He dropped out of school. Now he's livin' with a girlfriend who's on the welfare, jus' drinkin' up her money. Only one of her kids is his. That thief didn't steal just fifty bucks. He stole my brother's whole life.

"I finished school last month. I'm an apprentice down at the mill. I'm gonna be a tool 'n' die maker. Then I'm gonna get Sis and Momma outa there before Sis ends up on the welfare with a bunch of different guys' kids.

"And Judge, I ain't goin' to let some no-good steal my life, like they done to my brother. Don't try to tell me my property ain't as important as some no-good's life. You hear what I'm sayin'?"

Leahy held up his hand, palm out. "Young man, I can understand your feelings. When you've worked hard for something, only to see it disappear down the street in some burglar's sack, it can look like he's carrying away part of your life. However, I'm telling you what the law is, not what it should be. If you shoot him when he's no longer a threat to your life, you'll be charged with murder."

Tom spoke up. "What about us?" He gestured at Judith. "We were key witnesses in getting a dangerous criminal put in jail. He threatened to get revenge on us when he got out. He was released this past week. You've been telling us what we can do if he breaks into our house. But what about the rest of the time? Do we have to go around all the time scared that he'll ambush us somewhere? Do I have to worry that he'll go to the law office where she works and kill her? Do I have to worry that he'll be waiting for me in the parking lot at my plant, if I work overtime some night? What can we do to defend ourselves outside our home?"

"If you can verify the threat, the law says you can get a permit to carry a concealed weapon."

"I've been told that the police in my town won't issue permits. Is there anything I can do about that?"

"You can always sue the city. If you try, though, just remember you're fighting your own tax money. You'll go broke before they do. And carrying a gun without a permit is itself a felony."

"I'm not going to break the law by carrying a gun without a permit. But what can I do to protect myself when I'm outside my home?"

"Be careful. Avoid dark streets and dark parking lots. Go only where there's a lot of people. Don't fall into a pattern that's predictable. Vary the time you leave for work. Take a different route each day. Don't go to church at the same time every week. Keep an eye out for people and cars that don't belong in your neighborhood. And watch to see if anyone's following you."

"You're telling me I have to skulk around like some criminal, while he's free to come and go as he pleases. That's not right."

The judge held up both hands, palms out. "I didn't say it was right. I said it was something you might do. Until he commits an overt act, the law can't touch him."

"And if he does commit an overt act," Tom responded heatedly, "one or both of us will be dead. I'll bet he isn't sweatin' out any five-day waiting period, either. He probably had a gun before dark, the day he walked out of jail."

"To you, and to this young man here," Leahy pointed at George, "I can only say, I don't make the laws. As a judge, I just impose sentence when a jury decides someone has broken the law. If you don't like the laws, get your legislators to change them."

Baron broke in at that point. "Folks, that's all the time the Judge has. Take a quick break, have some coffee, and then we'll talk about defensive tactics inside your home."

Tom leaned over to speak to Judith. "From what the judge said, it sounds as though if Grubbs breaks into our house again and we have to shoot him, we'll be the ones on trial."

She frowned. "That's the way I felt last time. I'd rather be on trial for shooting him than go through that again."

With that she got up and headed for the coffee urn. Tom slowly followed her, a concerned look on his face.

As Tom stepped away from the coffee urn, he noticed that Judith was standing in the back of the room, talking to a woman who was wearing a safety-orange vest like Baron's.

George leaned across Judith's empty seat and spoke to Tom in a low voice.

"That judge, he's okay, I guess, but he don't understand how I gotta live. Drug pushers! Pimps! Numbers runners! All struttin' 'round my neighborhood, wearin' five-hun'erd-dollar suits. They all carryin' guns, but they ain't got no permits. And The Man? He don't do *nuthin'*. But if I carry a gun, wham! I'm in jail! It ain't right."

"It isn't right," Tom replied, "but like they say, you can't fight city hall. The only thing you can do is move. I hope you make it.

"That job of yours sounds like a good one," Tom went on. "How'd you get it?"

"My shop teacher. He made a deal with the comp'ny. If we stay in school, pass our shop courses 'n' graduate, they hire us."

"What's the job like?"

"First thing in the morning, they got a teacher come in to teach us to read and write, and do shop math. Then we learn to read blueprints. Then the rest o' the day I spend watchin' one o' the older workers, and doin' what he tells me. I been helpin' him set up the machines. This week he'll let me start runnin' 'em."

"You got to learn to read and write? But you said you graduated from school."

"I did." The bitterness in his voice couldn't be hidden. "But just 'cause I got a diploma don't mean I learned how to read."

Judith came back to her seat, still carrying a cup of coffee.

Tom nodded toward the woman in the orange vest. "Who was that you were talking to?"

"That's Gerry. She's a certified firearms instructor. I guess I'm still a bit nervous about this whole thing, but she was very encouraging. She was telling me about how she shoots in competitive matches. I never realized shooting was a competitive sport. She even said it was part of the Olympics"

"You never see much about it on TV," Tom replied. "Maybe the TV networks don't want people to know there's something good about guns."

Baron stood at the front of the room. "Take your seats, folks. Bring your coffee with you. We need to get started."

There was a general shuffling of feet and scraping of chairs as people started to seat themselves. When the room was quiet, Baron spoke again.

"Now we'll talk about defensive tactics. You have three lines of defense to your home. Your gun is only the third line of defense. Those first two lines of defense can help you avoid the kind of situations Judge Leahy was talking about.

"The first line of defense is your property line. Anyone has the right to walk on the sidewalk or drive on the street. It's when they reach your property line that you want to discourage them with that first line of defense. That means a fence of some kind."

A question came from behind Tom. "Does that need to be a chain-link fence?"

"No, it doesn't," Baron replied. "Even a picket fence or a hedge will mark off your property."

Tom leaned over to Judith. "One of the things I liked about our house was the hedge in front. I thought it looked nice. Looks like we made a good choice."

Judith replied in a low voice. "Our hedge marks off the front yard, but we need something in back. Especially if we want to keep a dog, and eventually have kids play there."

"Yeah, and a chain-link fence is probably what we want. Even if it makes the back yard look like a prison-yard. Maybe we ought to get that done soon."

Baron spoke again. "Okay, that leads to your second line of defense, your house itself. A determined burglar is going to get into any house. What you want to do is discourage him. Make your house a tough enough nut to crack that he'll go elsewhere.

"First, the doors. Make them tough to get through. And I mean every door. It doesn't make sense to put in a burglar-resistant front door, when your back door is an easy target. Even if you can't afford to spend much on doors, divide it between front and back doors. Make them equally tough to get through.

"Your outside doors should be solid, not the hollow-core doors they put on cheap houses. You can practically put your fist through a hollow-core door. It may keep the wind out, but it won't even slow down a burglar.

"Now, what about locks? Most doors have spring locks, the kind that snaps locked when you shut the door. The problem with them is that someone can spring them open with a credit card. You're better off with a deadbolt that you have to turn by hand."

"What about windows?" came from someone behind Tom. "Do you recommend bars on the windows? I see you have bars on the windows here in the cabin."

"I won't say you shouldn't put bars on the windows, but I don't have them on my own house. They'd give me the feeling I was in jail.

"This cabin is empty most of the week. We really want to make it tough to break in. But in your own house, I recommend locks on every window. Hang the keys near the windows, but not so near that someone could break a small hole in the glass, reach in, and get the key. If they insist on entering through a window, force them to break out the entire pane. That'll slow them down, and might make them decide to go somewhere else.

"An important addition to your second line of defense is a dog. A dog can alert you to someone in your yard, or inside your house. The sound of a dog barking may also discourage an intruder. The bigger the dog, the more the discouragement. But don't get a bigger dog than you can manage. Consider the size of your house, how much yard space you have, and so on."

Tom leaned over to Judith. "I hadn't thought about a watchdog, but that sounds like a good idea. I know you've been wanting a dog, but I thought it was just for a pet."

"We always had dogs around the farm. I miss having one. But they were working dogs, not just pets. Watch-dogs and rat-catchers. So yes, I'd like to get the yard fenced and get a dog."

Baron went on. "You should also consider a burglar alarm, if you can afford it. Alarm the doors and the windows. Don't forget the basement windows. Or at least alarm the basement door. And don't forget the door from an attached garage. It should be just as strong as the other doors, and it should be alarmed too."

Judith whispered to Tom. "Our first floor windows are too high for anyone to get in without a ladder, but they might get in through a basement window. Should we have a burglar alarm?"

Tom thought, *A burglar alarm wouldn't have done us any good the night Grubbs broke in. Once he was through the front door, he was already in the living room. Would a burglar alarm do us any more good if he attacked us again? But if he did attack, and we didn't have an alarm, I'd blame myself for not doing everything I could.*

"I guess we better have one," he responded. "It's probably just as important as the smoke detectors we have now. I'll talk to some dealers and try to get some prices."

Baron continued. "So, that's your second line of defense. First, discourage anyone from crossing your property line. Second, discourage them from entering the house. If you can't discourage them, slow them down.

"Now we come to your third line of defense, your gun.

"Okay, it's happened. You've been alerted to someone breaking in, either by your dog or by a burglar alarm. Where are you? Where's every other member of your household? Where's your gun? These things all determine the tactics you can use.

"First, your gun. If you ever need it, you'll need it in a hurry. It has to be where you can get it quickly. It has to be loaded and ready for use. You don't want to be unlocking a gun safe, or fumbling with a trigger lock or some such nonsense, or hunting for the ammunition and trying to load your gun, while someone's already in your house or maybe even grappling with you.

"Next, what about the rest of your household? What is everyone supposed to do when you're alerted to an intruder? You need a plan.

"You should have some part of the house designated as the retreat. Everyone goes there at the first warning of trouble. Make sure you have a phone there. A cell phone, if possible, so you don't have to worry about the wires being cut. Call the police and wait there until they arrive.

"When you have every member of the household accounted for, anyone else must be the intruder. If someone starts breaking open the door of your retreat, you can shoot, knowing that it's not one of your kids.

"Where should the retreat be? If you have a two-story house, I recommend putting it upstairs. Stairways are what we call a 'fatal funnel.' Anyone going upstairs is confined to that staircase.

They don't have much room to dodge or maneuver."

Judith whispered, "I'm glad we decided to use one of the upstairs rooms as our bedroom. We better figure on having the kids' bedrooms up there, too."

"Right. We can make ours the retreat, since it's at the end of the hall."

Baron continued. "What if your house has only one floor? A hallway can also be a fatal funnel. Make your retreat the room at the end of it, so the intruder has to pass through the hallway to reach you."

"Go over your house carefully. Think in terms of how to put an intruder at a disadvantage. Do you have anything that would be a fatal funnel? Is there anything that would give you concealment while allowing you to see the intruder? Can you take advantage of lighting, so you're in the dark while the intruder is in the light? Can you move the furniture so there aren't any blind spots where the intruder could hide? Once you've done that, you have the advantage. If the intruder comes at you, you have a clear shot."

A voice came from behind Tom. "Should we fire a warning shot? Should we try to wound him, or should we shoot to kill?" Tom turned to see who had asked the question. It was an older man, in the next row back.

Baron responded, "Let's take your last question first. You never shoot to *kill*. You shoot to *stop*. Remember what Judge Leahy told you. You are justified in using a gun to *stop* an attack on you. If the intruder is killed, that's his tough luck, but your intent was to *stop* him. If your first shot drops him to the floor, but you see he's still alive, *don't* shoot to finish him off unless you can see he's still holding a weapon. If he still has a gun in his hand, keep shooting until you're sure he's not going to use it. But as soon as he's out of the fight, you're no longer justified in shooting.

"Now about shooting to wound. That's tricky. What would you aim for? An arm or a leg? Even if your intruder is down with a hole in his leg, he can still shoot back. Besides, are you a good enough shot to hit a leg on a man running toward you?

"Your best bet is to shoot for the center of mass of the torso. That's the easiest to hit, it's usually effective in stopping the attack, and even a fight-stopping wound there isn't always fatal.

"Now, what about warning shots? That means you're going to shoot away from your attacker. That bullet has to go somewhere. It'll probably penetrate the wall of your house. Do you want to kill a neighbor, or someone who was walking down the street? Warning shots are only for the movies. Never fire a shot except at the person who's threatening you.

"Okay, I've told you the good news: you can give your house a defense in depth. Now the bad news. Let's say someone has broken into your house. You've been alerted by your dog or your burglar alarm. Your family has moved to your retreat. The bad guy is coming at you. You shoot him. He's lying dead on the floor. Next you call the police.

"Don't expect them to give you a medal. You've just committed homicide. Never mind how bad the guy was that you shot, the cops' job is to assume you may have committed a crime.

"They'll want a story from you. You'll end up telling it to the prosecutor. You might have to face a grand jury. You might even end up in criminal court, trying to convince a jury that your shooting was justified.

"All those problems are if the bad guy is dead. If he isn't dead, things could even be worse. Suppose your shot didn't kill the guy, but crippled him for life. You might end up in civil court. The bad guy's sleazeball lawyer will point at you, in good health, and at your victim, who'll be in a wheelchair for the rest of his life, and tell the jury you used excessive force. You could end up paying that intruder ten million bucks in damages. Even if you do win the case, you'll be out several thousand bucks in lawyer's fees, while the bad guy's sleazeball lawyer is working for a contingency fee.

"And if you think I'm exaggerating, consider this. Under the Constitution, the accused criminal has the following rights: right to due process; right to confront witnesses; right against self-incrimination; right to a jury trial; right to a speedy trial; right to counsel; and the right to be free from unreasonable searches and seizures.

"What rights do you as the victim have under the Constitution? None whatsoever. You don't have a right to be present at any proceedings such as the grand jury, or even be informed of them. You don't have a right to a speedy trial. Your attacker's lawyer can delay things until you give up. In fact, you don't even have a right to see the criminal get a trial at all. Ninety percent of criminal indictments never go to trial. The Prosecutor allows a plea bargain down to some lesser offense that makes life easy for him, and makes a mockery of justice. You don't have the right to be involved in any attempts at plea-bargaining. You don't have the right to be informed if your attacker is released or escapes from jail. You don't have the right to be present at any parole hearings.

"The criminal's Constitutional rights are intended to protect honest citizens against government tyranny. We wouldn't want to give them up. Nevertheless, the Constitution says nothing about the rights of victims. Starting with the Constitution itself, the law is stacked in favor of the criminal and against the victim."

Baron continued, "The police aren't the only people you'll have to deal with. You may have to deal with the press. Just remember, you don't owe them a single word. The First Amendment belongs to you, too, not just to them. You're within your rights to answer 'no comment' to any question they ask. Sure, they may crucify you on the eleven o'clock news, but if you don't say anything, you won't have to explain to a jury why you said what they videotaped you saying. Most reporters side with the gun-grabbers. They don't own guns, they don't like guns, and they don't like gun-owners. They'd like nothing better than to paint you as a wild-eyed lunatic who's been hoping for the chance to blow somebody away. They'll twist anything you say. It's hard for them to twist silence.

"Back to the aftermath of a shooting. After the reporters and the police are gone, you'll have more problems. You'll have a psychological reaction to shooting someone, whether you kill him or just wound him. It's called post-shooting trauma. Even cops go through it. That's why most police departments now require cops to undergo counseling after being involved in a shooting.

"I recommend that if you have to shoot someone in self defense, get counseling afterwards. Don't go to some pacifist clergyman who'll tell you that you should have turned the other cheek. But do get counseling.

"Now, am I giving you all this bad news to talk you out of shooting an intruder? No. But I want you to realize that the laws are stacked against you and in favor of the criminal. The laws are written by legislators who live in well-policed, low-crime neighborhoods. Those laws are interpreted by judges who live in those same low-crime neighborhoods, and who have armed guards around their courtrooms. These legislators and judges don't have any personal fear of crime, and they don't see why you should either. They start out with the assumption that you didn't need to shoot, and you have to prove you did.

"If it goes to a trial, your fate is going to be decided by a jury who will be second-guessing whether you really needed to shoot. And the lawyer for the other side will have done his damnedest to make sure that no one on that jury has ever been the victim of a violent crime. No one on that jury will have the experience of being robbed, or beaten, or having their person violated by a criminal. They won't have the experience of being frightened by an intruder, and having to make a split-second shoot or no-shoot decision. They'll take hours to discuss what you had to decide in an instant.

"So what to do? Just remember that it's better to be tried by twelve than carried by six. The whole point of defensive use of a firearm is to stop a fight that someone else has started. If the intruder is threatening you, shoot him. Then call your lawyer. And I mean a good criminal lawyer. Pick one out before you need him, and let him know you might some day have to call on him. Then don't say a word to the police until your lawyer is there with you."

Tom leaned over toward Judith. "Any good criminal lawyers

in your office?"

"Mr. Cohen is supposed to be one of the best in the city," she replied.

"Maybe you ought to ask him if he'd take our case if we ever needed a lawyer."

"I'll do that Monday. Getting legal help from members of the firm is supposed to be one of our benefits."

Baron continued. "Now, some final thoughts on defending your house.

"I said that your first line of defense is your property line. You can't control anyone on the street. However, that doesn't mean you ignore them. Look at your house through the eyes of a possible intruder.

"Does it look like an easy target? Can anyone on the street see anything, either through the windows or in the yard, that would tip them off that your house is worth robbing? Does your picture window show off an expensive painting or your rare coin collection? Is a gun cabinet visible through a window?"

Tom whispered to Judith, "Our two jalopies in the driveway ought to convince anybody our house isn't worth robbing." She returned a quick smile.

Baron went on. "Is there any place near your house where people might legitimately stand around? A bus stop? A convenience store? A pay phone? Even a park bench? Is your house visible from there? If so, go there and look at your house. Do it both in the daytime and in the dark. If someone is using those public places to scout out your house, make sure that what they see doesn't encourage them to break in.

Judith whispered, "What about the pay phone outside the Seven-Eleven on the corner?"

"I don't think anyone can see the house from the phone booth. The trees in the Scott's yard block the view. But I'm not sure about their parking lot. I always walk down there instead of driving. Our back porch might be visible. I'll take a look tomorrow."

Baron paused for a moment, then continued, "Well, folks, that's it for household defensive tactics. Have some coffee. Those of you who brought your guns get them now. Those who asked to use Academy guns come back to the storage room and we'll issue them. Then we'll show you how to hold them. After that we'll have lunch, and then go to the firing range."

• • •

Baron's voice cut through the chatter in the room. "Everyone finished with lunch? Load your gear on the back of the truck, and we'll haul it down to the range." He pointed out the door, where a pickup truck stood waiting.

Tom and Judith tossed the scraps from their hamburger and bratwurst sandwiches into a trash barrel, and joined the group that straggled down the hillside, ending at a shelter with a row of benches at the back. They picked up their gear from the truck and started to put it on.

Judith put the ear protectors over the top of her head, ready to pull them down over her ears when they were needed. Tom looked at her and burst out laughing. "Judy, with that pistol strapped on your hip, and those ears on your head, you look like a cross between Calamity Jane and Minnie Mouse."

She smiled and reached out to brush her fingers across the back of his hand. He grasped her hand and gave it a quick squeeze before releasing it. He thought to himself, *We haven't shared many laughs lately. Maybe this will help.*

Baron called out, "All right, shooters. Line up here in front of the shelter." A ragged line formed where he pointed. He waved at the end of the line to Tom's left.

"Start counting off."

"One."

"Two."

The rest of the line counted off, ending up on Tom's right.

"Odd-numbered shooters are relay one, even-numbered shooters are relay two. We'll have one relay on the firing line at a time."

"We're in different relays," Judith said.

"Yeah. I guess we can watch each other shoot."

Baron spoke again. "Now listen up, folks. This is important.

We run what's called a 'hot range.' That means after your first time on the firing line, your gun is always loaded.

"For you auto-pistol shooters, that means a round in the chamber, a full magazine in the magazine-well, and the safety on. For you revolver shooters, there should be a live round in each chamber, and the hammer should be down before you holster your gun."

"Now, we have reasons for wanting you to keep your gun loaded. First of all, an unloaded gun is nothing but an expensive iron club. If you need to use it, you need it to be loaded. We want you to get comfortable around a loaded gun. It won't shoot by itself. But it will be ready when you need it.

"Second, if you ever get in a shootout, you won't have us around to remind you to reload. We want you to get in the habit of reloading whenever your gun runs dry.

"You might be thinking, wouldn't it be safer to keep the guns unloaded except when you're on the firing line? Actually, it's safer the way we do it. If you always reload your gun and holster it before you leave the firing line, there's never any reason to draw your gun when you're behind the firing line. Those of you shooting don't have to worry that somebody's behind you, loading his gun, and creating a potential accident situation.

"Now, relay one line up at the five-yard marker. Pick a target and cover down on it. Revolver shooters on the left end of the line, auto-pistol shooters on the right. That way the revolver shooters aren't getting bombarded with empty brass."

Judith was in the first relay. Tom stood several yards behind her as she took her position.

The targets were human silhouettes, from hips to head, outlined in black on white paper, and stapled to a wooden frame.

"Okay, relay one, draw your weapons and load them. If you have any problems, raise your hand and an instructor will help you."

Judith raised her hand immediately. Gerry promptly stepped to her side and spoke. Tom could see Judith loading the revolver, apparently following Gerry's instructions. *Well, I won't have to ask how, now that I've seen her do it.*

Baron continued, "As soon as your weapon is loaded, holster it." When everyone on the firing line had holstered their weapons, Baron stepped in front of them.

"On my command, you'll draw your weapon, take up the stance and grip we showed you before lunch, and fire one shot at the target. When you've fired one shot, holster your weapon. Auto-pistol shooters, remember to safe your weapon before holstering it."

He stepped behind the firing line. "Ready on the firing line?" he called to the instructors.

"Ready on the left."

"Ready on the right."

Baron spoke again. "The firing line is ready. At your own pace, draw your weapon, fire one shot and re-holster."

Tom pulled the protectors down over his ears. He watched as Judith slowly drew her pistol, leaned forward, and extended both arms, as they'd been shown earlier. The sound of gunshots rippled up and down the firing line. He saw the gun buck in her hand. It didn't seem to bother her, as she straightened up and holstered the gun.

The smell of gunpowder wafted back to Tom on the slight breeze. It was an unfamiliar smell, but not unpleasant.

"Once more. At your own pace, draw, fire, and re-holster."

Baron took them through the drill until all the revolvers were empty.

"Reload, then holster your weapons."

After a brief interval, he called out, "Is the firing line safe?"

"Safe on the left."

"Safe on the right."

"The firing line is safe. Go forward, and patch your targets. You'll find rolls of white tape on the ground under the targets. Use that to cover each hole in your target. That leaves a clean target for the next shooter."

Tom followed Judith forward, to see how she'd done. There were two shots to the left of the silhouette, and four in the torso.

Three of these were in the chest area, one in the groin.

Gerry stopped by Judith's target. "For the first time you ever fired a gun, not bad at all, Judy. You kept them all on the paper, and each of those body hits would have been effective."

Judith picked up the tape and started to patch the holes. Baron came by, looked at her target, then looked at Tom. He pointed to the shot in the groin.

"Oh-oh, Tom, better watch it!"

Tom forced a grin, but his thought was bitter. *If you only knew . . .*

"Okay, relay two on the firing line. Load and holster."

Tom opened a box of ammunition and placed it the on the ground, swung out the cylinder of his revolver, squatted down and began loading the chambers. Off to his right he heard the *snick-slam* of auto-pistol slides being worked. He stood up, holstered his revolver, and faced the target. He shuffled his feet to get a stance he found comfortable.

"The firing line is ready. At your own pace, draw, fire one shot, and holster."

Tom drew his gun, extended his arms, and tried to line up the sights on the target. The gun wobbled, but he found he could keep it fairly well centered on the target. He pictured the face of Harry Grubbs on the silhouette, and squeezed the trigger.

The sound of the shot left his ears ringing. He suddenly realized he hadn't pulled his ear protectors back down after the first relay ended. He carefully holstered the gun, and pulled the ear-pieces over his ears. *All this is new, and there're too many things to think about.*

He looked at the target. His shot had gone in the left shoulder of the silhouette. The gun had wobbled more than he realized.

Baron ran them through the drill five more times.

"Reload and holster."

"Safe on the left."

"Safe on the right."

"Forward and patch."

Baron stopped by Tom's target. "You kept them all in the torso, Tom. Every shot would have been effective. Not bad for a first-time shooter. But they're pretty widely spread out. You need to work on your stance a bit, and concentrate on squeezing that trigger smoothly."

The first relay returned to the firing line. Baron put them through the same drill. This time, Tom noticed that Judith was leaning farther forward than she had before. Stepping slightly to the side, he recognized the look of intense concentration on her face. He had no doubt whose face she was seeing on the target.

This time her shots were all in the chest. A dinner plate would have covered them all.

"Forward and patch."

Tom walked forward with Judy, to examine the target.

"You really improved, honey. That's great."

"The first time I didn't know what to expect. This time I could concentrate on the sights and the trigger."

"Wow!" was Gerry's comment. "Keep that up and you'll be ready for competitive shooting."

"Relay two on the firing line."

Tom took up his stance, left foot slightly ahead of the right, facing square on to the target. Baron had them repeat the drill, six shots, one at a time. His first shot went left and high, beside the head of the silhouette. He kept the next two in the torso. He took a death-grip on the gun, and fired when he saw the sights were lined up with the center of the torso. The shot went wild, punching a hole in the left arm of the silhouette.

*What's wrong with you?* he demanded of himself. *Judy's hitting the target. Why can't you?*.

Baron's low voice behind him said, "Tom, you're jerking the trigger. You're trying too hard. Bring your arms forward smoothly, hold your breath, and *squeeze* that trigger. Try it again."

He tried to relax, and managed to keep the last two shots in the chest.

Relay one returned to the firing line. Baron stepped in front of them.

"By now you're keeping most of your shots in the preferred target area. That's good. But one shot may not be enough to stop an attack. This time I want you to fire two shots in succession each time. Don't rush the second shot so much you jerk the trigger, but follow up the first shot as quickly as you can and still keep it smooth."

He stepped behind them, then checked the line. "The line is ready. Fire!"

When the first relay was finished, Tom followed Judith up to the target. Again, she'd kept all her shots in the chest.

"I think I'm getting the hang of this," she said. "Just concentrate on the front sight, and squeeze the trigger."

"Relay two on the line. Two shots, then holster. Fire!"

Tom drew, and fired one shot. The recoil flipped the muzzle up. He was surprised at how long it took to get the muzzle back down on the target. He fired the second shot too early, and it went high. *So that's what the guy at the gun shop meant. I'm glad I didn't insist on getting a Dirty Harry gun.*

Both relays went through two more repetitions of this drill. Tom found that if he concentrated on keeping the front sight on the target while squeezing the trigger, instead of trying to trigger the shot as the gun wobbled past the center of the target, he could keep his shots where he wanted them. All of them stayed in the torso, with most in the chest.

As he returned from patching his target, Tom realized he was thirsty. He decided to get a drink while the other relay was on the line. The middle-aged man who had been seated on the end of the row beyond Judith was filling a cup at the water jug. His nametag identified him as Jim. Tom grabbed a cup, and Jim held the spigot open for him.

Tom asked, "You a new shooter too?"

Jim replied, "No, I've been doing competitive target shooting for years."

"Then why take this course?"

A wry smile crossed Jim's face. "One of my shooting buddies had a burglar in his house the other night. He fired six rounds at him and missed with every one. On the range, he's a crack shot, but he found out that self-defense shooting isn't like being on a target range. I figured if he could miss a burglar at twenty feet, I'd better take some self-defense training. So here I am."

Evidently everyone else was thirsty as well. Baron called for a break as the first relay left the firing line.

Judith came up to where Tom was standing. "How'd you do, honey?" he asked.

"Pretty well. I missed only one shot."

"I didn't see what you were doing. Still the same thing, two shots?"

"No, this was something Mr. Baron called 'body armor drill.' In case your attacker is wearing body armor, you put two shots in the chest and one in the head. I missed one of the head shots."

*Something else to worry about,* Tom thought. *Even if you hit the guy, you might not do any damage. At least a hit in the head should stop him.*

"Okay, shooters, relay two on line. Same thing as relay one did. Body armor drill. On my command, draw, fire twice at the chest and once at the head, then holster."

After checking the line, Baron called "Fire!"

Tom drew his gun, tried to control the wobble, and got off two shots to the chest. He raised the gun, fired at the head, and missed. *Slow down. Aim carefully. Judy's getting ahead of you.*

As he patched the target, he concluded the results were dismal. Three of the chest shots had hit. None of the head shots were good. *Looks like Judy can protect herself better than you can. Get that gun under control.*

When he returned to the firing line, Baron spoke to the group. "You're getting fairly good from five yards. Now let's see how you can do from ten yards. That's about the maximum distance you'd need to shoot inside your house. Relay one back to the ten-yard marker. We'll use the two-shot drill."

From ten yards, everybody's accuracy fell off. Even so, Judith got all her shots in the chest area of the target.

"Good work, Judy," Gerry said. "You're really making

progress."

"Relay two on the ten yard line."

Tom thrust his arms forward, locked his elbows, and tried to keep the gun from jittering. Three of his shots went wild. *Dammit, Judy's doing well, what's wrong with you?* Then the thought came to him, *What's the matter? Are you upset because your wife is shooting better than you are? She's the one who needs the protection. Be glad she can hit what she aims at.*

When Tom's relay was back on line again, Jack, one of the male instructors, stepped up behind him. "Tom, you've got to relax. Yes, you need your right elbow locked, and you need a firm grip on the gun. But that doesn't mean you should tense up. Remember, keep the front sight on the target, and squeeze the trigger. The shot should actually come as a surprise."

"Two shots. Fire!"

Tom took a deep breath, let it out, then drew. He leaned into the gun as he extended his arms. *Front sight, front sight, squeeze, front sight, . .*

*BANG!*

The muzzle flipped. He brought the gun back down. *Front sight, front sight, squeeze, . .*

*BANG!*

*Hey, that works pretty well,* he told himself in surprise. *Both shots in the chest, right where I wanted them.* After two more repetitions of the drill came the command "Holster. Forward and patch."

Tom was elated at the sight of the target. All six shots in the preferred area, even from ten yards. Better than he'd been doing at five yards.

Baron walked by, inspecting the targets. "Nice going, Tom. You're getting better."

The two relays repeated all the drills several times: one shot, two shots, body armor drill, at five and ten yards. As Tom's relay finished shooting, he started to reload and realized he was down to his last box of ammunition. As they started to move forward to patch their targets, Baron spoke.

"Don't bother patching. We're going to replace the targets. Take a break."

Tom wandered back to the shelter. The shade suddenly felt good after several hours of standing in the sun. Judith was already there, drinking a cup of water.

"I hadn't realized how thirsty I was," she said. "This has been a warm day. As Dad would say, it's a scorcher."

"Yeah, my face and arms are so gritty with salt they feel like sandpaper. A shower is really going to feel good tonight."

He got himself a cup of water, and returned to find Jim's wife, Carolyn, talking to Judith.

"You mean he never took you to a shooting range in all those years?" Judith asked.

"Oh, I'd go with him sometimes when he was shooting in a match. But I'd spend most of my time talking with the other wives. I never really wanted to shoot."

"Then what made you decide to come here?"

"Jim insisted on it. He said I'd better be able to defend myself, since he couldn't be there all the time."

"I guess that makes sense."

"Yes, but I wish he'd told me years ago how much fun this is. I really enjoy it. There's a skill here I can take some pride in. I doubt I'll ever end up competing in matches like he does, but you can bet the next time he goes to the range to practice, I'll be there shooting with him. And I won't be talking to other non-shooting wives."

Tom spoke up. "Maybe you should talk to them. Let them know how much fun you think it is. Their husbands might even thank you for getting their wives interested in shooting."

"Do you really think so?"

"I only know I was really worried about going home to Judy and saying I thought she ought to get a gun. I was afraid she'd even be upset by my getting one."

"It worried you?" Judith asked. "I didn't know that."

"I wasn't going to tell you it worried me, but it sure was a relief when you agreed to go to the gun shop."

Baron's voice boomed out. "Relay one to the ten yard line."

"Looks like we're ready to start again."

Baron spoke to the assembled relay one. "This is your final exam, folks. We've put up clean targets. At your own pace, fire six shots, two at a time, then reload and holster. Then six more shots in body armor drill. When everyone's finished, you'll move up to the five-yard line and repeat both exercises. After that, do not reload. Auto-pistol shooters should fire your weapons dry and remove the magazine. After the line is safe, you can take down your target and keep it. Then relay two will go through their final exam."

Tom followed behind Judith as she moved through the various stages. She wore a grim look on her face as she fired. Even at ten yards she kept all her shots in the target. At five yards her shots were well grouped in the chest. There was a look of triumph on her face as she carefully pulled her target off the frame and rolled it up.

*I haven't seen Judy look so happy in a long time. But I wonder if she really wants a shot at Grubbs, or if she's just trying to be sure she can defend herself? Does she hope he'll come back so she can blast him? I never want to see him again.*

After the targets were replaced, Tom's relay formed up at the ten-yard line.

*Okay, never mind trying to outdo Judy. Outdo yourself. Keep your front sight on the target and squeeze that trigger!*

He didn't outdo Judith, but he did keep all his shots well inside the preferred target area. He felt a warm sense of satisfaction as he took his own target down. The training here had been intense, but it seemed to work. He had no doubt that with some warning as an intruder broke into the house, he could give a good account of himself. But his elation was promptly swamped by a storm of doubts.

*If someone breaks in, will I get enough warning to get my gun? Will it happen like it did the last time, so fast I can't react? And what if Grubbs has a gun next time? What if he shoots first? Can I really carry out my promise to protect Judy? And what if the attack comes when we're outside the house? We won't even have our guns then.*

Depressed, he rolled up the target and didn't even bother showing it to Judith.

Baron's voice cut through his gloom. "Back to the cabin, everyone. I have a few more things to cover, then we'll hand out your certificates while you're cleaning your guns."

Once back at the cabin, they all took their seats. Baron strode to the front of the room.

"We have your certificates of completion ready, folks. You may be thinking, what do I need a certificate for? Believe me, it isn't just another piece of wallpaper. If you ever have to shoot someone who has attacked you, your certificate can help you convince a prosecutor, or a jury, that you've prepared yourself to know when lethal force is justified and when it isn't. That should help you defend yourself against a charge of excessive force.

"Also, you've been trained in firearms safety, and been taught good shooting techniques. That should help you defend yourself against a charge of reckless discharge of a firearm.

"So keep your certificate in a safe place. You may need it again. In addition, I or any of the other instructors here will testify on your behalf regarding the training you've received, if you need to defend yourself in court.

"Shooting is like any other skill. If you don't practice it, you lose it. You can repeat this course for refresher training if you want. Whether you do that or not, you should get to a firing range regularly, and practice shooting. I recommend you choose a range that has silhouette targets, not just bulls-eye targets. You want to practice defensive shooting, not competitive target shooting. You're not likely to be attacked by a bulls-eye in your home.

"Also, don't overlook dry firing. Make sure your weapon is empty, and practice getting the right sight picture and squeezing the trigger. I like to dry-fire at the people on a TV screen. They move around, so you get some practice tracking a moving target, but they don't move so much they're impossible to follow."

"We hardly ever have time to watch TV," Judith whispered.

"Maybe we ought to make time for it. That's something we can do together." A smile crossed his face. "We can both sit on the couch and dry-fire at the TV."

She frowned. "No, that would mean both of our guns would be unloaded at the same time."

*Judy's not the same person she was yesterday. She wouldn't have thought of that before she took this course. And even now I didn't think of it.* "Well, okay, we can take turns dry firing."

Baron continued. "One final thing. We've taught you how to shoot, and we've taught you some tactics for defending your house. But the biggest part of defending yourself is your mindset. If you're going to succeed in defending your house, you must have the right mindset, the right mental attitude.

"It's your house. You have a right to defend it. The intruder has no right to be there. If he's a threat to you, you have the right to defend yourself, using lethal force if necessary. You must be determined to exercise your right to defend yourself.

"If you don't really intend to use your gun, don't try to bluff with it. The intruder is experienced in dealing with householders. He'll spot your bluff and call it. Then you'll be worse off than if you hadn't made an empty threat. So if you're going to keep a gun, make up your mind that you'll use it if you need to.

"The intruder may be armed, too. Your first shot might not stop him. He may even get in the first shot. What do you do if you're hit? That's where your mindset is even more important. Both as a cop and in Vietnam I've seen people give up the fight after a superficial wound. I've also seen people get a nonsurvivable wound and continue to fight right up until they dropped dead. Mindset made all the difference.

"You need to make up your mind you want to live more than your assailant wants to live. Even if you're wounded, you must have the determination to keep going until you finish off your assailant. You need to make up your mind that no matter what happens, you're going to keep fighting as long as you can point your gun at the attacker. With that mindset, you have a good chance of stopping your assailant and surviving the fight.

"That's my final word, folks. I've enjoyed working with you today. If you feel the course was worthwhile, tell your friends."

Next Jack came to the front of the room. "Folks, you need to clean your guns after shooting. You don't want powder residue and lead to crud up the barrel or the action. Follow along as I demonstrate." He began to field-strip an auto-pistol. Throughout the room, people imitated him. Soon the room was filled with the pungent smell of gun-cleaning solvent.

Tom said to Judith, "Why are we practicing how to clean a revolver? We're getting auto-pistols."

"Simple. The Academy wants its guns cleaned before we turn them back in. And look at the auto-pistol shooters. They're swabbing out the barrels the same way we are. But I guess we'd better get some instructions on how to clean our own guns when we get them."

Baron came up behind them and placed their certificates on the table. "You two did real well today. You can already shoot better than most crooks. Keep practicing, so you'll have confidence in yourselves."

"I certainly intend to, Mr. Baron," Judith said

"Me too," Tom added.

Tom turned in their borrowed gear at the storage room. He looked around the cabin, and spotted George. He approached the black man and extended his hand.

"George, best of luck to you. I hope you make it at the mill. I'm a machinist, and I really enjoy my work. There's a lot of satisfaction in taking a chunk of metal and making something useful out of it."

George clasped his hand. "Thanks, man. I 'ppreciate it."

Where was Judith? He started to look around. There she was, talking with Gerry. He walked toward them.

Judith said, "Thanks so much for your help, Gerry. I was pretty nervous about this whole thing. It was a big help to have you as one of the instructors."

Gerry smiled. "That's why they have me here. It reassures the women to see me as an instructor. And I get a big kick out of helping them get over their worries. You can feel proud of yourself. Don't forget to keep practicing."

As they walked toward the door, Judith said, "Having Gerry here made a big difference. I think I'd have managed without her, but not as easily."

They walked to Tom's car. He opened the door for her, then went around to the driver's side. As he was about to get in, he noticed a piece of paper under the windshield wiper.

He unfolded it. There was a message printed with a low-quality dot-matrix printer. At the top there was what appeared to be a telephone number, then some text.

WE MAY BE ABLE TO HELP YOU WITH YOUR PROBLEM. MEMORIZE THIS NUMBER, THEN BURN THIS PAPER AND SCATTER THE ASHES. CALL THE NUMBER. LEAVE A NUMBER WHERE YOU CAN BE REACHED, AND THE PHRASE "INVOICE NUMBER 70085."

THE JUSTICE COOPERATIVE

He looked around. No one was near the car. Whatever the message meant, whoever had left it didn't want to be known.

"What is it?" Judith asked. He handed her the paper.

She read it, then turned to him, eyebrows arched. "It sounds mysterious. What is the Justice Cooperative? And is that invoice number a password?" She waved the sheet of paper. "What's this all about?"

He shrugged. "I haven't the foggiest idea."

"Are you going to call the number?"

"I guess I'd better, just to find out what it's all about."

"Better burn the paper, like it says. Whoever it is evidently doesn't want anything that could be traced to them."

"Yeah. It could be traced to us, too. We both have fingerprints on it now."

She frowned. "Do you suppose it's something illegal?"

"I don't know what to think. But I'm going to follow instructions. Except I'm not going to take a chance on forgetting this number."

He copied the phone number and the invoice number down

on a scrap of paper from the glove compartment, and slipped it under the floor mat of the car. He went to the charcoal grill that had been used to cook lunch. The coals were still hot. He stuffed the message into the grill, watched it flame up and blacken, then stirred the ashes around with a stick. He then got into the car and started the drive home.

# FIVE

Tom hauled their gear in from the car and dumped it on the living room floor.

Judith went to the kitchen and came back with a box of frozen pizza. She asked, "Shall I start warming this pizza?"

"Let me try calling this number first." He unfolded the paper on which he'd written the number of the Justice Cooperative. He punched in the number. After four rings, an answering machine responded with "You have reached" and repeated the number. "At the tone, leave your name, a number where you can be reached, and the subject of your call."

Tom waited for the *beep*, then spoke. "My name is Tom Borden." He gave his home phone number. "I'm calling about my order on invoice number 70085." Then he hung up.

"Who answered the phone?" Judith asked.

"I got a recording. I guess we'll have to wait to see who calls back."

"Okay, I'll start warming the pizza while we're waiting."

"Now I better get rid of these numbers." He took an ashtray from the cupboard, burned the paper, then flushed the ashes down the garbage disposal.

They had barely sat down at the kitchen table when the phone rang. Tom jumped from his chair and grabbed the instrument after the first ring.

"Hello."

A muffled voice spoke quickly. "You called about invoice number 70085?"

"Yes."

"Get to a pay phone and call this number within the next 15 minutes."

The voice repeated a number, then the phone clicked off. Tom scrambled to write the number down before he forgot it.

"What did they say?"

"They want me to call another number from a pay phone."

"That must be so the call can't be traced to our home phone."

"That's probably it. I'll go down to the pay phone at the Seven-Eleven on the corner to make the call." He took his keys out of his pocket and put them on the table. "Make sure it's me before you open the door. I'll knock three times."

"Knock three times and say 'Joe sent me,' huh?"

"Yeah." Somehow Judith's attempt at levity didn't raise his spirits. Going out the door meant exposing himself to unknown risks. Was Grubbs already watching the house? Was he laying in wait for them? In any encounter outside the house, Grubbs would most likely be carrying a gun. The law didn't allow Tom Borden to carry a gun.

The night was clear, but the city lights dimmed the stars. A fitful breeze rustled the leaves in the trees. The smell of the city air was a distinct contrast with what he'd smelled all day at the Self Defense Academy. He walked briskly down the block, determined to get this over with.

The pay phone was in use. He stepped back and leaned against the corner of the convenience store. While he was waiting, he decided to check how much of his house was visible.

*Just as I figured. The trees in the Scotts' front yard block the view. Nobody can see our house from here.*

Finally the phone was free. He stepped to it, dropped in a

quarter, and punched the buttons. The phone rang once, then a voice responded.

"Who is this?"

"I'm Tom Borden. I'm returning a call to this number."

"Okay. What's your story?"

He paused to think. "I got a message to call you. I think it was because I said my testimony had put a man in jail. He threatened to get me when he got out. He's out now, and I'm worried he's going to carry out the threat."

"What's his name?"

"Harry Grubbs."

"What did he do?"

"He ...," Tom said, then paused. Did he have to tell that story all over again? But it had been in the papers. It wasn't any secret. He blurted out the reply. "He knocked me out and raped my wife."

"When did this happen?"

The date was burned into his memory. He might forget Judith's birthday, he might forget their wedding anniversary, he might even forget his own birthday, but not that date. He stated it.

"Are there police reports, or was there anything in the papers?"

"It was in the papers. They didn't print her name at the time, but during the trial they did print the details. Name, address, everything."

"And Grubbs was found guilty?"

"Yes. But he got the shortest possible sentence, and now he's been let out to reduce crowding in the jail."

"He served his sentence. Isn't that enough? What's your beef?"

Tom almost shouted. "That sentence was ridiculous. He was already out on parole from another rape conviction. He should have been put away for life, or even hanged. We didn't get justice. He threatened revenge for our testimony against him. Now he's out of jail and my wife and I are both in danger. That's my beef!"

"Then what do you want?"

"I want justice! I want to live in peace! I don't want to spend the rest of my life watching over my shoulder in case Grubbs is following me." Reflexively, he threw a glance behind him. There was nothing. "And I don't want to spend the rest of my life worrying that he's stalking my wife, either."

"Okay, we'll check out your story and get back to you. Don't try to call us until you hear from us. Good-bye."

*Click!*

# SIX

"There it is," Judith said as she pointed. "On the right, just beyond the TACO KING sign."

"I see it now. Thanks."

He pulled in beneath the small, discreet sign that read THE SHOOTING GALLERY.

"Don't seem to be many cars in the parking lot," he remarked.

"It's a weekday night. We probably wouldn't be here either if we hadn't just picked up our guns."

The sign beside the door was a little more informative:

The Shooting Gallery
Indoor Pistol Range
NRA Certified Instructors

They entered through a heavy, windowless door. Inside, the atmosphere seemed bright and cheerful. Facing the entrance there was a long glass case filled with guns. To one side there was a door labeled "Office." At the end of the counter was another door under a sign "Range." They could hear a faint sound like distant fireworks.

The man behind the case spoke. "Can I help you folks?"

"Yes," Tom said. "We'd like to practice with our new guns."

Judith added, "This is our first time here. We don't know how your system works."

"It's simple. You pay a fee to use the range. The fee includes some targets. You can rent guns, and we sell you ammunition. You have to use our ammo because we don't want you using something exotic that might damage our backstop or put lead dust in the air."

"Does the fee cover both of us?" Tom asked.

"It covers one station. You can have as many people as you want using that station. If you use two stations, that's two fees."

"I guess we'll use just one station tonight."

"Do you have your own ear protectors and shooting glasses?" the manager asked.

Tom held up a gym bag. "Yes. We brought them with us."

He paid for one station, and received a tag with the station number on it. They entered the door to the range, to find themselves in a small foyer. A sign on the second door read, EYE AND EAR PROTECTION MUST BE WORN BEYOND THIS DOOR! Below it was another sign, CLOSE THE DOOR BEHIND YOU BEFORE YOU OPEN THIS ONE.

"Time to put our on eyes and ears, I guess," Judith said.

"Yeah. It looks like this double-door thing keeps the noise out of the cashier's area, too."

They stepped through the inner door. The range was brightly lighted. Despite the audible *whirr* of the exhaust fans, the air had the pungent smell of gunpowder. Three stations were in use, and there was a steady crackle of gunfire.

Tom checked the number on the tag. "We're supposed to use station six." He looked around, then pointed. "There. That's it."

The station consisted of a small chest-high stand on a pedestal. It was separated from the adjacent stations by sheets of plywood.

"That's only quarter-inch plywood," Tom remarked. "That's not going to stop any stray bullets."

"They don't have any bullet holes in them, though, so maybe they don't need to."

Tom placed their boxes of ammunition on the stand.

"You folks know how to operate the target carrier?"

Tom turned to look behind him. A man in dark coveralls stood there. The name "Carl" was embroidered over his right breast pocket.

"This is our first time here," Judith said.

"Okay, there're two buttons on the side of your equipment stand. The one with the F on it moves the target forward, to the other end of the range. The one with the B on it moves it back towards you.

"Now, what kind of target do you want? Bullseye or silhouette?"

Tom and Judith looked at each other. Finally Tom spoke. "Silhouette."

"Okay, bring the target carrier all the way back."

Tom pressed the button. The target carrier moved smoothly toward him, then stopped. He let up on the button.

Carl showed them how to hang the target. Tom looked a Judith. "Want to try it at ten yards?"

"Okay."

He moved the carrier downrange until it was even with the ten-yard marker. "Thanks for the help," he said to Carl.

"That's what I'm here for. Call me if you need anything more."

Tom turned to Judith. "Want to go first?"

"You go ahead."

"Okay. Let's see if I remember what Mr. Baron taught me."

He loaded the gun and took up his stance. Then his thoughts returned to the training session of the previous Saturday.

• • •

Once everyone had obtained their guns, Baron had returned to the front of the room. "Okay, folks, I want to go over some pistolcraft with you. I'll cover how you hold the gun, the sight picture you'll want, and trigger management."

He briefly demonstrated various grips and stances. "Don't try to be purists about these things, folks," he said. "You want a grip that holds the gun steady for you, and you want a stance that will allow you to resist the recoil. Choose a grip and a stance that are comfortable for you and that give you good control of your gun. We'll give you a chance to try several things in a few minutes."

He then sketched the proper sight picture on the blackboard. "Your guns have a blade front sight, and a notch rear sight. You want to center the blade in the notch, with the top of the blade level with the top of the notch. The target should sit right on top of the blade."

Baron continued, "Okay, you have your sights properly lined up on the target, now you have to pull the trigger. The biggest cause of bad shots is jerking the trigger. Your trigger finger has to squeeze the trigger back smoothly, while the rest of your hand remains still. Your finger has to pull the trigger straight back, not push the gun to one side or the other. It's a bit tricky to get the hang of it. But if you do it right, your sights will stay on the target as the trigger moves back and the hammer falls on the firing pin.

"Now, let's everyone line up around the walls of the room. Spread out. Face the center of the room."

There was a scraping of chairs being slid back, and a shuffle of feet. After everyone was lined up, Baron spoke again.

"Jack," he pointed at one of the instructors, "and I will be around to check each of your guns to make sure it's empty. Revolver shooters, swing the cylinder out. Autopistol shooters, lock your slides back."

Tom fumbled at his gun, then looked at Judith. She was doing the same. The man next to her pointed to the catch that released the cylinder. "Here, push that."

The two instructors went around the room, stopping at each person. They reached Judith. Baron took her gun, examined it, then passed it to Jack.

"Yes, it's empty," Jack confirmed.

They repeated the inspection with Tom's gun, then went to the next person in line.

After everyone's gun had been inspected, Baron walked to

the center of the room. "Okay, close up your guns. What I want you to do is try some of those grips and stances I showed you. See which one suits you best.

"And something else I want you to do. Most of you were probably taught as kids, never point guns at people. That was probably drilled into you. Even those of you who do target shooting probably aren't used to pointing your gun at someone. If you're going to defend yourself with a gun, you must be willing to point it at the bad guy. We need to break whatever psychological blocks you may have against pointing guns at people. So pick someone across the room from you, take up your stance, and put the sights on them. Center the front sight in the middle of their torso, about halfway between their armpits and their elbows. That's where you'll want to be shooting.

"Then pull the trigger. Auto-pistol shooters, rack the slide if you need to cock your weapon. Keep dry-firing like that, and try to hold the rest of your hand steady while the trigger finger puts increasing pressure on the trigger."

Tom looked across the room, to see a couple of guns pointing right at him. *I'm sure glad they double-checked to make sure those things aren't loaded*, he thought. He decided to point his gun right back at one of the people targeting him. He got a broad grin in response.

All around the room there came the *snap, snap* of guns being dry-fired. Finally, Baron strode to the center of the room.

"Okay, folks, that's all for now. Holster your weapons. It's time for lunch."

• • •

Tom shook his head to break the reverie. He'd proven he could point an empty gun at someone and pull the trigger. He'd proven he could point a loaded gun at a paper target and pull the trigger. But if he was threatened, could he point a loaded gun at a living person and intentionally pull the trigger? *If it's Grubbs, I'd better be able to do it*, he told himself.

He pointed his gun at the target. The sight seemed to wobble back and forth, up and down, with no particular pattern.

*Don't fight the gun. Focus on the front sight and squeeze that trigger.*

The shot caught him by surprise. *Well, at least I didn't jerk the trigger.*

The spent case bounced off the plywood partition and hit the floor with a metallic ring. *Okay, so that's what the plywood is for. All it has to do is keep the empties from hitting the guy in the next station.*

He kept his arms extended and the sights on the target, as he'd been taught, while he scanned the target. *Not bad. Missed the heart, but his lung'd be bleeding now.* He then brought the gun back to the chest-ready position and held it there for a moment.

He extended his arms and emptied the magazine, as rapidly as he could recover and get the gun back on the target.

As he reloaded, Judith stepped up behind him. "That looks good, honey. You kept them all in the chest. Mr. Baron would be proud of you."

"Yeah. At least I feel confident about what I'm doing now. Last Saturday it was all new."

He proceeded to fire off the entire box of ammunition, then brought the target back. *A couple of complete misses. A couple of hits in the arms. But the rest in what Baron called the preferred area. Okay, maybe next time I'll try some head shots.* He turned to Judith. "Ready to try it, honey?"

She nodded and opened another box of ammunition.

"Want a new target, folks?" They turned to see Carl standing behind the station, a broom in his hands. "And let me get that brass swept up, so you don't slip on it."

"Yes, let me have another silhouette target," Judith said.

When the target was back in position, Judith started shooting. Tom stood back and watched.

*Maybe Gerry was right,* he thought, as she emptied the first magazine. *She might make a good competitive shooter. But that's not why we're doing this. She's got to be able to protect herself. And I've got to be able to protect her.*

He heard a voice next to him. "She's doin' pretty well."

*Pretty well for a woman, is that what you mean?* He thought. *She does better than I do.*

He turned to face the speaker. "Yeah, she is. And I'm glad."

"Don't blame you. Wish I could get my wife interested in shooting." He extended his hand. "I'm Hank Towers."

"Tom Borden."

"You folks come here often?"

"No, we just took up shooting. This is our first time here."

"It's a good place. Not many people here tonight, but shooters are a friendly bunch. You'll make friends among the regulars if you keep comin' back."

"That's good to know. We'll definitely be back."

"Say, you see that piece in the paper tonight about the gun turn-in?"

"No, what's that?"

"The police chief talked the city council into puttin' up money for a gun turn-in program. You turn in a gun to the police and they pay you fifty bucks, no questions asked. Supposed to reduce crime by takin' guns out of circulation."

Tom slapped his gun case. "This gun cost me several times that much. How do they expect anyone to turn in any good-quality guns?"

"A lot of the guns turned in'll be junk. Oh, there'll be a few good guns turned in by widows whose husbands never saw to it they learned to shoot. But most of the good guns turned in'll be stolen ones. Just like that, steal a gun, turn it in to the cops with no questions asked, and you got fifty bucks to buy drugs with."

"I guess that beats hocking it at a pawnshop," Tom said. "The pawnshop owner might ask you to prove it's yours."

"Yeah. It turns the cops into a bunch of fences. And you know what's the worst part of it?"

"What's that?"

"The cops'll destroy the guns without trying to find the owners. They find a stolen TV, they try to locate the owner. They recover a stolen car, they get it back to the owner. But they get their hands on a stolen gun, and they melt it down for scrap." He shook his head in disgust.

"Well, good talkin' to you," Towers said. He turned to leave. "I'm goin' to get me another box of ammo." He went out the doorway to the cashiers' area.

Tom turned back to Judith. She fired the gun dry, removed the empty magazine, and brought the target back.

"Hey, not bad, honey." The shots were all in the chest area, and could have been covered by a saucer. "Want another box of ammunition?"

"No, I think I've done all I want for tonight. Are you going to shoot again?"

"I don't think so. I'm satisfied my gun shoots okay. But I want to get back here often enough to get good at it."

"Yes. We've got to keep practicing."

# SEVEN

"Here, King," Judith shouted. The half-grown collie stopped sniffing around the chain-link fence and ran toward her. She gave a biscuit an underhanded toss. The dog snatched it out of the air, gobbled it, wagged his tail, and pushed his nose into her hands, looking for more.

"No more now, King," she said as the raised both hands over her head. Disappointed, the dog approached Tom. Tom squatted down, grabbed the dog's ears, and scratched behind them, as he'd seen Judith do. "Good doggie, King. Good doggie." The dog licked his forearms.

"See, he likes you," Judith said.

"He just likes the salt on my arms."

"Oh, you! It's too bad you never had a dog when you were growing up."

"You're right. I wish I'd had a dog. But where would we have put him? The apartment was too small, and there wasn't any yard. The nearest park was ten blocks away."

"You might have had a small dog."

"I don't think that would've worked either. My best friend Jim's family had a terrier in their apartment. Every time I went over there to play with Jim, the place always smelled of dog, and it was full of dog hairs. I don't see how his mother stood it."

"I guess you're right. It wouldn't have worked. But you missed out on grass and trees and a place to run, too. Maybe a place where you can't have a dog isn't fit for human beings, either."

He laughed. "Maybe so. My father's dream was always to move to a house in the suburbs, with a big lot where us kids could play. By the time he finally could afford it, my older brothers were all grown, and I'd just gotten out of high school. I lived there only a few weeks until I got this job and moved back into town."

"At least he and your mother could enjoy it themselves, even if you kids were grown."

"I don't think they would've enjoyed it much longer. The big yard was getting to be too much for him and mother to take care of. He was talking about moving back to an apartment just before the accident."

Tom fell silent for a moment, a glum expression on his face. He continued to scratch King's ears as though he were on autopilot.

"It still hurts, doesn't it?" Judith asked.

"Yeah. Damn that drunken driver! Why wasn't he in jail? Why did they let him off with a reduced charge so many times? Why was he still driving, even though they'd taken away his license?

"I keep asking myself, what's wrong with this country when law-abiding folks like Mother and Dad have so many restrictions on them, while crooks get away with murder? Dad's barbershop was crawling with inspectors, and he was buried under regulations that told him every move he could make. And yet convicted drunks drive around without licenses. It isn't right!"

He shook his head, knowing there was no answer, and stood up. King tossed his head, ran across the yard, and came back carrying a rubber ball in his teeth.

"He wants you to throw it for him," Judith said.

Tom eyed the saliva-covered ball with distaste, then grasped it and tugged it out of the dog's mouth. He threw it to a far corner of the yard, then wiped his fingers on the grass. King promptly returned with the ball gripped in his teeth. Resigning himself to being a dog-owner, Tom grabbed the slimy ball again and threw it. He kept it up until King finally returned the ball, dropped it on the ground, and flopped down, panting. Tom reached down to scratch the dog's head.

"You've tired him out. That's what you need to do, to keep him in good shape."

"That's okay, so long as he doesn't wear me out too."

"At least with a yard this size, you don't have to take him for a walk."

"Yeah. He'd be tugging at the leash and dragging me around."

With King temporarily satisfied, Tom stood, hands on hips, and slowly scanned the yard. The chain-link fence surrounded the back yard on three sides and connected to the house and the garage. A gate beside the garage allowed him to get in and out with the mower. King could be kept in the house at night. In the morning he could be let out through the sliding glass patio door right into the back yard. With a burglar alarm installed on all the doors and windows, Tom felt the house was as secure as anyone could reasonably ask. And they had their guns as the final defense.

Tom turned to Judith. "How about those flower gardens you want to put in? Should we put a fence around them, to keep King out?"

"Let's wait and see. If King starts digging up the flowers, we can put up some fences."

"I wonder if he'll scare away the squirrels that come in our oak tree?" He pointed to a tree just inside the fence at the back of the yard, whose branches hung over the fence. "But maybe the fence will keep them out anyway."

"I've seen the squirrels traveling up and down the block on the power lines that come through the back alley. They can reach the tree that way, without ever touching the ground or climbing the fence. I don't think King will keep them away. It'll be fun to watch him chase them, though."

Tom headed for the back door, and reappeared in a few minutes, carrying a dish of dog food. "Here, King, time for dinner." He placed the dish in front of the doghouse. The dog immediately ran over, ignored Tom, and started gulping the food. Tom thought, *No wonder Mother always said to eat slowly or I'd look like a dog. I wonder how she knew how a dog eats.*

"Come on, Tom, it's time for our dinner, too," Judith said. He followed her into the house.

# EIGHT

Tom parked the car in the driveway, locked the door, and strode to the fence where King was leaping and bounding about. He reached over the fence.

"Here, King. Good doggie." He scratched King's ears, then rubbed the dog's neck vigorously. As he straightened up, he thought, *Never dreamed I'd see the day when I'd pet my dog before I kissed my wife.*

He unlocked the front door. "I'm home, honey."

Judith's voice came from the kitchen. "Hi!"

He went to the kitchen, where she was seated at the desk. He put his lunch pail on the sink, kissed the back of her neck, and put his arms around her.

She turned her head toward him. "Hi, darling, how was your day?"

"Not bad. Two rush jobs, but we got them on the truck on time. How'd your day go?"

"Same as usual. Tons of mail to sort and route. And then I come home to find our mail full of the month's bills."

She picked up one envelope from the stack. "Did you charge some gas to your oil company credit card while we were visiting my folks the last time?"

"Yeah. Didn't I give you the receipt? I must have left it in my suitcase. I'll get it."

"Don't do it right now. Here's something else. What did you want with a water purifier?"

"What water purifier?"

She handed him a large envelope. The return address read ACME PLUMBING, with a street address in town. In the lower left quadrant of the envelope was the inscription, HERE'S THE WATER PURIFIER INFORMATION YOU ASKED FOR, and the hand-written initials *TJC*.

"I sure never asked for that."

"It's addressed to you."

He reached over her shoulder, brushed his hand across her cheek, then picked up the letter opener. He spilled the contents of the envelope on the kitchen table.

The top sheet was printed in faded dot-matrix letters:

BURN THESE PAPERS AFTER READING THEM. CRUMBLE AND SCATTER THE ASHES.

"Hey! This stuff's from that Justice Cooperative outfit."

Judith was thumbing through the Yellow Pages. "That plumbing company isn't listed here. I'll bet there's no such address as the one on the envelope, either. Those TJC initials must be the giveaway."

"Okay, so they disguised the stuff they sent me. They must not want anyone to know where they are."

She stepped up beside him. "What's it say?"

He spread the pages out on the table and they began reading.

YOUR CASE HAS BEEN REVIEWED. IT IS CLEAR THAT YOU DID NOT RECEIVE JUSTICE FROM THE GOVERNMENT. THE THREAT TO YOUR SAFETY MAY JUSTIFIABLY BE REMOVED. READ THE ATTACHED INFORMATION ABOUT THE JUSTICE COOPERATIVE. IF YOU WISH TO JOIN, FOLLOW THE INSTRUCTIONS ON THE LAST PAGE.

Tom grasped the corner of the page, and gave Judith an inquiring look. She nodded. He moved the first page aside and began to read the next page.

SOME QUESTIONS AND ANSWERS

WHAT IS THE JUSTICE COOPERATIVE?

The Justice Cooperative is a group of people who have been victimized by criminals and denied justice by the legal system. The types of victimization include physical assault, rape, injury, or the death of a close relative. The forms that denial of justice have taken include reducing the seriousness of the charge, inadequate jail sentences, early release from a jail sentence, and probation for repeat offenders.

HOW DO I JOIN THE JUSTICE COOPERATIVE?

You join by requesting the help of the Justice Cooperative in obtaining justice in your case. You must identify the person who victimized you, the nature of the victimization, and the way in which justice failed to be done. Your case will be reviewed to determine that an actual crime was committed against you, that you have correctly identified the guilty party, and that the government failed to do justice. A determination that an actual crime was committed will be based on a finding that the guilty party was convicted in a court of law, or that a prosecutor accepted a plea to a lesser offense. A determination of failure to do justice will be based on a finding that the charge was reduced by too great a degree or that a sentence was too lenient. If the review verifies that you have a valid claim of injustice, you will be admitted to the Justice Cooperative.

WHAT DOES THE JUSTICE COOPERATIVE DO?

The members of the Justice Cooperative repair the government's failure to deliver justice by carrying out justice upon the criminal who victimized you. The usual form of this is execution of the criminal. The execution will be carried out by another member of the Cooperative, at a time when you can fully account for your whereabouts. This execution will be carried out AFTER you have carried out an execution on behalf of some other member of the Cooperative.

ISN'T THIS TAKING THE LAW INTO OUR OWN HANDS?

On the contrary, it is returning the law to its origin. As the Declaration of Independence states, governments are instituted to protect rights, and they derive their just powers from the consent of the governed. If you didn't already have the right to protect yourself against actual or threatened attacks, the government could have no just authority to protect you. If you didn't already have the right to avenge an injustice done to you, the government could have no just authority to punish a criminal. If the government fails to fulfill its function of protecting you, you have every right to reclaim those powers for yourself. Therefore the Justice Cooperative is not usurping any legitimate powers of the government. On the contrary, it is reclaiming the legitimate powers of the citizens because the government has failed in its primary obligation to protect the rights of its citizens and avenge violations of those rights.

WHY DO WE NEED TO RECLAIM OUR RIGHT TO JUSTICE?

Because the government has failed in its obligation to protect us. Sixty-three percent of all violent felony defendants are put back on the streets during their trials. Over ninety percent of all criminal prosecutions result in plea bargains instead of trials. Of those felons who are convicted of a violent crime, forty-seven percent are never sent to jail. Those violent convicts who do go to jail are, on average, released before they serve half their sentences. Forty-five percent of all violent offenders in jail were on probation or parole at the time they committed their latest offense. Over ninety percent of jail inmates are repeat criminals. This is not justice. This is a complete abdication of the government's obligation to protect its citizens and administer justice.

HOW WILL I KNOW THE PERSON I'M TO EXECUTE DESERVES IT?

You will be provided with copies of public records that will verify that the criminal in question deserves execution, and that the government has failed in its obligations. Since these are public records, you may check them for their validity.

HOW SOON WILL I SEE JUSTICE DONE FOR MYSELF?

You will undergo a period of testing to assure the other members of the Cooperative that you have a good chance of carrying out your assigned mission. Once the testing is completed, you will be assigned a mission, and provided with the information you need to carry it out. Once your mission is completed, another member of the Cooperative will be assigned the mission of carrying out justice on your behalf.

WILL I MEET OTHER MEMBERS OF THE COOPERATIVE?

Under no circumstances will you meet other members, or know who else is a member. This is for your own protection as well as for the protection of the other members.

THEN HOW DO I COMMUNICATE WITH THE COOPERATIVE?

All communication from the Cooperative to you will be through mail under false cover. When a reply from you is expected, you will be given a phone number to call.

HOW DO I LET THE COOPERATIVE KNOW I'VE DECIDED TO JOIN?

Tie a red ribbon around a lamppost or tree somewhere in your block, preferably not in front of your own house. Leave it up for 24 hours. Then replace it with a green ribbon. After another 24 hours, remove the green ribbon. You will then be contacted.

REMEMBER TO BURN THESE PAPERS!!!

Tom turned to Judith. "It wouldn't bother me to knock off Harry Grubbs. Knocking off some other crook in return for getting Grubbs killed seems like a fair bargain."

"No!" Her voice was sharp. "If Grubbs comes into this house and you shoot him, you can claim self defense. If you go out somewhere else and shoot somebody, you can call it a fair bargain if you want to, but the police will call it murder. And if you do it as part of this Justice Cooperative, that's conspiracy to commit murder. If you join, you're an accomplice to every murder they commit."

"You've been working in that law office too long, Judy. You sound like a lawyer. Look, I'd be doing this for you. You're the one he hurt."

"And you're the one who feels like you let me down. Well, you didn't. You did everything anyone could reasonably ask. We just had bad luck. Now we've prepared ourselves. We have a sturdy house, we have a dog, we have guns and we know how to use them. That's enough. Grubbs is not likely to get away with repeating his attack. Don't go putting yourself on the wrong side of the law.

"Look, Tom, I don't want to spend the rest of my life married to a jailbird. Or worse yet, be widowed by the gas chamber. Grubbs got away with a light sentence. You wouldn't be so lucky. Remember what Mr. Baron said. The law is stacked against the law-abiding people."

"I'm not worried about dealing with Grubbs here," Tom responded. "What about outside the house? Do we spend the rest of our lives dodging him? What happens when we have kids going to school? Do we have to worry about what he'll do to them?"

"We'll go on being careful for now," she replied. "As for the safety of our children, we'll cross that bridge when we get to it."

Tom remained silent for a long moment. He opened his mouth to speak, then clamped it shut again. He grabbed the papers from the Justice Cooperative and tore them into shreds.

"I'm taking these out back. I'll burn them in the barbecue grill."

"Don't forget to crumble the ashes. Simply having those papers could be evidence against you."

# NINE

Tom slammed the car door and ran to the fence. Judith was in the back yard throwing a ball to King.

"Judy! Get cleaned up! We're going out tonight!"

"What's going on?"

"I got tickets to the *Alabama* concert at the Arena."

"But they were all sold out when you called. I hope you didn't pay a scalper for them."

"A guy in the shop had two tickets. His wife's folks dropped in for a surprise visit, and he couldn't go. He sold 'em to me for what he paid."

"That's wonderful. Give me a few minutes to change. I'll put supper back in the fridge and we can eat on the way there."

Half an hour later they were on their way.

"Where do you want to eat?" Tom asked. "A TACO KING sound okay?"

"Sure. I'd go for some Mexican food."

"Okay, there's one a few blocks farther along."

He pulled into the restaurant's parking lot. He looked around the lot, then picked a parking space that was under a light and as close to the entrance as possible. Before opening the car door, he carefully scanned the parking lot for anyone standing around or looking suspicious. Satisfied, he got out, locked his door, and opened the door for Judith.

Inside, they went to the counter, looked over the menu posted on the back wall, and placed their orders. Tom then picked a table where he could face the door, and could watch his car through the window.

Shortly their ticket number was called, and Tom retrieved their meals and brought the tray to their table.

Judith asked, "How much time do we have?"

"Over an hour yet. The Arena is only about twenty minutes drive from here. We don't have to hurry. They won't even open the doors for another half hour."

Judith finished a taco, picked up another, then put it down. "Tom, is something wrong? You've hardly looked at me since we sat down."

"Sorry, Judy. I'm keeping an eye on the door and on our car. I don't want any surprises."

"Don't let this business of watching around you become an obsession. You can't let it dominate your life."

"I won't. I'm just being careful."

He picked up a taco, bit into it, and said, "Hey, these are pretty good. Lots of chili powder in them. I like that."

"I thought you would."

"Too much for you?"

"I wouldn't use that much if I were making them, but they're okay. I like them."

"Good. Maybe we ought to try a Chinese place some time. They usually give you a choice of how much hot stuff you want."

"That sounds like a good idea. I like Oriental food. I recall Dad saying that's one of the things he missed after coming home from Vietnam. Mother tried to cook some Oriental meals from time to time, but somehow she never got it quite like Dad remembered it. Every once in a while we'd go to a Chinese restaurant so he could have the real thing."

Tom sipped at his coffee. "Not bad coffee for a fast food place.

Certainly better than what I get out of the coffee machine at work. Not as good as yours, though," he added hastily. She grinned but said nothing.

Their meal finished, they walked out. Tom stopped just outside the door and looked over the parking lot carefully. Then he headed straight for their car. He kept looking around as he opened the door for Judith.

Once on the street, he felt he could actually relax. Traffic was light enough not to be a problem, and they were on a major street. It wasn't likely they could be attacked there.

At the Arena he drove through the parking lot, seeking a well-lighted spot near an entrance. He finally found one and parked the car.

Inside the arena, they located their seats. Tom looked around at the crowd.

"Hey, these people are really dressed up for this show," he said. "Look at all the cowboy boots." He lifted up one sneaker-shod foot. "I almost feel out of place. And look at all the blue jeans, and the loud shirts. And even a few bandannas."

"But no black hats."

"Right. This is *Alabama*, not Garth Brooks."

Judith stood up and looked around, then turned to Tom.

"Where were we sitting the night we met?"

Tom pointed. "Right over there, I think."

"That's right. I recall it being near the concession stand." She chuckled. "I remember you asking me if I'd like a beer."

"Yeah, you said you'd rather have a Coke."

"I wasn't going to accept a beer from a total stranger, but you looked kind of cute and I didn't want to turn you off." She smiled at him.

"I'm glad," he replied. "That concert ticket was the luckiest ticket I ever bought. Meeting you was even better than winning the lottery."

She smiled and reached out to brush her hand across his. "That was a Hank Jr. concert, wasn't it? If he ever comes back here, we ought to go." She laughed. "Never would have guessed

I'd think of a Hank Jr. concert as romantic. You know, it's a shame this is the first time we've been back here since then. We ought to come here more often. There's lots of other good shows here."

"Right. We need to get out more often. But I need the overtime and the money, too."

The warm-up act came out on the stage and went into their first number.

Tom exclaimed, "Hey, that's real foot-stompin' music."

"Right. I'd like to square dance to that. You ever do any square dancing?"

"Nope. We never even heard of it where I lived."

"When I was in high school we had square dances almost every Saturday during the winter. I miss that."

"Well, maybe we can find some square dancing around here. I guess I could learn."

After a few more numbers the main act came on stage. They began with their latest hit. The crowd roared its approval, and began to clap in time to the music. By the time the performers broke for intermission, the crowd was in a lively mood.

As people around them got up, Tom turned to Judith. "Excuse me, ma'am, would you like a beer?"

She laughed. "Yes, I guess by now I know you well enough to let you buy me a beer."

He got up and headed for the concession stand. There was a long line, but it seemed to be moving rapidly.

The man behind him remarked, "Did you see the ruckus in the parking lot just before the concert?"

"No. What happened?" Tom asked.

"Bunch of punks tried to crash the gate. Looked to me like they was high as a kite. The cops stopped 'em. One of 'em pulled a knife. He didn't last long. A cop poked him with a flashlight and he just sort of folded up."

"Good. I don't want some punks spoiling the concert. I came here for a good time, not to see a fight in the stands."

He got two paper cups of beer and a bag of pretzels. He carefully threaded his way back through the crowd, trying to avoid slopping the beer or dropping the pretzels.

"Here, honey."

He sat down and Judith held his beer while he tore open the plastic bag of pretzels with his teeth. Then he held out it to Judith.

They had just finished their beer and pretzels when the musicians returned to the stage. Again the crowd let out a roar.

Tom remarked, "They sure like these guys, don't they?"

"Why not? They're making good music. I'm really glad you were able to get tickets. I'm having a great time."

"Too bad Bob couldn't use the tickets. I'll have to let him know tomorrow what he missed."

"Don't make him feel bad. Next time he might sell his tickets to someone else instead of to you."

Finally the concert was over. The crowd roared and clapped through two encores, then began to leave. As he and Judith left the Arena, Tom scanned the parking lot. No sign of any problems. Still, he led Judith directly to the car, got in quickly, and locked the doors.

They arrived home without incident. Tom checked the front of the house. Everything seemed in order. At the front door, he found that the burglar alarm was still set, as he'd left it. No one had tried to break in. He opened the door, to King's enthusiastic greeting. Everything was fine. His second line of defense was working.

Judith remarked, "Better let King run in the back yard a bit before we close up for the night."

"Okay."

He slid the patio door open. King rushed out and quartered the yard, sniffing here and there. Tom stood and idly looked around the neighborhood. Everything seemed quiet. The night was clear, with a crescent moon. A slight breeze rustled the leaves of the oak tree. All in all, it had been a good evening. He thought, *Maybe this is going to work out after all. So long as we're careful, we shouldn't have any problems. Judy was right. I don't need the Justice Cooperative.*

# TEN

Tom wriggled his way under the front bumper of his car and brought his head next to the left front wheel. He grabbed a rag, reached up and wiped the dirt off a grease fitting. He coupled the grease gun to it, and pumped the handle until grease started to ooze out of the joint. He wiped the excess grease on the rag, and repeated the process on the next fitting. Then he squirmed sideways and greased the right wheel.

He twisted his head around to look at the crankcase drain. The oil had stopped dripping out. He groped around, found the drain plug, and screwed it back in. He groped again, picked up a wrench, and tightened the plug. Then he put the cap on the jug holding the used oil. He'd drop that off at the recycling center in the morning.

He slid out from under the car, grabbed a new oil filter and the filter wrench, and crawled back under. He clamped the wrench around the old filter, loosened it, then twisted it off by hand. He started the new filter onto the threads, and spun it until it was tight.

He crawled out once more, stood up, and wiped his hands on a rag. He went into the garage, loaded his arms with five quart jugs of oil, and returned to the car. As he poured the oil into the filler neck, he thought, *Too bad Judy's car isn't ready for an oil change, too. I could do 'em both and not get dirty twice.*

As the last can of oil emptied itself, he glanced down the street. *Hey, that's Judy's car. She's back early from the grocery. And how come she's drivin' so fast?*

Judith squealed the brakes as she came to the driveway. The car lurched over the curb and screeched to a stop next to Tom's.

Judith flew from her car and left the door standing open as she cried in a shrill voice "I saw him! I saw him!" She ran to Tom, clasped him fiercely, and burst into sobs.

"Easy, honey, you'll get grease all over yourself. Who did you see?"

"Grubbs! Harry Grubbs!"

"You're sure? Where?"

"Yes, I'm sure. At the grocery." She choked back another sob. "He was standing at the end of the aisle. He was already watching me when I saw him. He had the most evil look on his face I've ever seen."

"What did you do?"

"I left my cart sitting there and ran. I got in my car and came straight home."

"Did he follow you?"

"I don't know! I don't know!" She gasped for breath, then spoke more slowly. "I didn't even think about watching to see if he followed me. I just wanted to get back here as fast as I could." She burst into sobs again.

"Take it easy, honey. We can defend ourselves here."

"Yes, but we've got to have groceries." She sniffed, then pulled a tissue out of her purse, and wiped her eyes.

"I'll get cleaned up, and we'll go back and get them."

He went into the garage, pulled a wood chisel off the rack, switched on the grinder, and with a shower of sparks, put a sharp edge on it. *There, it may look funny, me carrying a big wood chisel, but it'll make a good spear. Wish I could carry a gun, but this'll have to do.*

Minutes later, Judith was at the wheel of her car, heading back to the grocery. As she pulled into a parking space, Tom slid the chisel up his left sleeve, with the handle at the heel of his hand. *I won't be able to bend my left arm, but maybe nobody'll notice.*

They found the cart where she'd left it.

"Any sign of Grubbs?" Tom asked.

She looked around carefully. "I don't see him anywhere. Maybe he left when I did."

Tom looked at the contents of the cart. "Anything in here that needs to be cooled?"

"No, I hadn't gotten to the meat or the eggs yet."

"Okay, you just keep on going, and I'll walk behind you and watch for him."

They finished the shopping with no sign of Grubbs, then returned home. Once in the house, Judith collapsed into a chair.

"Could you bring the groceries in, Tom?"

"Yeah, I'll get them. You just take it easy."

He brought the last bag into the kitchen, then returned to the living room, where Judith was still slumped in a chair.

"You okay now, honey?"

"I guess so. But that was a shock. For a moment I was just paralyzed. I couldn't move. Then I wanted to scream, but couldn't. Then after what seemed like forever, with him staring at me the whole time, I just turned and ran."

"We're safe here. You just rest. I think there's still a pizza in the freezer. I'll warm that up and we can eat. And after this, I guess I'd better go to the grocery with you. You shouldn't have to risk running into him by yourself."

"I hate to burden you with the shopping," she replied.

"No help for it. It's part of what that judge talked about at the Self Defense Academy. We just have to watch where we go, and not be predictable."

# ELEVEN

Judith cleared the last of the dinner dishes from the table, then spoke.

"Tom, I've got to make a decision tonight about my job."

Tom took a sip from his coffee cup and put it down on the saucer. "What's that, honey? Something wrong at your office?"

"No. Just the opposite. Mr. Abernathy, our office manager, told me today I could have a promotion. The firm would pay for me to take a word processing course. If I did well, they'd transfer me to the word processing section. I told him I'd let him know tomorrow if I'll do it."

"Do you want the job?"

"Yes. I'd like it. It'd pay better than being a mail clerk, and the job'd be more interesting."

He moved his chair back and turned to face her.

"It sounds like something you could always use, too. What's the problem?"

"I'd have to take the course at the community college downtown. Three nights a week for three weeks. I took a course there once, several years ago. American literature. I liked the course, but the college is in a pretty run-down neighborhood. There's not enough parking space on campus. Lots of times I had to park on the street off campus." She paused for a moment. "And Tom, I'm afraid. I don't want to be walking around there at night, thinking Harry Grubbs may be lurking in the next alley, or that he's broken into my car and is waiting for me."

He paused in thought for a moment. "If you turn down this chance for a promotion, they probably won't ever give you another one."

"That's what I thought, too."

"Okay, so we've got to find a way to get you to and from the college safely. Then you can take the course, get the promotion, and be back on your normal schedule."

"But how can we do it?"

"What time is the class?" He asked.

"Seven-thirty to nine-thirty."

"Then I guess I'd have to take you to and from the class. Even if I have to work overtime, I'm hardly ever that late."

"What will you do while I'm in class?"

"I'll drop you off at the door to your class building, find someplace to park, and then pick you up at the door after your class. It's only for three weeks. I can manage that."

"But will you be safe yourself while you're waiting in the car? What if you have to park off campus?"

"I'll have my gun with me."

"But that's against the law! You don't have a permit to carry a gun, and without a permit you're not allowed to have a loaded gun in your car."

"No one will ever know I have a gun unless I have to use it. And then, Mr. Baron had it right. I'd rather be tried by twelve than carried by six. I'd rather take my chances explaining to a jury why I carried a gun without a permit than have you call the undertaker."

• • •

Tom waited at the exit from the campus, looking for an opening in traffic. *All this traffic must be because it's class change time,* he thought. As he waited, he looked around. The area did look run-down. Broken bottles on the sidewalk. A few trash cans, all overflowing. Scraps of paper blowing around. A couple of houses with the windows boarded up. *It looks bad enough in twilight. I sure wouldn't want Judy walking around here after dark.*

Finally there was a break in traffic. He pulled out, headed down the street, and then made a turn that took him to the McDonald's he'd spotted earlier.

*Wouldn't you know it. The first day of Judy's class, I have to work overtime and barely make it home in time to take her.*

He'd called from the plant to let Judith know he'd be later than usual. She'd microwaved a TV dinner and eaten it before he got home.

He pulled into the restaurant's parking lot and got in line at the carryout window. He inched forward, following the cars ahead. He finally reached the window.

"Cheeseburger, small fries, and a vanilla 'shake."

*Judy'd have a fit if she heard that. She'd say all that fat isn't good for my heart. It probably isn't, but I like it. I guess I'm glad she cares, though.*

He took the bag of food and drove to a parking space. The aroma of grilled hamburger filled the car. He opened the bag and began to eat. *Maybe this stuff isn't good for me, but it sure smells good. Nothing like the smell of a hamburger to make a guy hungry.*

He finished the meal, tossed the remains in the trash barrel, and drove back toward the campus. He had over an hour to wait yet. After driving around several blocks, he found a parking spot and pulled in.

He pushed the seat back, picked up the evening paper he'd grabbed before he left the house, and started reading. The headlines were about the latest Mideast crisis. He read the first paragraph of the story, decided it didn't affect him, and turned the page. The City section had the news that was a lot closer to home. The headlines were all too familiar.

"STORE OWNER BEATEN AND ROBBED"

"CLERK SHOT IN HOLDUP"

"TEENAGER SLAIN IN GANG TURF BATTLE"

"DRUG BUST NETS THREE SUSPECTS"

*Wait, here's one that's different.*

"STORE CLERK SHOOTS ROBBER"

He decided to read that one.

Nicholas Stavropoulos, owner of NICK'S QUICK SHOP, shot and wounded a robber late last night. Stavropoulos was getting ready to close his convenience store when a man came in, held a knife to Stavropoulos's throat, and demanded the contents of the cash register. Stavropoulos opened the cash drawer, but came up with a .38 revolver instead of money. He fired twice, wounding the robber. The suspect, William Flowers, no fixed address, was treated at Mercy Hospital for gunshot wounds. He has been charged with attempted robbery. According to police records, Flowers has been charged with robbery several crimes, usually pleading guilty to a lesser charge. He has served a total of three years in the state penitentiary.

Stavropoulos, who came to the United States in 1960, said, "I fought both the Nazis and the Communists in Greece. I wasn't going to let this guy get away with threatening me."

Police Chief Harold Cates stated that Stavropoulos's gun has been seized as evidence. Prosecutor Thomas Benning stated that no decision has yet been made about whether to file charges against Stavropoulos. Benning noted that even if no criminal charges are filed, Flowers still has the right to file a civil suit against Stavropoulos, charging use of excessive force.

*Well, score one for the good guys. Too bad he didn't kill that sonuvabitch. Then the crook couldn't sue him. And what's he gonna do now that the cops have his gun? It'll take him a week to get a new one. Until then he's cold meat for any other crooks who come to his store. Hope he has another gun stashed away somewhere.*

Tom suddenly became aware of a car standing beside him. Startled, he almost reached for the gun he'd placed under the seat when he spotted the shield on the side that identified it as a police cruiser. He rolled down his window.

"What is it, officer?"

"Is there something wrong, sir? Are you having car trouble?"

"No. My wife's in class at the college. I'm just waiting to go pick her up."

"Very well, sir. We're just checking."

"Thanks for checking. This looks like a pretty tough neighborhood."

"It is. We get several calls here every night. It's not really a good place for the students."

He rolled the window up as the police cruiser drove off.

*It's a good thing the cops are patrolling around here. That might cut down attacks on the students.*

Then he had another thought. *Wait a minute. That cop never asked for my ID. I could be Harry Grubbs, sitting here in Judy's car waiting for her, and they'd never know anything was wrong until they found her body.*

Then another thought came to him. *But do I really want the cops asking everybody for ID, and stopping everybody they meet on the street? That's no way to live either.*

He shook his head. *Even running the country like a jail wouldn't stop crime. In jails they still have beatings and killings and rapes. They even have drugs in jails. The cops can't do the whole job, not even by clamping on all kinds of restrictions. The only way we can be free to move around is if we can defend ourselves against the crooks.*

He glanced at the clock on the dashboard. *Time to go pick up*

*Judy.  It's gettin' too dark to read anyway.*

# TWELVE

Tom marked the pillar with a pencil, then unrolled the steel tape and measured the distance from the floor to the pencil mark.

"What're you doin' that for, Tom?" Anderson, one of his helpers, asked. "You already measured it once."

"A rule I learned when I was an apprentice. 'Measure twice, cut once.'"

"But you ain't cuttin', you're drillin'."

"Same idea. No point in goin' to all this work, then havin' that OSHA guy tell me to move 'em again."

The assistant foreman, Sven Gunderson, nodded in approval. "Okay, Tom. Drill those holes, and we'll hang this fire extinguisher. Only one more extinguisher to go. Then we can get back to the work that brings in the money.

"Damn stupid jerk. Those fire extinguishers've been hangin' at that height for twenty years now and nobody ever had any problem with 'em. Now this inspector comes in and says we got to raise 'em by three inches. That's what the OSHA regs say. Occupational Safety and Health Administration? Hah! Official

Stupidity and Harassment Administration, if you ask me."

Tom finished hanging the last extinguisher, then folded the stepladder and took it back to the tool crib.

"Okay, Tom," Sven said. "Honda needs those parts, and their truck'll be here at five-thirty. Can you make up for the time we lost movin' those damn' fire extinguishers?"

Tom glanced at the wall clock. "Yeah, we can make it, so long as the foundry gets the castings to me right away."

"Here they come now," Gunderson said. He pointed at a fork-lift bringing a pallet loaded with castings into the machine shop.

"Okay, let's get started." Tom got his helpers busy loading castings on the conveyor while he completed the setup on the first machine in the cell.

*This is going to be tricky. Wish I could have finished the setups on the machines before I started on the fire extinguishers. The parts could've been running through while I was moving fire extinguishers. But that guy from OSHA said it had to be done right away or he'd fine the company. After all, he says, it's for my safety. Don't want anybody bumping those fire extinguishers if we have to evacuate this place in a hurry. Wish that was my biggest worry. If the government'd do its job of keeping Judy and me safe from Harry Grubbs and people like him, I'd be willing to take my chances on bumping a fire extinguisher.*

Finally the parts were through all the machines in the cell. Tom called out "Pete! Get your lift over here. We're ready to go!"

Pete wheeled his forklift to the cell, loaded up the pallet of parts, and took them off to the loading dock. The wall clock showed it was just past five.

Gunderson said, "Tom, the packing crew can't handle it all. You want some overtime? Help 'em lash those parts down on the shipping pallets."

"Sure, Sven. I need the money. Besides, after bustin' my back to get 'em done on time, I don't want 'em sittin' on the loading dock while Honda gripes about needin' 'em."

The express truck showed up a few minutes later. Tom, two of his helpers, and the regular packing crew got the last pallet on the truck just before the five-thirty deadline.

Tom grabbed his lunch pail and headed for the parking lot. He stopped at the plant entrance and scanned the lot carefully. The shift was over. Most of the lot was empty. The entire lot was clearly visible. The only people in sight were a couple of workers getting into their cars. There didn't seem to be any threats visible.

*It's summer. There's still plenty of light when I get off work. Come winter, though, it'll be dark even at regular quitting time. I'll have to be even more careful then.*

Once in his car, he had to decide on a route. *I'm late getting off work. If I take the longer route down South Street, I'll be even later getting home. But I took the direct route on Market yesterday. I've got to avoid following a pattern. Especially a pattern that says I'll take the short route on days I'm late. Okay, South Street it is.*

He turned onto the street that led to his subdivision, then entered the cul-de-sac on which his house was located.

*This business of changing routes is silly. I live on a dead-end street with only one entrance. If anyone wants to ambush me, they can do it here at the entrance, no matter what route I take. They could even park in the 7-11 lot and I'd never know they were laying for me until it was too late.*

He slowed as he approached his house, and turned into the drive. *Something's wrong. Judy's car is in the drive, but King's not in the back yard.*

He hastened to the front door, stuck his key in the lock, and was about to open it when he noticed the alarm light was on.

*Why's the alarm set at this hour, and with Judy home?*

He pulled the barrel-shaped alarm key from his pocket, disarmed the alarm, unlocked the door, and entered.

"Judy! I'm home! What's going on?"

King bounded into the hallway, followed by Judith, who was holding her gun at chest-ready position.

"Oh, thank God you're home, Tom," she burst out. "Lock the door and set the alarm."

"What is it, Judy?"

For answer, she handed him a sheet of paper. On it were letters evidently cut and pasted from newspaper headlines, ransom-note style.

## i KnOw WhEre yoU ArE

"I found this in the mailbox when I got home. It has to be from Harry Grubbs. He's taunting us!"

"Okay, this is the last straw. We take this to the police. Let's go!"

• • •

Tom parked in a visitors' space at the police station, and entered.

The desk sergeant asked, "What can I do for you?"

"We've received a threatening note." He handed over the message.

The sergeant examined the message briefly. "Lieutenant Callahan is the only detective on duty this shift. He'll be with you in a couple of minutes. Just have a seat." He pointed to a row of chairs.

"Thank you."

Shortly a man in civilian clothes approached them. "I'm Detective Lieutenant Dave Callahan, folks. Sergeant Black tells me you have a threatening note. Come back to my desk and let me hear your story."

He led them to a battered wooden desk near the wall, grabbed a couple of chairs from nearby desks, and pulled them over.

"Sit down, folks. What's the problem."

Judith spoke up. "I'll give it to you quickly, and then you can ask for details about any part you want. We were attacked by a criminal who was then put in jail because of our testimony. He threatened to get revenge on us when he got out. He was released a little over a month ago. I know he's been stalking us because I've seen him. Just last week I spotted him watching me in the grocery store where I often stop on the way home from work. Today when I got home I found this note in the mailbox."

Callahan examined the message. "Who was the criminal?"

"A man named Harry Grubbs."

Callahan seemed to recognize the name, but didn't comment on it. He finally asked, "How do you know this is from him? It's not signed."

"It doesn't need to be signed," Tom said. "I know who's after my wife."

"Did anyone else see him when you say he was in the grocery store? Did you point him out to anyone who might identify him from a mug shot?"

"No. All I could think of was getting out of there." She then recounted the incident in detail. "He was gone when we got back."

"I see. All we have, then, is your word that you saw him."

At that moment the station house door banged open. Three uniformed policemen entered, dragging a man whose left shirtsleeve had been torn off and whose upper arm had been splinted and bandaged.

"Oh-oh," Callahan said, "this looks like an emergency. Excuse me, folks, I'll be back as soon as I can."

Callahan walked toward the group and spoke to the prisoner. In the small room, his voice carried to Tom and Judith.

"Well, Sam, did you finally get caught in a drug bust?"

"I'm clean, Callahan. You won't find no drugs on me."

The detective turned to the police sergeant in charge of the detail.

"What happened?"

"We got a call about a shooting at the Empire Bar and Grill."

"I know the place. Lots of wholesale drug deals go down there, but never any stuff actually on anyone."

"When we got there, Sam here," the sergeant nodded toward the prisoner, "had just emptied a Ruger .357 Magnum into another drug dealer and his 'muscle.' Sam claims to have gotten the word that the other dealer was going to, quote, 'take him out.' Evidently some dispute over territory.

"Sam was in the Empire when the other dealer came in. According to several patrons, the other dealer called him some unprintable names, knocked his hat off, then left. According to the bartender, Sam waited a while, then when he evidently thought it was safe, he walked out the door. He walked right into an ambush. He took a slug in his left arm. He drew his gun, dispatched the other drug dealer, who was hiding behind a car, and emptied his gun at the two other guys who were shooting at him. They got away, but we have descriptions. One may be wounded.

"We took Sam here to the ER at Mercy Hospital. They pulled a slug out of his arm and bandaged him. Here's the slug. Nine millimeter hardball. It broke a bone in his upper arm, but didn't penetrate beyond that. He's lucky it broke his arm. If it'd missed the bone, it'd have gone through his chest."

Callahan spoke. "Sam, where'd you get the gun?"

"Bought it on the street. A hundred bucks for the gun and twelve bullets."

"The gun's probably stolen. Very convenient for you. No waiting period, no ID, no background check, no nothing. And at a price much lower than you'd pay a gun dealer. You want to tell us who sold it to you?"

"Don't give me no jazz 'bout waitin' periods, Callahan. If I hadn't bought that gun, I'd be dead right now. The guy who sold it to me did *you* a favor. You rather be investigatin' my murder instead of my self-defense shootin'?"

"Speaking personally, Sam, and not for the Department, I don't really care which of you two drug dealers shot the other. Either way, the city temporarily has one less drug dealer, and I have a shooting to investigate."

He turned to the officer in charge. "Book him, give him his one call to his lawyer, and lock him up. Write up your reports, and I'll open the investigation. It doesn't look like there'll be much to investigate, though, unless we can catch those other two."

The officer shook his head and replied, "His lawyer will have him back out on the street before I've finished filling out the paperwork on him."

"I know, but we've got to do it anyway."

He returned to where Tom and Judith were sitting.

"Sorry for the interruption, folks. We get at least a couple of these every night." He sat down at the desk.

"Interesting problem Sam faced there," Callahan went on. "Apparently his other two attackers were still on their feet when his gun was empty. He'd never practiced one-handed reloading. With his left arm shattered, he couldn't reload. The additional six rounds in his pocket were totally useless to him. If our guys hadn't arrived when they did, he'd be dead too. Probably no great loss.

"Well, at least it takes two drug dealers out of action, and takes a gun off the street. Sam'll be locked up for a while, and the gun'll be melted down."

Tom thought, *That guy at the gun range was right. The cops know that gun was stolen, but they won't even try to return it to its owner. They'll destroy it.* However, he said nothing.

"Now," Callahan continued, "about your problem. I'm not disputing the truth of what you've told me, Mrs. Borden. You have to realize, though, that you haven't given me much to go on.

"You may actually have seen Harry Grubbs in the grocery store. Even if you did, he has a perfect right to be there. He's served his sentence and been freed under court order. And in any case, it'd be your word against his. You don't have any other witnesses.

"As for this message, Mrs. Borden," he pointed at the paper, "I have only your word that you found it in your mailbox. I'll have it checked for fingerprints just in case. But Grubbs isn't stupid. If he actually prepared it, he probably wore gloves. Only your prints will show on it. His lawyer would say you made it up to try to get him, and you'd have the expense of fighting a lawsuit claiming you fabricated evidence against him. Even if you won, could you afford it? And if you lost, could you afford that?"

Wordlessly, she nodded in the negative.

"Okay then," Callahan went on, "the best advice I can give you is to watch very carefully. If you see him again, try to get witnesses. Then go to court and request a restraining order and a peace bond, for him to stay away from you." He stood up. "And I'll let you know if the fingerprint lab finds anything. We'll need your prints, Mrs. Borden, and yours as well, Mr. Borden. If it's convenient for you, they can take your prints right now."

Judith remained silent through the fingerprinting, the walk to the car, the drive home, and the walk to the house.

Once inside the house, she finally spoke.

"Tom, I can't take any more of this. He's stalking me. He's playing cat-and-mouse. I can't live with this house becoming a bunker, where I carry a gun around all the time I'm home. I can't go on watching behind every tree and jumping at every shadow when I go out. *I just can't take it.*" She put her hands over her face and started to sob.

Tom stood silently for a moment, then said, "You got any red ribbon in your sewing basket?"

She swallowed, then said in a small voice, "Yes. And some green ribbon, too."

# THIRTEEN

"Some more coffee, Tom?" Judith's mother asked. "How about you, Jim?  Sally?"

They were seated on the front porch of Judith's parents' house, just having finished breakfast, and looking forward to a Fourth of July with her family.

"Yes, thank you," Tom replied. "I could use another cup."

"Still have some, Mom," Jim said as he held up his mug.

"No more, thanks, Mom," Sally said.

As she went back into the house, Judith's father said, "How do you like your new job, Judy?"

"Just great, Dad. It's much more interesting than my old one was. Just sorting mail, day after day, got pretty boring."

"Back when I was in the 'Nam, we used to say that the most powerful man in the Company was the clerk in the mailroom. He decided where all the official correspondence went."

"I'm afraid that doesn't work in my law office," she replied. "I had to get each letter to the right attorney. Routing it wrong could have meant missing a filing date or something like that. It was important to get it right the first time."

"Is the new job any easier?"

"Actually it's even more critical, but the pressure is less. I get a hand-written draft or something from one of the attorneys, then I have to type it up. Or I may get a marked-up draft they want changed. But I know where it's supposed to go, and I know how fast it has to be done. So far they haven't given me any unreasonable deadlines."

As Judith's mother returned with the coffee, a faint sound of drumbeats came from up the street.

"Sounds like the parade is starting," her father said.

"How come you're not in it, Dad?" Tom asked.

"This year the VFW is providing the color guard. The Legion's turn was last year. I was with the color guard then. I'll be back in it next year, when it's the Vietnam Vet's turn. Then I get another year off when the Gulf Wars guys take their turn."

The parade came around the bend in the street. It was led by the color guard. Judith's father snapped to Attention as the flag passed. Tom set his coffee cup down carefully and stood up.

The color guard was followed by a convertible carrying the parade marshal. A hand-written sign stuck on the side of the vehicle bore his name.

The local high school band came next, with the drum major in front, walking backwards and keeping time with a baton. A row of snare-drum players kept up a steady beat. The rest of the band members simply held their instruments.

"Back when I was in school," Judith's father growled, "they played those horns while they was marching. Kids have it too easy nowadays."

Tom suppressed a smile. His father-in-law might be right, but it still sounded funny. *When I have kids*, he thought, *I'll probably tell them how easy they have it compared to when I was young, too. That is, if Judy and I ever get things straightened out so we can have kids.*

The band was followed by a series of convertibles carrying local politicians.

"You know it's an election year," Judith's father said. "The parade is about twice as long as other years. Those politicians are just hypocrites. They want to ride in a Fourth of July parade as part of their election campaign, but when they get in office, they vote more taxes on us than George the Third ever put on the American colonies."

"That isn't all they do," Jim said. "They keep taking away our rights, little by little. Sneaking things into bills, then saying they didn't know it was there. Liars!

"Say, Dad, what ever happened about that gun registration thing your police chief wanted?"

"The city council voted it down."

"That's good."

"Yeah, but by only one lousy vote. Five to four. Of the nine people on the council, four of them wanted to turn my right to own a gun into a privilege, something I had to ask their permission for.

"One of the votes for gun registration came from the councilman from this ward. I'm going to see he has opposition next time he's up for election. I'll run myself if I can't get anyone else to. He's going to be sorry for that vote. Even if he's re-elected, it's going to cost him money he didn't expect to spend."

The last unit in the parade went by, and Judith's father sat down again. Tom picked up his coffee cup and sat down.

Judith's mother turned to Jim. "We need some ice for the cooler for this afternoon. Would you get some?"

"Sure."

"Better go before they close down the store."

"Good idea. Want to go, Tom?"

"Sure. Let's go."

• • •

Tom leaned back in the chaise lounge, hamburger in one hand and a bottle of beer in the other.

"These hamburgers are great, Mom. What do you put in them?"

She smiled. "That's my secret. If I told you, you'd make them yourself and not come back."

"I'd see that he came back, Mother," Judith said. "But anyway, keep it a secret, or he'll be wanting me to make them all the time."

"Okay, be that way," Tom growled.

"The bratwursts are done," Jim said, as he picked them off the grill and stacked them on a plate. "Get 'em while they're hot."

Tom heaved himself out of the chair, picked up a bun, inserted a bratwurst, and slathered it with mustard.

*I better stop after this one,* he thought, *or I'll get Judy upset. I know she won't say anything here in front of her folks, but she'll be thinking it. And she's right. I don't want to get overweight.*

He sat back down and started munching on the sausage.

• • •

As the fireworks display ended, Tom and Judith said goodbye to her family and headed for their car.

"Can't you stop by the house before you go back?" Judith's mother asked.

Tom replied, "Sorry, Mom, but we've got to get home. We both have to go to work tomorrow. But we had a great time."

"We'll try to get up for a weekend some time," Judith said.

As Tom maneuvered the car through traffic towards the Interstate, he felt depression settling over him. They'd had a wonderful Fourth of July, free of worries. Now they were heading back into what he thought of as the danger zone. *Will I ever get over this?* he asked himself. *Will life ever be normal for us again?*

# FOURTEEN

Tom tugged at his collar. "This thing is choking me. I hate wearing a suit and tie. The last time I wore a necktie was at our wedding, and the last time before that was when I graduated from high school."

"Oh, quit making a fuss over it," Judith said. "I made a point of buying a clip-on tie, so you can't complain it's the tie that's choking you."

He took another tug at his collar, then shrugged his shoulders to straighten out his coat. He picked a piece of lint off the coat, then glanced at Judith.

*Judy sure knows how to dress. I know she didn't pay much for that outfit, but on her it sure looks classy. I want to look sharp for her sake. I don't want the folks she works with to feel sorry for her, thinking she's married to a slob.*

They entered the hotel lobby and checked the directory, to find the location of the party they were going to.

"Here it is," Judith said, pointing at the board. "Jones, Cohen, and so on. It's in the Pine Room."

"Just what's this party about? Tell me again." Tom said.

"Mr. Hardesty, one of the firm's lawyers, has been admitted as a partner. He's now a full member of the firm."

"And this party is to celebrate that?"

"Yes. For a lawyer, that's an important step forward in his career."

"Okay. I just want to understand what's going on."

They entered the ballroom where the party was already in progress. People were milling about, circulating between the buffet and the bar.

A short, balding man stepped toward them. "Good evening, Judy. I'm glad you could make it."

"Good evening, Mr. Abernathy. Tom, this is the office manager. My husband Tom."

"Glad to meet you, Mr. Borden."

"Nice meeting you," Tom replied.

Abernathy said, "Your wife has been doing excellent work in the word processing section. I understand you went to considerable trouble to make sure she could take the training course."

"I'm glad to know she's doing well. I wanted to do what I could to help her."

After some further small talk with Abernathy they excused themselves and stepped up to the bar. "I'll have a beer," Tom said. He turned to Judith. "What would you like, honey?"

"I'll have a glass of white wine."

They carried their drinks toward the buffet. Judith spoke to a man standing there.

"Hello, Mr. Cohen. Tom, this is Mr. Saul Cohen. He's the criminal lawyer I mentioned."

"Good to meet you, sir."

"Nice meeting you, Mr. Borden. I think your wife made a good decision to talk to me. If I ever have to defend you in a self-defense shooting, it will be a big help that I already know you."

Another man stepped up. Cohen introduced him. "This is Paul Hardesty, the new member of the firm, and the guest of honor tonight. Paul, you already know Mrs. Borden. This is her husband Tom."

After they exchanged greetings, Hardesty said to Cohen, "I heard you say something about a self-defense shooting. Is that the new client you have?"

"No, this was about the fact that I've agreed to defend the Bordens if they're ever involved in a self-defense shooting."

"Oh. Well, I hate to talk shop at a party, but I don't see you very often at the office. I wanted to ask you how you were planning to handle that new case. Are you going to advise her to plead temporary insanity?"

"I'm not sure yet," Cohen replied. "I may end up doing that, but right now I'm leaning toward a plea of self-defense."

"But how can you get away with that? She walked into a bar, pulled a gun from her purse, and emptied it into her ex-husband. It was as cold-blooded and deliberate a killing as any gang execution."

"You're looking only at the event itself," Cohen replied, "not at what went before it. He had a long history of beating her up before she filed for divorce. Even after the divorce, he got drunk, broke into her apartment, and beat her up again.

"She got a restraining order from the court, but that didn't help any. He kept going to where she worked, and trying to see her. She nearly lost her job when her employer got tired of the guy coming around.

"She bought a gun, and while she was sweating out the waiting period, he broke into her apartment once more. The neighbors called the police when they heard her screaming. The judge fined him only fifty dollars for violating the restraining order. When she finally got her gun, she used it. I think I can convince a jury she had ample provocation."

"But wouldn't a temporary insanity plea be safer?" Hardesty asked. "The odds are you'd get a directed verdict. She'd never even face a jury."

"But then she'd spend months in and out of mental hospitals, being checked out by psychiatrists. And she'd have that insanity judgment hanging over her forever. People would always be wondering, is she stable? Is she going to go berserk again and kill somebody? She'd have a tough time getting another job, especially if it was a position of trust. If I can succeed with a self-defense plea, she's home free. What she did would be seen as justified, and there would be no question about whether she'd slip a cog and shoot someone else."

"Well, maybe, but it's risky."

"I agree it is," Cohen responded. "I may have to recommend an insanity plea if the self-defense case turns out to be weaker than I think it will be. But there are plenty of witnesses to his abusing her, and to his harassing her at her job. In addition, I have witnesses who were at the bar before she showed up, and who will testify that he repeatedly said that he'd, quote, 'get that bitch.' I don't think there's much doubt that she was in real danger."

"But do you really want to succeed with a self-defense plea?" Hardesty asked. "She took the law into her own hands. He wasn't physically threatening her at the time. She searched him out. She made a preemptive attack. We don't want to encourage that sort of thing. We don't want people bypassing the courts and engaging in vigilante justice."

"You're missing something, Paul." Cohen gestured vigorously, nearly spilling his drink. "*The courts failed her*. When her ex-husband violated the restraining order, he wasn't jailed. He wasn't even fined enough to deter future violations. He was turned loose with what amounted to a slap on the wrist, and told not to do it again."

"But even so," Hardesty replied, "nothing he did would warrant capital punishment. She appointed herself judge, jury, and executioner. She carried out a sentence far more severe than anything a court could have imposed. Even if that judge had imposed a proportionate punishment for violating the restraining order, he couldn't have imposed a death sentence."

"True but irrelevant." Cohen started to make a dismissive gesture, hesitated, then finished his drink and handed the empty glass to a waiter.

"She felt threatened," he continued. "In fact, she felt she was in danger of her life. His history shows that her fear was warranted. My argument will be that she didn't have to wait until he came through the door again. She was in danger, and the legal system wasn't protecting her."

"But even if she had to protect herself, couldn't she have gotten a pistol permit in case he attacked, instead of attacking him herself? Sounds as though she fits the requirements of the law perfectly."

"She tried to get a pistol permit."

"Was her application denied?"

"The police wouldn't even give her an application form. Worse yet, the cops have this crazy idea that confiscating the guns in the house will put a stop to violence. So if she'd survived the next beating, the cops would have taken her gun even if she did have a permit.

"It's really stupid. The vast majority of women killed by their husbands or boyfriends are either beaten to death or strangled. The vast majority of men killed by their wives or girlfriends are shot. The gun is the equalizer. It offsets the disparity in strength. All removing a gun really does is disarm the victim. It just means that the next time there's a fight, it's the woman who will end up dead, not the man.

"Anyway," Cohen continued, "I'll argue that she felt sufficiently threatened that she concluded she had to act before she was permanently maimed or even killed."

"You might have a tough time getting a jury to buy that," Hardesty said, a dubious look on his face.

"That's true. I might. If it looks like that, I'll recommend a last-minute change to a plea of temporary insanity. But on the basis of the facts I have available, I think it's worth trying a plea of self-defense."

"Okay, I just wanted to find out what you were planning." Hardesty turned to leave. Cohen turned back to Tom and Judith.

"As you may have gathered, this is going to be an interesting case. I think I can convince a jury that the woman acted in self-defense, but the prosecution will undoubtedly try to make the case Mr. Hardesty was making, that the punishment was too severe for the crime. Of course, I can only recommend a plea to her. She'll have to make the final decision."

Tom spoke. "It sounds as though you're the man we'd want defending us if we ever had to shoot to protect ourselves."

"Thank you for your confidence. It was nice meeting you, Mr. Borden."

Tom and Judith sampled some of the buffet, then Judith introduced him to her co-workers in the word processing section. All were women. Several had their husbands with them.

"Hi," Tom said to one of the men, as he extended his hand. "I'm Tom Borden. That's my wife Judy over there."

"Dan Smith. I'm Carol's husband. What d'you do?"

"Machinist. And you?"

"Drive a beer truck. I make deliveries to bars around town."

Another man joined them. "I'm Pete Hanover. My wife Cindy's standing there with Judy. She just introduced me to her."

"What do you do?"

"Drive a pizza delivery truck."

"Carry-out pizzas?"

"No, I deliver frozen pizzas to groceries."

"Hey," Tom said, "if we could just get you two together, we could have a real party. A truckload of beer and a truck full of pizzas would handle even a bigger crowd than they've got in this room."

"Beer and pizza. Sounds good," Hanover said. "Beer and pizza and a ball game on TV. That's really livin'. Say, did you watch last night's game? How 'bout them Dodgers, huh? Seven to nothin'. They keep that up and they'll go all the way."

"Nah, they won't make it," Smith responded. "Their lead's been shrinkin' ever since the All-Star Game. They'll be in second or third place by the end of the season."

They spent the next several minutes debating the merits of each of the teams. Then Hanover said, "I'll hate to see the end of the baseball season. Football's just not the same."

Smith responded, "Yeah, but fall's when I start doin' things.

That's when the bowling leagues start, and then there's huntin' season. Either of you do any huntin'?"

"Not me," Hanover said.

"Not me either," Tom said, "but I do some pistol shooting."

"Where at?"

"A range on the south side."

"Ever go out to the Deer Hunters Club? They got a pistol match every Sunday afternoon. Combat shootin', not just bangin' away at a target. I've watched 'em a few times while I've been out there for rifle matches. Looks like fun. You ought to try it."

"But I've never hunted deer or anything else."

"You don't have to be a hunter to join. And you don't even have to join to shoot in the matches. Just pay your five bucks entry fee. And if you decide you want to join the Club, I'll sponsor you."

"Maybe I'll give it a try. Where is it?"

Smith gave him the directions, just as Hanover's wife stepped up to the group.

"C'mon, you guys, quit hidin' in a corner and talkin' sports. You need to meet some of the other people here. Right, Judy? Right, Carol?"

As Tom followed her, he noticed a black couple entering the room.

"That's Jenetta Brown," Judith said. "She's the new mail clerk they hired when I was promoted."

She and Tom walked toward the newcomers.

"Hello, Jen, it's good to see you."

"Hello, Judy. This is my husband Sam."

"And this is Tom."

The two men shook hands.

Tom said, "You look about as uncomfortable in that suit and tie as I feel in mine. What kind of work do you do?"

"I'm a carpenter for a building contractor. And yeah, I sure don't wear this kinda clothes on the job."

"And I sure don't wear a necktie in the machine shop where I work. Wouldn't want it to get caught in a lathe or a boring mill."

They both laughed.

"I'm sorry we's late," Sam said, "but I was scared to leave the house."

"What happened?"

"The guy who bought the house down at the end of the block runs the numbers. Every evenin' he got lots of people parkin' in his driveway or on the street. Most of 'em're prob'ly crooks. I tol' the police 'bout him, but they won't do nothin'. Said they didn't have enough cops to go after it 'less it was a crack house. Anyway, after I tol' the police, the guy said he'd get me. There was a big mob at his place tonight, and I didn't want to leave until they was gone."

"Sounds like you picked a bad neighborhood to move into," Tom said.

"Wasn't bad when we moved in. Bunch of FHA houses on that street. People couldn't pay off their loans. FHA took 'em over. We could buy in cheap. The house we bought was a real fixer-upper. Needed lots of work inside. Figured I could do most of it myself. Most of the houses went to people like me. People who got jobs but who can't afford real nice houses. Like me, they seen a chance to buy in to a good house that somebody'd let run down. Fix it up an' you got a nice house. Prop'ty values'd go way up all along the block.

"Then that numbers runner come in. Bought a house cheap. Di'n't bother fixin' it. It's a real eyesore, an' it's runnin' down the value of all the other houses. It ain't right."

"What'd you do to your house?" Tom asked.

"Had a guy paint the outside. I did some carpentry in his house to pay him back. Then Jen 'n' me stripped the walls down to the plaster. It's a real old house. Still got plastered walls, not plasterboard. Patched the plaster 'n' painted the walls, 'n' then I built in some cabinets. Paneled the whole livin' room. Looks real nice now. I even built a cabinet for my huntin' rifles."

Dan Smith had already joined the group. He spoke.

"You do much huntin'?"

"Go to Michigan every year for a deer. Upper peninsula. I

like deer meat. All natch'ral, no preserv'tives." He chuckled.

"Ever go out to Wyoming for some antelope or elk?"

"Not on my pay. Leastways, not while I'm fixin' up a house. You?"

"Not yet, but I keep tellin' myself I'm goin' to go. Ever'body at the Deer Hunters says that's the real challenge."

Judith took Tom by the elbow and gestured toward a woman across the room. "Tom, that's the lawyer who gives me most of my work. You should meet her." They headed across the room.

"Mrs. Stryker, this is my husband Tom."

"I'm pleased to meet you, Mr. Borden. Judy has been doing a fine job for me since she moved into the word processing section."

"Mrs. Stryker does mainly civil rights work," Judy said. "She has a couple of interesting cases now."

"I do indeed. One age discrimination case, and one race discrimination case. In that one, I'm defending a landlord who evicted a minority tenant because the tenant was leaving garbage around. The house was attracting roaches and rats. Naturally the tenant screamed race discrimination. I think we'll win that one easily. The owner had the good sense to videotape the house right after the tenant left, and put a TV set in the middle of one scene. The tape showed the weather channel, with date and time, and the mess all around the TV set. It'll be hard for the tenant to squeak out of that one."

"I'm glad to know Judy's doin' good work," Tom said. "I was real proud of her when she got the promotion."

• • •

At the end of the evening, as they were leaving, Tom spoke. "I don't mean anything against the lawyers you work for, but I felt a lot more at home with the guys who're married to the women you work with. They're more my kind of people."

"Nothing wrong with that, Tom. The other women in the section are more my kind of people than the lawyers are, even the women lawyers. But even so, most of the members of the firm are very nice people. They've been very kind to me, even if they do live on the other side of town."

She lapsed into silence, and seemed preoccupied as they drove home. Finally she spoke.

"I've been thinking about what Mr. Cohen said about that woman client of his. She may be able to plead self-defense. She has witnesses to all kinds of things. But if you were to go and shoot Harry Grubbs, you'd have a tougher time pleading self-defense. We don't have any witnesses. He's made no open threats since he got out of jail. We can't prove that note came from him.

"And if you go shooting someone else, like the Justice Cooperative talks about, you'd have no defense at all. Mr. Cohen would have to have you plead temporary insanity."

"Okay, what do you want me to do? The Justice Cooperative hasn't responded to our green ribbon yet. When they do, should I tell 'em we don't want their help? They'd probably never contact us again, even if we did change our minds.

"And you heard what Mr. Cohen said about that woman. The legal system failed her. They can't have a cop follow her around all the time, and they wouldn't remove the threat. She had to remove the threat herself. We're in the same fix. We have to take care of Harry Grubbs before he takes care of us. We either do it ourselves, or we do it through the Justice Cooperative. We don't have any other choices."

She was silent for a long moment, then said quietly, "I know. I know. We don't have any other choices."

# FIFTEEN

Tom looked at his watch for what must have been the hundredth time. The numbers seemed to creep as they changed. *My watch can't be broke. It wouldn't show anything at all if it was. I never thought a minute was this long.*

It had begun two nights before. When he came home, Judith handed him a letter. On the outside there was a notice advertising a waterbed sale.

"This looks like junk mail," she said, "but I didn't want to open it in case it came from the Justice Cooperative. I looked up that store. They're not in the Yellow Pages."

He opened the envelope. "You're right. It is from them."

CONFIRM THAT YOU RECEIVED THIS MESSAGE BY GOING TO A PAY PHONE AND CALLING THIS NUMBER BETWEEN 7:00 AND 7:15 PM EITHER OF THE FIRST TWO EVENINGS AFTER YOU RECEIVE THIS.

He noted that the phone number was a local one, but didn't recognize the exchange. He continued reading.

LOCATE ALL THE PAY PHONES WITHIN TWO BLOCKS OF YOUR HOUSE. YOU WILL NEED TO MAKE

REPORTS USING THEM. DO NOT USE THE SAME
PHONE TWICE IN SUCCESSION.

FROM TIME TO TIME YOU MAY NEED TO STAND
BY AT A PAY PHONE TO RECEIVE A MESSAGE. YOU
WILL BE INFORMED OF THE LOCATION OF THE
PHONE AND THE TIME TO BE THERE. THE INFOR-
MATION WILL BE CONVEYED IN A "WRONG NUM-
BER" CALL TO YOUR HOME TELEPHONE.

THE ENCLOSED PAGE GIVES A LIST OF BLOCKS
WITHIN THE CITY. TWO DAYS AFTER YOU CONFIRM
RECEIPT OF THIS LETTER, YOU ARE TO DRIVE PAST
THESE BLOCKS BETWEEN THE HOURS OF 8:00 PM
AND 9:00 PM. SEE WHETHER THERE ARE ANY RED OR
GREEN RIBBONS ON LAMPPOSTS OR TREES IN THESE
BLOCKS. USING A PAY PHONE, CALL THE NUMBER
AT THE BOTTOM OF THE PAGE BETWEEN 9:45 PM
AND 10:00 PM THAT NIGHT AND REPORT WHAT YOU
FOUND.

Again, the phone number was a local one.

"I don't know of any pay phones around here besides that
one at the Seven-Eleven. I'll use that to call them tonight. But I
guess I'd better locate some others near here for future use."

"Are you going to make that check for them?"

"I don't see why not. After all, this is just looking for ribbons.
It's no big deal. This must be how they check people out before
they trust them with more information."

"But up to now, Tom, you haven't really taken part in this
conspiracy. This may not seem like a big deal, but legally it commits you. Once you do that, legally you're as guilty as the people
who have already killed someone."

"What choice do I have, Judy? It's this or kill Grubbs myself."

"I know. We've already been over this. We don't have any
other choices. But it still scares me."

• • •

Now he was making the rounds for the Justice Cooperative.

He'd located the blocks on a city map, and plotted a route that took him past them. He had pulled into a convenience store parking lot near the first block on the list, to wait until 8:00 PM.

Finally the hour changed, and he pulled out of the lot. The first one was the even-numbered 300 block on Elm Street.

*That lamp post is clear. So's the next one. How 'bout that tree? Nothing. Wait. What's that? Yep. A red ribbon around that tall tree down the block.*

He made a checkmark on the list, then continued to the next block on the list. He found nothing there. Nor on the next one. He finally completed the survey. Out of ten blocks, two had red ribbons and one a green ribbon.

*Wonder how many people there are joining the Justice Cooperative? Am I the only guy making a survey tonight? Evidently they have leads on ten people that I'm checking out. If this's a typical night, there must be lots of people who can't get justice through the system and are desperate enough to get it for themselves. It shows I'm not alone.*

Having completed the survey, he drove into a convenience store and pulled up next to the pay phone in the parking lot. He dropped in a coin and punched in the number.

"Hello," a male voice said, and repeated the number he'd called.

Tom read off the code number at the top of his list of blocks, then the sequence number of each block on the list, with a "yes" and the color, or a "no," after each number.

"Thank you. You will receive further information by the usual means. Good-bye."

*Click!*

*Well, that was short and sweet. Even if anybody was listening in, they wouldn't learn much. If they were intentionally tapping the wire, though, they'd already know what was going on. I sure hope no cops have found out. Judy was right. I can't back out now. I'm in the game, and I've got to see it through.*

• • •

Two nights later he was back on the streets again, with a new list of blocks to search.

*That first list of blocks they sent me was in pretty decent neighborhoods. This time they're sending me through some pretty crummy places. Hope I don't run into any trouble. This sure would be a bad place to have the car break down.*

The first block on the list had two houses boarded up. The rest looked rundown, with peeling paint, sagging porches, and unkempt lawns. All but one of the street lights were broken. The curbs seemed to be lined with broken glass.

*Wonder what kind of person here needs the help of the Justice Cooperative? Some poor slob like that guy George at the gun training course, who got robbed or whatever, and can't get the cops to do anything?*

He slowly cruised the length of the block. In the dim light it was hard to see the trees and lampposts. He slowed by each one, to let his headlights illuminate it.

*Nothing here. The next block on my list is two streets over.*

The next block was more of the same: rundown houses, broken street lights, broken glass. With one addition. Ahead of him there was a man lurching down the middle of the street, screaming unintelligibly at the top of his voice. Tom crept forward, alternately eyeing the man and looking for colored ribbons. As the man staggered briefly to the left, Tom gunned the engine and slipped past him. The man appeared to give no notice, continuing to lurch down the street. Tom was about to turn to another block when he spotted something at the end of the street.

*That last tree. It has a green ribbon.*

He made the turn, went halfway down the block to make sure the screaming man wouldn't catch up with him, then checked off the block he'd just surveyed.

The next block on his list was still in a rundown area. This street had another feature besides the blighted houses. There was a man standing on each corner. They stared at Tom's car as he slowly drove by. Suddenly they all faded away, moving into alleys or into nearby houses. Tom glanced in his rear-view mirror. He caught the tell-tale look of a light bar on the roof of a police car as it passed under an unbroken street light.

*My God. Those guys must be drug dealers. I hope those cops don't think I'm down here trying to make a drug buy.*

Despite his concern, he cruised the block slowly. There were no ribbons on any of the lampposts.

*That's it. Last block on my list. Now I got to get out of here and report in.*

He turned onto a street that would lead him back to the main part of town. To his distinct relief, the police car did not follow him. He reached an area where all the street lights worked, and the houses looked well-kept.

*Boy, that's a relief. I'm sure glad to get out of that part of town. I hope the Justice Cooperative doesn't send me back there again. The cops probably got my license number, and they'll have me on record as a suspicious character. They see me down there again, they'll stop me for going too slow, or going too fast, or not signaling, or some damn thing. They'll say I fit a profile, and haul me in. And what excuse am I going to give them for being in that crummy part of town at this time of the night?*

As he pulled in to a convenience store to make his report to the Justice Cooperative, he suddenly realized he'd been sweating heavily. The armpits of his shirt were soaked, and his heart was still racing. He stopped the car and took several deep breaths.

*Boy, am I all worked up. But I got through it. I hope that means I can get through the rest of it, including shooting some guy I don't even know.*

# SIXTEEN

Tom removed the program tape from the numerically controlled machine and installed another tape from the cabinet. He checked the cutting heads racked at the back of the machine. Two of them looked worn. He pulled them out, replaced them with newly- sharpened heads, and tagged them to go back to the tool crib. As he stepped back from the machine, Sven Gunderson approached him.

"Tom, the office got a call from your wife." He read from a message slip. "She says it's not an emergency, but call her at her office before her quittin' time."

Tom glanced at the clock on the wall. "Thanks. I'll get back to her soon's I finish settin' up the last machine in the cell."

With the setup finished and the parts flowing down the conveyor, where the robot arm picked them up one by one and ran them through the machining steps, he nodded to Miller, one of his helpers.

"Keep an eye on the machines, Jim. Stop 'em if somethin' goes wrong. I got to make a phone call. Be right back."

He went to the pay phone near the vending machines, and

called the number Gunderson had given him. He waited while Judith was called to the phone.

"What's up, honey?" He asked when she got on the line.

"Remember the Browns that you met the night of Mr. Hardesty's party?"

"Yeah."

"They've got a real problem, and I think maybe you can help. I'm going directly to their house from work. Meet me there." She gave him the address.

"What's wrong?"

"It's too long to describe. Just come."

"Okay. See you there. Looks like I'll be done here at the regular quittin' time, so I'll see you about 5:30."

• • •

He had taken his now-customary precautions at the employee parking lot, then drove to the main thoroughfare across town. He turned off the boulevard and took a side street that lead to the neighborhood where he was to meet Judith. As he got closer to his destination, the houses looked shabbier and more run-down, the yards were more ragged, and the streets became dirtier.

*I don't know what's going on, but I don't like the idea of Judy being in a neighborhood this crummy.*

He turned onto the street Judith had named. Suddenly things looked better. The houses were freshly painted. The yards were mowed. Neat fences had been put up around the houses. The street was free of litter.

*I see what that Brown guy meant. These places can be fixed up with a little work, and they look real nice.*

As he came to the block with the address he was looking for, he passed a ratty-looking house that had cars in the drive, cars parked on the lawn, and cars parked up and down the street.

*That must be the place where the numbers-runner hangs out. He really is hurting the neighborhood. I wouldn't want somebody running down the value of my place like that either.*

He reached the address Judith had given him. There were four cars in the drive, one of them Judith's. There was no room for him to pull in, so he parked on the street.

As he reached the front door, he saw that the door handle had been smashed and the striker plate ripped out of the frame. Even that didn't prepare him for the wreckage he saw as he pushed the door open.

"My God, what happened?" he exclaimed. "It looks like a tornado went through here."

Judith responded. "Not a tornado. Just a SWAT team from the Drug Enforcement Administration."

About half the paneling had been ripped from the living-room walls and lay jumbled on the floor. A smashed cabinet door hung on one hinge.

"They did all that?"

Sam Brown spoke in a tired voice. "They done more'n that. They really tore up the whole place. Jen 'n' me, we spent the whole day puttin' things back together."

"Yes," Judith added, "Jen called in today to say she couldn't come to work. Her house had been wrecked. I couldn't believe how bad it was until I saw it."

"Well, just what happened?"

Jen replied, in a voice that revealed she was tired of telling the story.

"Last night me 'n' Sam was just settin' down t' supper when we heard this bangin' on the door, and somebody yellin' 'Open up.'"

Sam added, "Yeah. I thought, them crooks down the street is finally comin' after us."

Jen took up the story again. "There was a crash, and the door come flyin' open. I thought, it's the Klan bustin' in. Then I thought, no, the Klan'd be wearin' white sheets. The guy standin' in the doorway holdin' a sledgehammer was wearin' all black, even a black mask.

"There was this huge flash of light an' a bang that broke out all the livin'-room windows and lef' me standin' there so I couldn't move."

Judith said, "Mrs. Stryker called it a flash-bang grenade. She says police use it to stun the people in a room before they come in."

Jen continued. "That's what they done. Half a dozen of 'em all dressed up in that same black outfit come pourin' into the room, pointin' guns at us. They all shoutin' at once. I couldn't make out what they was sayin. B'fore we could even move, they knock us down on the floor and put their guns to our heads.

"One of 'em yells, 'Okay, where is it?'"

"Where's what?" I say to him."

"'Where's the drugs?' he say."

"I don't know what he talkin' 'bout. We ain't got no drugs here. So he say, 'If'n you don't tell us, we'll find 'em our own selfs."

Tom doubted that was an exact quote, but he figured she'd conveyed the essence of the message.

"Two of 'em stand there holdin' their guns to our heads. The rest run through the house. They pull out every drawer in the whole house an' dump it on the floor. They open every closet 'n' cupboard 'n' they pull everything out on the floor. They turn over the chairs, they rip open the sofa cushions, they even rip open the pillows on our bed. Then they get some pry-bars and start rippin' the panelin' off the wall. I so shocked I can't say nothin'."

Sam added, pointing to the wrecked cabinet door, "They even busted open my gun cabinet and conf'scated my huntin' rifles. Evidence, they say."

"Evidence of what?" Tom asked.

"Beats me. Evidence I owned some rifles, I guess. That ain't illegal, last I knowed."

Jen continued. "After they done rippin' up the house, they say, 'We got a tip you're dealin' drugs here. We di'n't find any, but we're gonna keep an eye on you.' Then they leave. I just sit down on the floor 'n' cry. Sam, he so mad he start throwin' things."

Sam spoke up. "Then what could we do? Door smashed open, we can't even lock it. Windows all busted out, can't lock them neither. Anybody could come right in. An' I ain't even got my rifles. We start pickin' things up, puttin' 'em back in the draw-ers. Fin'ly I push the sofa across the front door an' we go to bed. This mornin', we can't leave the house. No way to lock it. I miss a day's work, Jen misses a day's work, while we clean up."

"But where'd they get the idea you were dealin' drugs?"

"I ain't sure, but I bet that numbers runner gave 'em the tip. This's his way of gettin' back at me. The cops done a good job for him."

Just then a woman carrying a video camera entered the living room. Tom recognized her as the lawyer whose work Judith typed.

"Hello, Mrs. Stryker."

"Hello, Mr. Borden. I'm glad you're here. That bunch of rack-eteers down the street makes me nervous." She turned to the Browns. "I wish you'd given me more details this morning, or even called me last night. I'd have liked to get videos of the dam-age before you started cleaning up. Even as it is, though, the evidence is pretty damning."

Tom asked, amazement in his voice, "Can drug cops bust in like that and smash things up?"

"They can indeed. They had a 'no-knock' warrant. What's more, under the law, they can confiscate anything that they claim was used in dealing drugs, or was bought with the proceeds from the sale of drugs. It's called 'taking the profit out of crime.' Most police departments are now setting quotas for seizures, as part of their budgets.

"They don't even have to prove you're guilty in order to con-fiscate your property. A common trick is to check your money for traces of cocaine. Since over eighty percent of all the cash in circulation has traces of cocaine on it, they can claim it's your profit from drug dealing, and seize it. They've developed a cute trick there. If you protest, they demand that you prove the money is yours by telling them the serial numbers on it.

"Even if a court finds you not guilty of drug charges, you'll play merry Hell getting your property back. I doubt Mr. Brown will ever see his guns again. Somehow they'll have been lost from the police evidence room."

She turned to the Browns. "For whatever consolation it is, be glad they didn't confiscate your cars. At least you can still get to work.

"I recommend you sue. I think these videos of the damage they did will be pretty convincing to a jury. No matter what, they weren't justified in doing all this damage."

Tom was incredulous. "Wait a minute! You mean anyone can turn in a drug tip and the cops'll come bustin' in like that?"

"Sure. The DEA depends on drug dealers to rat on each other. The dealers get rid of competitors that way. It may be handy for the DEA, but it's a violation of the Fourth Amendment, which requires sworn testimony before a search warrant can be issued. It's gotten so bad that some judges even sign blank warrants and give them to the police, so they can make a raid as soon as they get a tip.

"This whole thing has really gone too far. Behind the smokescreen of a war on drugs, the government is really making war on our civil liberties. The idea that the government can confiscate your property on the suspicion that it was paid for with drug money, even before they get a conviction, is a violation of the Fifth Amendment. Even drug dealers are still citizens, and they're protected by the Constitution."

"But Mrs. Stryker," Tom protested. "We can't let drug dealers go hidin' behind the Constitution. Look how much damage they do. Look at how much that numbers-runner down the street has lowered the value of every house on this block. S'pose it was a crack house instead. It'd be even worse."

"Can't we, Mr. Borden? Suppose you tear a hole in the Constitution to make it easier to get drug dealers. Then you tear another hole to get the pimps, and another hole to get the people in the numbers racket, and another hole to get the people peddling Sneaky Pete, and so on. The Constitution will end up looking like a Swiss cheese. What are you going to hide behind when they come after you?"

*The Constitution sure as Hell didn't do the Browns much good,* he thought. *If they come for me, I'll still have my gun, unless they take that away first. But no, like the bumper sticker says, they'll have to pry it from my cold dead fingers. But even my gun won't do me much good if they swarm over me like they did the Browns last night. If Sam'd gotten out a gun, he might have shot one or two of them, but he'd be dead now. If they came after me that way, I'd need lots of friends with guns.*

"Okay," he said, "I guess there wouldn't be much to protect me."

"Right. There wouldn't be. We must protect everyone's rights, or none of our rights are safe. I have no brief for drug dealers, but there ought to be a sentence from a court before any property is seized or any punishment imposed. Just causing Jen and Sam to lose a day's pay each is a pretty severe fine when they haven't been found guilty of anything, never mind the cost of the repairs they'll have to make to their house."

*Yeah, the Constitution would be better than using our guns, if we could get it back to protecting the honest people instead of just the crooks. But like that judge said at the gun training course, we need our guns to protect the Constitution. If we're unarmed, the government will run right over us, just like these drug cops are doin'.*

Mrs. Stryker turned to leave. "I want to get these videos duplicated and a sealed copy notarized. Will you be at the office in the morning, Jen?"

Jen turned to Sam, a questioning look on her face.

Sam answered. "I think I can get these windows boarded up tonight yet, and I'll pick up a hasp and padlock at the hardware. That'll let me lock the front door when we go out."

As Mrs. Stryker left, Tom asked, "Judy, what'd you want me here for?"

"They're going to need something more permanent than just replacing the windows and fixing the door. Maybe next time it will be those racketeers from down the street. They need bars on the windows, and something to make the door stronger. You're a metal-worker. I thought you might have some good ideas."

"What they really needed is a welder, not a machinist, but yeah, I think I can help."

Sam said, "Guy down the block is a welder. He made a real nice fence 'round his front yard. You tell me what, and he'll do it. He been after me to make him some doors anyway. I'll trade him some doors for some weldin'."

Tom and Sam walked around, looking at the window-frames.

"You don't want to feel like you're in jail," Tom said. "You want some nice-lookin' bars on the outside. They got to be mounted inside the frame, though, so somebody can't just take 'em off with a screwdriver."

He examined the frame closely. "Yeah, there's room here between your window and the storm window. Got some paper and a pencil?"

Sam handed him a sheet. "You want somethin' like this," he said as he sketched. "You want a grille that goes across the window, then bends back inside where it's screwed down to the window frame. That way they can't get at the screws."

Sam said, dubiously, "That gonna cost me a lot o' money?"

"You buy it at a store, and it sure will. But down at the plant we got a lot of scrap steel rod about the right size. I can get it for you at scrap metal price. Then your welder friend can put it together."

They went to look at the door. "You have to repair that lock. But then put an eye-bolt into the door frame on each side of the door, and slip a steel rod through 'em, and nobody's goin' to get in like those guys did last night. They'll have to bust out the whole doorframe. It may not stop 'em, but it'll slow 'em down. I'll get you some scrap rod for that, too."

"Okay. Thanks, man. You 'n' Judy been a big help."

"And one more thing, Sam. First thing tomorrow, you go buy yourself a pistol. Get the clock runnin' on that waitin' period right away. Then while you're waitin' for the gun, go get some training." He gave him the contact for the Self Defense Academy.

"Yeah. I better do that."

"Have Jen take the gun course too. Get her a gun too if you can afford it. Have her talk to Judy if she gets nervous about the idea."

He turned to Judith. "Okay, Judy. We better get on home. King is goin' to be pretty anxious to get out."

Tom got in his car and led the way, with Judith following in hers. As he wound his way through the run-down area on his way to the boulevard, he noticed a dark gray, battered-looking car following Judith's. At first he paid it no attention, but it continued to follow them up one street and down another. As he stopped for the light at the boulevard, the driver of the car allowed another car to pull in between his car and Judith's. Tom turned right; Judith followed; the car immediately behind her turned left. The mysterious car turned right.

*Is that guy following us? He's been tagging along too far for him just to be going the same way.*

After a couple of blocks, Tom signaled for a right turn. Judith started signaling to follow him.

*Bet she wonders what I'm turning for. Wish we had cell phones or radios so I could tell her. Maybe we ought to get cell phones. Nearly everyone else has them. They'd sure be handy when we have both cars out.*

He slowed after making the turn. Judith slowed to match. The mysterious car continued to follow them. Tom made two more right turns to circle the block, and came back out on the boulevard. The mysterious car pulled up behind Judith's car as Tom waited at the stop sign. As an opening appeared in the passing traffic, Tom made a right turn back onto the boulevard. Judith followed. The mysterious car waited at the stop sign, then began signaling for a left turn.

*He had to be following us. Going around the block like that was too much to be coincidence. He had to know he'd been spotted when I circled that block. Has he given up, or has he handed us off to another car that I haven't spotted?*

He kept watching his rear-view mirror, but none of the cars he saw seemed to be following him. As he turned into the cul-de-sac where his house was located, he slowed to a crawl. No one turned in from the boulevard behind them.

After they entered the house, Judith asked, "Tom, what was that all about? Driving in a circle like that?"

"Sorry, Judy, I had no way to let you know what was going on. I'm sure we were being followed. The guy quit when he knew I'd spotted him."

"Harry Grubbs?"

"I don't know. I don't know what kind of car Grubbs drives, and I've never seen that car before."

"Who else could it be?"

"It might be those guys from the gambling house down the street from the Browns."

"Do you suppose they'd give the police a phony drug tip about us?"

"I don't know, but from what we saw at the Browns, that's a good way to get back at somebody."

"We can't go on like this, Tom. We can't be watching the rear-view mirror the whole time we're out driving."

"Yeah. Grubbs was enough of a problem. We don't need to make any new enemies. I sure wish the Justice Cooperative would move quicker."

# SEVENTEEN

Tom casually lowered the paper he was pretending to read. He reached for the sack of popcorn sitting on the park bench beside him. He lobbed some popcorn toward a squirrel that had boldly approached him. The squirrel darted away, halted, then started grabbing up the kernels. Tom raised the paper again and pretended to be reading it while he watched over its top.

For nearly two weeks, the mail from the Justice Cooperative had been coming regularly. Every second or third day, Tom was patrolling a series of blocks to check on red and green ribbons. Two days ago, there was another piece of advertising from a store they couldn't find in the Yellow Pages. Tom expected it to be another list of blocks to check. It was something new.

THERE IS A ROOMING HOUSE IN THE MIDDLE OF THE 2200 BLOCK OF SYCAMORE AVE., BETWEEN PARKVIEW AND WOODLAND. THERE IS A SMALL PARK ACROSS SYCAMORE, FACING THE ROOMING HOUSE. THE NIGHT AFTER NEXT, BE IN THAT PARK FROM 7 PM TO 8 PM. BE PREPARED TO LOOK AS THOUGH YOU ARE SIMPLY RELAXING IN THE PARK.

WATCH THE ROOMING HOUSE FRONT DOOR. YOU ARE LOOKING FOR A HEAVY-SET MAN 5'8" TALL, WEIGHT 190 POUNDS, THINNING BROWN HAIR. A PICTURE OF HIM IS ENCLOSED WITH THIS MESSAGE. IF YOU SEE HIM LEAVE THE ROOMING HOUSE, GO TO THE PAY PHONE AT THE INTERSECTION OF PARKVIEW AND SYCAMORE. DON'T GO SO QUICKLY THAT IT'S APPARENT YOU WERE WAITING FOR HIM, BUT DON'T DELAY EITHER. CALL THE NUMBER AT THE BOTTOM OF THIS PAGE. IF HE TAKES A BUS, GIVE THE MESSAGE "THE LETTER HAS BEEN SENT." IF HE GETS INTO A CAR, GIVE THE MESSAGE "THE PACK-AGE HAS BEEN SENT. IT'S IN A (COLOR OF THE CAR) WRAPPER." THEN RETURN HOME. BE SURE TO AR-RIVE AT THE PARK EXACTLY AT 7 AND LEAVE EXACTLY AT 8 IF YOU DON'T SEE HIM.

MEMORIZE THE PICTURE, THEN BURN THIS MES-SAGE AND THE PICTURE.

"I wonder why they're so particular about when I arrive and leave," he'd said.

"Probably so you don't see who was watching before you're supposed to get there, and who'll be watching after you leave," Judith had responded. "After all, you don't want anyone to spot you, either."

• • •

Tom glanced at his watch. It showed half past seven. *It's into August already. It's getting dark earlier now. In another month there won't be much light at this hour. I don't know how I'd do any watching then. I hope the Justice Cooperative gets me fixed up before then.*

He threw some more popcorn at the squirrel that had again approached the bench. The squirrel kept a wary eye on him as it grabbed the popcorn in its paws and ate it. It was soon joined by another squirrel. Tom threw some more popcorn at them, then picked up the paper. He opened it and again pretended to read as he looked over it, towards the rooming house.

The front door of the rooming house opened. He tried not

to show he'd noticed, but watched carefully. An elderly woman came out and went down the front steps, holding the railing in one hand and a cane in the other. She hobbled up the sidewalk, evidently heading for the carryout store on the corner. Tom returned to gazing over the top of the paper.

A woman with two small children, a boy and a girl, came by on one of the walkways that crisscrossed the park. One of the squirrels on the walkway glanced over its shoulder, saw the children coming, and moved a few feet farther along the walk. The children kept coming. The squirrel gave them an annoyed look, as if to say, "Why are you following me?" and moved a few more feet. The children advanced some more. The squirrel dropped the piece of popcorn it was holding and ran for a tree. It leaped up to the trunk, scuttled around to the other side, and looked around the trunk to see if the children were following.

Tom tossed some more popcorn to the remaining squirrel, which was still sitting in the grass. The children stopped to watch the squirrel eat the popcorn. "Don't get too close," Tom said, "or you'll scare it away."

The boy, evidently the bolder of the two, said, "C'n I feed the squirrel some popcorn?"

Tom gave the woman a questioning look. She gave an affirmative nod.

Tom held out the bag of popcorn. "Take a handful. But don't eat it yourself. It's for the squirrels."

The boy toddled up to Tom, reached a hand into the bag, and came out with some popcorn.

The woman spoke. "Thank the nice man for the popcorn."

The boy looked at Tom and lisped out a sing-song "Fank you."

"You're welcome."

The boy toddled toward the squirrel and gave the popcorn an awkward overhand throw. The popcorn fell short of the squirrel. The squirrel, startled by the approach of the child, ran for a tree, scooted up the trunk, and climbed out onto a branch. From there it watched the tableau below.

They boy had a disappointed look on his face. The woman spoke. "Move back. Maybe the squirrel will come down again."

The children and the woman moved back along the walkway. Shortly both squirrels climbed down and returned to the popcorn. The family watched for a few minutes, then the woman spoke.

"All right, children, it's time to go." The woman gave Tom a friendly wave, then she and the children continued along the walkway. The squirrels watched them warily, but continued to eat.

Across the street, the elderly woman came out of the carryout store. Her left arm clutched a brown paper bag, about the right size to hold a wine bottle, against her side. She hobbled down the sidewalk, reached the front steps of the rooming house, and leaned against the railing as she climbed up. She transferred the cane to her left hand and opened the door, then went inside.

"Hi, there."

Tom looked up. An elderly man stood beside the park bench. "Don't remember seein' you before. You come here often?"

"Not very often," Tom said, with narrow truth. He added, "Only when the ol' lady's havin' a fit. When she calms down, I'll go home."

"When my ol' lady used to get upset, I'd take a walk. Got lots of exercise that way." He grinned. "But I hated it when she got mad durin' the winter. Walkin' was no fun then."

The man sat down on the other side of the popcorn bag.

"Nice day, ain't it?"

"Yeah."

"Too hot to go walkin' in the middle of the day. Right now's a good time. When fall comes, then I can take my walk in the middle of the day.

"Say, you read that piece," he pointed to Tom's newspaper, "about that guy gettin' mugged in a park in broad daylight?"

"No, I haven't finished the paper yet."

"Real bad. He's one of my buddies from the VFW. He was takin' a walk through a park down on the south side. Nice park.

I been there. Bicycle paths, hiking paths, nice flower beds. Anyway, he was walkin' along one of the paths when a bunch of young punks jumped him. Took his wallet, beat him bloody, and left. Some guy come along right behind him, found him, 'n' called the cops. They found the punks. Not only fit his description, but still had his wallet. Turned out they'd all been in trouble with the cops, but they been treated as juveniles. No convictions. If the guy dies, they'll be tried as adults. If he lives, they're back to bein' treated as juveniles. Means they'll be back out on the street, ready to mug somebody else.

"Real shame. He survived the Japs on Guadalcanal, on Mindanao, and on Okinawa. Then he nearly gets killed by a bunch of American punks."

"Doesn't seem right, does it?" Tom said.

"Nope. Shouldn't need to have somebody get killed before a bunch of punks can be locked up. Gettin' so a body can't take a walk nowadays without worryin' about . . ." Tom tuned out the oldster. He'd caught sight of the door opening across the street. A man poked his head out, looked both ways, and started down the steps. *That's him! The guy I'm looking for. Same face, same haircut. Now what's he doing?*

The man paused at the foot of the stairs, then walked directly to the curb. He started watching to his left. A car approached, slowed, and halted in front of him. He got in, and the car accelerated away.

*Okay, I've got to report that. But first I've got to get rid of this old-timer without making him suspicious.*

". . .think the police'd do somethin' to protect us," the old-timer droned on, "but they claim they're too busy chasin' drug dealers. Drug dealers never bothered me, but muggers, now, that's diff'rent. I'd carry a gun if I could get a permit. Used to be pretty good with a gun when I was in the Army. You ever been in the Army?"

"No. My dad was in Korea, but I never was in."

"Well, I was in the big one, sonny. Double-you double-you deuce. From Guadalcanal right through to Okinawa. Last time we ever really won a war. Ever since then, we either flat out lost, like Vietnam, or quit before the other guy lost, like the first time in Iraq."

Tom ostentatiously glanced at his watch. "I'd better make a call home. See if it's safe for me to come back."

"Oh, she'll take you back, sonny. Leastways, mine always did. Just take her some flowers or somethin'."

Tom picked up the sack of popcorn, emptied the few remaining kernels into his hand, and tossed them out toward the squirrels. He wadded up the bag, dropped it into a trash barrel, and slowly ambled toward the pay phone.

He punched in the number for the Justice Cooperative. A voice repeated the number he'd called. He delivered his message. There was a click at the other end. He hung up the handset. He turned and walked past the park bench.

"I'm headin' home now, old timer. Good talkin' to you. I'll take your advice and get some flowers." He continued walking to where he'd left his car.

• • •

The TV sitcom was ending. Tom picked up the remote and switched channels, to get the 11:00 o'clock news. The commercial ended, and the studio news desk appeared on the screen. The two anchors, a man and a woman, spoke alternately. "At the top of the news, the latest on the Mideast crisis. We'll hear from the UN ambassador."

"And a local killing has police baffled. More after this."

Another commercial, then the news desk reappeared. The woman spoke. "The American ambassador to the UN today urged that a peace-keeping force be placed between the disputing parties on the Golan Heights."

The news desk was replaced by a clip of the ambassador, with some sound bites that must have been the highlights of his speech.

As Tom listened, the thought came to him, *Do you suppose there's a school they send these diplomats to, so they can learn to talk in long sentences without saying anything? How else do they get so good at it?*

The male anchor spoke up. "And on the local scene, a man has been killed in what police suspect is a gang slaying. The deceased had a long criminal record, with several convictions for violent crimes." The picture showed a man lying on the ground, his shirt soaked with blood.

"My God! That's him!"

"That's who?" Judith said as she looked up from her book.

"That's the guy I was watching for this evening. The one at the rooming house. When he came out and got into a car, I called the Justice Cooperative. They must have alerted somebody who was laying for him.

"My God! That means I fingered him! I set him up to be killed. If the cops track down the killer, they're going to find me!"

"Yes, and this probably isn't the last killing you'll have a hand in. I told you, once you're in the conspiracy, you're as guilty as all the rest. The police'll call you an accessory to murder."

"But it isn't murder, Judy. It's an execution. You heard what the announcer said. He'd been convicted of violent crimes. And then he'd been turned loose again. He should've been locked up for good after the first conviction. Then he wouldn't have done anything more."

"You can call it an execution, but the police will call it murder. I know we don't have any choice, Tom. The government won't defend us, so we have to defend ourselves. But I'm still scared."

• • •

Tom stared into the darkness of the bedroom. He couldn't sleep. The image of a man in a blood-soaked shirt wouldn't go away.

*Why am I so upset? I didn't pull the trigger. Somebody else did. I only spotted the guy leaving his apartment. That doesn't matter, though. The man who eats the meat is just as guilty as the butcher. I put the finger on him. I gave the warning to the guy who did pull the trigger. I might as well have pulled the trigger myself.*

*But dammit, am I guilty when they hang a murderer? Is the*

*man who's safe from criminals as guilty as the hangman? I don't feel guilty when they strap some murdering bastard into a chair and turn on the gas.*

*But that's different. That guy has been tried and convicted. A judge has sentenced him to die. The guy who turns the gas valve is only carrying out the law. The Justice Cooperative is going outside the law.*

*No, dammit, it isn't different. The creeps the Justice Cooperative kills were tried and convicted too. But justice wasn't done. They got a light sentence, or they were turned loose early, or some damn thing. That creep I helped kill tonight caused an awful lot of misery for a lot of people before he was stopped. He won't cause anyone any trouble again. If the government had given his first victim justice, there wouldn't have been any more victims.*

*That's the point. The government isn't doing its job. And we don't have to sit still and let the crooks run over us just because the government sides with them. We still have the right to defend ourselves. If the government won't defend us, we have no choice but to get rid of the crooks ourselves.*

*It's just a damn shame we have to sneak around like this to get the justice the government should be giving us. What're governments for anyway if they aren't to protect us against crooks? Judy and I have suffered enough from what that crook Grubbs did. It's time we got justice, and I'll take it wherever I can get it.*

With that he turned over and went to sleep.

# EIGHTEEN

The road wound around a hill, then dipped into a valley. Tom watched the odometer carefully. "Smitty told me it was exactly one and a half miles from the main road. We ought to be almost there."

Judith pointed. "There's a sign, over on the left just before the bend."

"I see it now. Yeah, that's it."

A rustic sign over an open gate read DEER HUNTERS CLUB. A graveled lane led back into the woods. Tom turned through the gate and followed the lane.

After a short distance the woods thinned. They entered a cleared area. There were several cars parked alongside a cabin. Next to the cabin there were two flagpoles, one flying the American flag and another flying a plain, bright red flag.

Tom parked next to a pickup truck bearing a DEER HUNTERS sticker on the back window and a bumper sticker that read FEAR A GOVERNMENT THAT FEARS YOUR GUNS.

A man was just getting out of the truck. Tom opened the door and called to him.

"Excuse me. We're looking for the pistol match."

"Follow me. I'm headin' that way myself. It's around the side of the hill. Better bring your guns and ammo with you."

"What're the rest of these ranges?" Tom asked, gesturing around the cabin.

The club member pointed. "The one over there on the left's for trap shooting and rifle matches, the next is a hundred-yard range for sighting-in hunting rifles, and that one's for pistols and .22 rifles. We got room for all kinds of shooting."

Tom opened the trunk of his car. He put his eye protectors on, leaving them over his forehead. He hung his ear protectors around his neck. He picked up their gun cases and boxes of ammunition. Judith carried her ear and eye protectors.

The man from the pickup truck reached over the tailgate, pulled aside some netting, and lifted out a black canvas bag.

"This way, folks."

Tom slammed the trunk lid and started to follow him.

Judith said, "If we're going to do this very often, we ought to get range bags like he has."

"Yeah, you're right. Carryin' all this stuff loose isn't very smart. And that gym bag I used at the indoor range is too small for all this gear."

They followed their volunteer guide around the side of a hill until they reached the range. What they saw was a series of wooden panels braced with two-by-fours that had been staked to the ground. One panel had a door, another a cutout the size of a window. One was low, about waist-high. Tom noticed a doormat on the ground in front of that one. Beyond the panels were several cardboard silhouette targets, with scoring areas marked on them. One target was placed just beyond a table, at which there was a single chair facing the target.

"It looks almost like a false-front set for a Western movie," Judith said.

"It sure does."

There was a row of picnic tables across the entry to the range. A man was seated at one of them. There was a short line of people waiting in front of him.

Their guide put his range bag down on a picnic table. Tom and Judith unloaded their gear next to the range bag. When Tom's hands were free, their guide extended his hand.

"I'm Paul Cameron."

"Tom Borden. And my wife Judy."

"Good to meet you. You folks new here?"

"This is our first time. Dan Smith told us about it."

"Oh yeah, Smitty's out here for most of our rifle matches. Don't believe I've ever seen him at one of these pistol matches, though."

Tom gestured at the stage-sets on the range.

"What's this all about?"

"These matches go by the rules of the Practical Shooting Association. They put you in the kind of realistic situations you'd face if you were a cop or security guard, or if you had an intruder in your house. You're scored on both accuracy and speed. You got to get the bad guys before they could get you. Now let's get registered."

Tom paid the registration fees, then watched one of the participants going through the course of fire.

The shooter stood behind a blank panel, and held his right arm raised, with the palm flat against the panel. Behind him stood a man holding a small gray metal box. Behind them was a man with a clipboard.

Cameron spoke. "When he hears the BEEP from the timer, he draws his gun, steps around the wall, and engages the first set of targets. After his last shot, the recorder takes down the elapsed time. After he's fired each of the stages of the match, the recorder will score each one, then the targets'll be patched.

"They're ready to start. Better get your ears on."

Tom hastily pulled the goggles down over his eyes, then adjusted his ear protectors.

There was a faint electronic BEEP, then the shooter drew his pistol, stepped to the edge of the wall, pointed his gun, and began firing at the targets.

Tom said, "He's bracing his hands against the edge of the wall. Is that allowed?"

"It's allowed, but it's a bad idea."

"How come? Doesn't it steady your hand and help your accuracy?"

"It does. That's why he's doing it. But in a real fire-fight, it'd be dangerous. You don't know if there's anyone hidin' on the other side of the wall. Somebody there might grab your gun, or smash your wrist with a tire iron. Besides, the bad guys might be shooting back. If the wall is brick or concrete, your hands'll get spattered with chips, and maybe with lead splashed from the bullets. You could end up with some nasty wounds on your hands."

*There's so much to think about. Shooting looks so easy in the movies. The more I learn, the harder it looks. But getting this practice is better than learning the hard way. Wonder how many cops got their hands torn up before they learned not to stick them out like that?*

He watched as the shooter moved to the next stage, then turned to Cameron.

"I noticed the bumper sticker on your truck. What's that all about?"

"Just what it says. The only government that needs to worry about people's guns is a bad one. The bulk of the people won't rebel against a good government. Instead, they'll defend it against anybody who tries to overthrow it. When the government is afraid of the people's guns, that means they're up to no good. They're planning to rip you off or kill you, and they want to make sure you can't defend yourself.

"So if they're afraid of your guns, you ought to be afraid of them. Get rid of them while you still have your guns. Once they take away your guns, you can kiss all your rights good-bye. You've got no way to defend yourself."

"But what about the Bill of Rights?"

"Listen, old Joe Stalin gave the Roosskies the best-sounding Bill of Rights any country ever had. On paper, it was even better than ours. But he had all the guns. So the Roosskies good-sounding Bill of Rights was just on paper. It didn't stop old Uncle Joe from hauling millions of people off to Siberia.

"Or how 'bout Adolph Hitler? D'you think he could've killed six million Jews in concentration camps if they'd had guns to fight back with? The Nazi gun control law of 1938 specifically said Jews weren't allowed to own guns. It even said they couldn't own knives and clubs. Hitler knew what he was doing."

Cameron continued, "If anybody tried to copy what Hitler or Stalin did here in the good old U. S. of A, he'd have a real fight on his hands from seventy million gun owners. That's why those clowns in Capitol City and down in Washington are so eager to take away our guns. Then they can do anything they want to us."

"Do you really think we've got a bunch of would-be Hitlers in Washington?" Tom asked.

"Prob'ly not. The guys we got now're more like Al Capone than like Adolph Hitler. Just like Capone charged you for protection you didn't want to buy, they just want to tax you to death for the benefit of their friends. But once the Capones take away your guns, then the Hitlers and the Stalins crawl out from under the rocks. Remember, Hitler won more votes than any other candidate in the last free election the Germans held."

"Yeah," Tom said. "The politicians're chargin' us for protection all right, but we're sure not gettin' it. All we get is a bunch of laws and regulations and inspectors. Maybe I ought to be afraid of the government, instead of just mad at it."

He turned his attention back to the range. The shooter on the line was firing at what looked like a bowling pin perched on a post. After several shots he knocked it off. He cleared his gun and holstered it. The recorder began scoring the targets, and the timekeeper patched the holes as the recorder finished with each target.

The rangemaster called out "Next!"

Tom turned to Cameron. "You were ahead of me."

"Go ahead. I like to see what the other shooters did before I try. I do better when I've got a tough score to beat."

Tom walked to the first stage, where the timekeeper was waiting.

The timekeeper gave instructions to Tom. "At each stage, I'll ask, 'Shooter ready?' Let me know whether you're ready. Don't feel you have to rush, if you need to reload or something. When you're ready, the next command is 'Stand by.' When you hear the BEEP from the timer, draw your gun and engage the targets you've been given. After your last shot, the recorder will write down the total time. Then you'll move to the next station and reload. All clear?"

"I think so."

"Okay. At this first stage you start behind this wall. On the BEEP, draw your gun and engage the three targets numbered 1, 2 and 3, in that order. Two shots at each target. Take a look to see where they are."

Tom stuck his head around the edge of the wall. "Yeah, I see 'em."

"Okay, load and holster your gun."

The timekeeper stepped behind him.

"Shooter ready?"

"Ready."

"Stand by."

*Don't try to be Fast-Draw McGraw, or you'll shoot yourself in the foot. Do everything just as careful as you run those machines down at the plant.*

*BEEP!*

He drew his gun, stepped to the side just enough to see around the wall, and brought the gun up, being careful not to let the muzzle go beyond the wall. He aimed at the first target.

*Front sight, front sight, front sight, . .*

*Bang!*

*Bang!*

*Got to learn to get that second shot off quicker.*

He swung the gun to the second target and fired twice.

*Would I really be this calm if those targets were shooting back?*

He swung to the third target and fired, then holstered the gun. He glanced behind him. The timekeeper was holding up the timer and the recorder was reading the elapsed time.

The timekeeper led Tom to the next stage, the wall with a window in it.

"You start by standing to either side of the window. At the signal, you draw, step to where you can fire through the window, and engage three targets, two shots each."

"Okay, I see the targets."

"Better reload now, so your gun doesn't run dry in the middle of the string."

"Oh! Yeah, I better. Thanks."

*One more thing to think about. How do cops manage to keep track of all this when somebody's shooting back at 'em?*

He stepped to the left of the window. At the signal, he drew, stepped to the window, and began firing.

*These are just cardboard targets. But the Justice Cooperative wants me to shoot at a real, live person. Can I do it as easy as I'm doing this? And what if the guy is shooting back? Can I handle that? I better be able to.*

The next stage was the panel with the door in it.

"In this stage you stand either behind or beside the door, your choice. At the signal, draw your gun, open the door, put one foot through the door, and engage the three targets on the other side. Two shots each."

Tom pulled the door open and located the targets.

*In a real fight I couldn't do that. I'd have to open the door without knowing where the people are on the other side. And they'd be shooting at me as soon as I opened the door. This could get real scary. BEEP!*

He drew with his right hand as he turned the knob and opened the door with his left. He fired one-handed at the closest target. By the time he swung to the second target, his left hand was up to steady the gun. He fired at it, then turned to the third.

After his time was recorded, the timekeeper led him to the low wall.

"In this next stage you start off crouched down behind this barrier. At the signal you bring your gun up and engage the two targets on the other side. Body armor drill. Three shots each, two in the body and one in the head."

*So that's what the doormat is for. You can kneel on it without getting muddy.*

He knelt with one knee on the mat, and leaned forward to bring his head and shoulders below the top of the barrier.

*This is more like shooting from ambush, where you're trying to catch somebody by surprise. I wonder if that's how the guy I fingered was knocked off. Did somebody nail him from ambush? And how did they get away afterwards? Could I just calmly wait to shoot somebody I don't even know? I've got to, though, or nobody will take out Grubbs for me. I'd have to take him out myself. One way or the other, I have to ambush somebody.*

On the signal he rose just enough to bring his gun above the barrier and began shooting.

*Keep your head low. If this was a real fight, you wouldn't want to give them any more of a target than you have to.*

He put two shots into the torso of the first target, then elevated his gun.

*Damn! The gun's wobbling so I can hardly hold it on his head. Steady, steady. Front sight, front sight, . .*

*Bang!*

He repeated the maneuver on the next target, then stood as the recorder took down the time.

*If I'd really been shooting from ambush at somebody, and he was wearing body armor, I don't think I'd have been able to hit his head. He'd have been moving. It's tough enough holding steady on a target that's standing still. Hitting the head of a moving target must be damn near impossible. But cops must learn how to do it. I need more practice. I hope I don't have to take out somebody who's wearing body armor.*

The timekeeper led him to the next stage.

"In this stage, you're seated at this table, with your gun on the table and cards in your hand." He handed Tom a sheet of cardboard to represent the cards. "At the signal, drop the cards, pick up your gun, and engage the three targets across the table.

Two shots each."

*This must be somebody's idea of a Western movie scene. But I better think of it as somebody in my house. What would I do if someone broke in, and I had my gun handy?*

He seated himself in the chair, and held the "cards" in both hands.

"Shooter ready?"

"Ready."

"Stand by."

*BEEP!*

He dropped the cards and grabbed the gun. He braced himself on the table with his left hand while firing at the nearest target one-handed. He kicked the chair back with his right leg and dropped to his right knee. He rested both elbows on the table and began firing at the other two targets.

"Hey, not bad," the timekeeper said. "Most people don't think of knocking the chair out of the way. They just start blazing away."

"Maybe I been watching too many late night movies."

The next stage was a tall, narrow panel.

"Here you start behind the wall. At the signal, fire around the right side of the wall at the three targets there. Three targets, two shots each."

"Just like the first stage?"

"That's right. But in the second half, you'll fire around the left side of the wall."

At the signal, Tom moved to the right, drew, and fired at each of the targets.

"Okay, now you repeat that, except that you fire around the left side."

At the signal, Tom stepped to the left far enough that his right shoulder cleared the wall. He began firing.

*Hey! I'm almost completely exposed here. There's got to be some way I can hide most of me behind the wall and still shoot. Maybe I ought to practice shooting left-handed. I don't want to end up like that drug dealer at the police station, who was out of the fight because one of his arms was broken.*

"Now the final stage," the timekeeper said. "There's a bowling pin sitting on top of that post. Stand at the firing line. On the signal, draw, and keep shooting until you knock the pin off the post. Reload if you have to."

On the *BEEP* he drew, fired once, and missed. He hit the pin with his second shot.

*I was in too much of a hurry on that first shot. I've got to aim carefully, even if it means taking more time to get the shot off.*

The recorder then checked each target, writing the number of hits and the points for each on the score sheet. After he'd recorded the last target, he turned to Tom.

"You're going to finish out of the money. There's already four people with better final scores than yours. But your raw scores, just for bullet placement, are pretty good. It's the time that's hurting your final score. The people ahead of you were shooting much faster, even if their accuracy wasn't any better than yours."

"I guess I've got to work on speed."

"Don't do it at the cost of accuracy. Remember what they say, speed is fine, but accuracy is final. It's the first hit that counts, not the first shot. It's better if you can do both, but work on the hits before working on speed. You can't miss fast enough to win a gunfight. And don't feel bad. You did pretty well for your first time on this course of fire."

Tom watched as Judith went through the course. He couldn't tell how she was scoring, but she didn't seem to be rattled or upset. She wore the look of determination that always seemed to appear on her face when she was shooting.

*I'm sure glad Judy has taken to shooting the way she has. I don't have to worry so much about her. But her deadly seriousness worries me. She must still be really upset about Grubbs.*

*Damn! I wish the Justice Cooperative would move faster. We've got to get this thing finished up. We can't go on looking over our shoulders all the time thinking Grubbs may be after us.*

As Judith finished shooting, Cameron spoke to Tom. "What do you think? You like this shooting?"

"Yeah. Actually it's fun. Even if I'm not winning a prize."

"Well, I hope to see you out here again. Get some practice and you'll work your way up to some prize money."

Tom thought, *Yeah, it's fun, and it's more realistic than shooting at that indoor range. But the different things they're putting us through here seem to fit cops and people defending their homes. They don't fit what I'll have to do for the Justice Cooperative. Or what I'd need to do if I had to take out Grubbs myself.*

*What I really need is some training in assassinating people. All the different situations here assume the other guy has done something and I have to respond. But I don't want to respond to what somebody else is doing. I want to take him out when he doesn't even know I'm around. I want him dead before he even knows he's been attacked. I guess I'd have to get him from ambush. This stuff isn't really helping me with that.*

After Judith's score was computed, she came back to where Tom was standing.

"How'd you do?" He asked

"I got good hits, but I was too slow."

"Same here. I guess we need to work on that."

"I think you're right," she said. "But even so, I've gotten a lot more confidence in myself since we've started shooting. I think I'll be able to give a good account of myself the next time I have to defend myself."

The words stabbed at him. *You mean you don't think I can defend you? You think I let you down once before, and you can't count on me?*

But then calmer thoughts prevailed.

*Nuts to that! You want her to be able to defend herself. You can't be around her all the time. Be glad she can do it.*

Then another thought crept in.

*She talked about defending herself the next time she's attacked. But I'll have to attack somebody, not just defend her. That means more than just hitting what I shoot at. I'll have to shoot somebody I don't even know, and who never hurt me. That's a lot different from shooting somebody who's trying to hurt me. Will I be able to do it?*

Judith pointed to the clubhouse. "It smells as though they're cooking some barbecue over there. You want to get some lunch?"

"Yeah. I'm ready to eat. Then we can watch the rest of the shooting."

• • •

Inside the clubhouse, they got in line at the kitchen, picked up plates of barbecue sandwiches and coleslaw, then looked for a place to sit.

"That table has only one guy at it," Tom said, nodding his head toward a table near the door.

He walked toward the table. "Mind if we sit here?"

"Come ahead. Plenty of room here."

Tom held a chair for Judith, then sat down.

"I'm Tom Borden. This is my wife Judy."

"Glad to meet you. I'm Mike Masters. I don't remember seeing you folks here before."

"This is our first time here. Dan Smith told us about it."

"Okay. Smitty'll probably be out here later when the rifle match starts. He comes out pretty regularly.

"I'm the Club secretary. Are you folks interested in joining? You can get a family membership for not much more than the cost of a single membership."

Tom looked at Judith, then turned to Masters. "I think we'd like to join. We enjoyed the shooting today, and want to get more practice. Dan Smith said he'd sponsor us."

"Okay. After lunch I can give you the applications. Fill them out and I'll have Smitty co-sign them when he comes.

"You folks done much shooting?"

"We're new to it," Judith answered, "but we've really become interested. We figure we need it for self-defense."

"Wish I could get my girl-friend interested in it," Masters said. "She really needs it. But I think she's finally convinced the cops can't protect her."

"What happened?" Tom asked.

"She was bein' stalked by some guy from work. She'd dated him a few times, but quit because he was a creep. He wouldn't take 'no' for an answer. He kept after her. Last weekend he broke into her house. Right in broad daylight. She locked herself in her bedroom, called the cops and then called me."

He held up his left arm. It was scraped and scabbed from wrist to elbow.

"See that? That's from the cops."

"What'd they do?"

"Soon as I get her call I jump on my Harley and zoom off to her place. I come pullin' up on my Harley just as the cops show up. They come pilin' out of the squad car, pointin' their guns at me. They're all shoutin' at me. 'Freeze!' 'Down!' I'm sittin' there in the saddle like, wait a minute, what's goin' on here? They push me and the Harley over. I get this road rash from the cinders, even though I'm standin' still. I get a burn on my leg from the Harley's exhaust. That still hurts. They're all shoutin' at me. I'm tryin' to tell them my girlfriend called me, but they're all screamin' and not listening. I see somebody run out of her house. I try to point at the guy, and a cop stomps on my wrist with his combat boot. Lucky he didn't break it. Finally my girlfriend comes out, grabs one of 'em, shakes his arm until he stops shoutin' and listens to her. She points to where the guy has run off. They let me up. No apology, no nothing. They take a report from her, and that's it."

"Did they get the stalker?" Judith asked.

"They told her she'd have to come down to the station house and swear out a warrant. I was in no shape to take her on my Harley. She drove us down there. I backed up her story that this guy had been stalkin' her for weeks. The guy had to post a peace bond, but that's it. He's still runnin' around. Fat lot of good that peace bond is goin' to do if he kills her. I'm tryin' to convince her she needs a gun and needs to learn how to use it."

"Wonder if it would help if I talked to her?" Judith said. "I'm being stalked too. That's why we got into shooting."

"Can't do no harm to try. I'd be grateful if you could talk her into it. We have our monthly dinner meeting here at the clubhouse next week. I finally convinced her to come with me." He smiled. "Deer meat stew, from last huntin' season. Hope she likes it."

"We're joining the Club, we ought to come," Judith said. "If she's here, I'll talk to her."

"Okay. Let me get you those application forms now."

• • •

Later, as they walked to the car, Judith spoke. "I really enjoyed that. The shooting was fun, and the people here are very nice. You want to come back next week?"

"Yeah, I do. This was fun, besides being good practice. And you're right about the friendly people. I'll get us a couple of range bags this week," he said as they reached his car.

# NINETEEN

om stopped at the plant door and scanned the parking lot carefully. There was no sign of anything out of order. He had hung back for a few minutes after the quitting whistle, giving the parking lot a chance to clear and reduce the number of places where somebody could hide.

He checked the tires on his car, verified that the hood was still latched down, and looked through the windows to make sure no one was hiding behind the front seat.

After getting in, he stopped to think about a route home. *I took the short route down Market yesterday. Should I take South today? That's a pattern itself; long route one day, short route the next.*

He pulled a quarter out of his pocket and balanced it on his thumb.

*Heads I take Market, tails I take South.*

He flipped the coin. It came up heads.

*Okay, I'll be home sooner. Maybe I'll even beat Judy home.*

When he reached Market, he carefully nosed his car into an opening in traffic. Once into the traffic stream, he relaxed and simply followed the cars ahead of him.

*The traffic lights're well timed tonight. I'm hittin' all the greens.*
His thoughts drifted to his and Judith's unsolved problem.

*What's Grubbs up to? He made a point of letting us know he's found us. I keep watching for him, but either he's invisible or he's laid off us. Maybe he's waiting until we get tired of watching, and relax. Then he'll jump us.*

*I know we've got to be alert the rest of our lives. Grubbs isn't the only crook out there. But he's the one who's specifically after us. The rest of the crooks're just looking for somebody easy to hit. If we make ourselves hard to hit, the rest of the crooks'll leave us alone. But Grubbs'll be after us until he takes us out, unless somebody takes him out first, no matter how hard to hit we make ourselves.*

He looked ahead, through a break in traffic.

*Hey! That's Judy's car up ahead. Looks like we'll get home about the same time.*

He checked the left-side mirror, pulled into the left-most lane, and started to pass the line of cars behind Judith's, to catch up with her. Suddenly something caught his eye.

*That gray car a couple of places behind Judy's. It looks like the car that followed us home from the Browns the other night. It must be following Judy.*

He picked an opening in traffic and eased back into the same lane as Judith's car.

The gray car stayed put, never more than two or three cars behind Judith's car, but never making any move to catch up with her either. It followed her as she turned off the boulevard. It followed her through several turns down side streets.

*Traffic is light here. There aren't any other cars he can hide behind. But he's keeping a steady block or so behind Judy. I wonder if he's spotted me following him yet?*

Judith turned into the cul-de-sac on which they lived. The gray car turned in, then slowed. Tom made the turn, then hesitated.

*Whoever he is, he has to come back out this way. Should I wait for him here? But what if he's after Judy? I'd better be there in case she needs me. Damn! I wish I had my gun with me. If he's a crook, he's probably got a gun with him. It's only the honest people who obey the gun laws.*

He continued to follow Judith and the gray car. Judith pulled into their driveway. The gray car slowed as it passed their house, then went by. Tom pulled to the side of the street. The gray car continued to the dead end of the street, where it made a U-turn, and came back toward him. The car slowed again as it passed their house. It was still creeping along as it passed Tom's car. He got a good look at the driver.

*Grubbs!*

As Grubbs caught sight of him, the gray car suddenly accelerated. Tom's first reaction was to whip his car into a U-turn and follow Grubbs.

*No! That would mean leaving Judy alone. I'd better get home and call the cops.*

His tires squealed as he braked to a stop behind Judith's car. He dashed past King, who stood with forepaws on the fence and looked imploringly at him.

"Judy! Did you know that Grubbs followed you home?"

"What? No! Are you sure?"

"I'm sure." He recounted his drive home behind her car. "He was already following you when I first spotted you on the boulevard."

"But I take a different route home each night, just like you're supposed to. How did he find me?"

"Maybe he's been waiting every day on that route, and finally got lucky."

"Or maybe he followed me all the way from work. That's really scary. What's the point of taking different routes, like they tell you to do, if someone's waiting for you right at the start."

"Or what if he's waiting for you right here at the end? What could you do if he was waiting here to ambush you?"

"If I saw him I guess I could just turn around and leave."

"But what if he's parked his car somewhere else and walked here. We've made sure there's no place he could hide in our yard, but he could be hiding behind some car parked partway down the street. By the time you got the alarm turned off and the door unlocked, he might be able to run up here and grab you."

"I've thought of that. I take a good look around before I open the car door. I make sure I have one hand free, even if that means I'll have to make several trips to the car to bring things in. The first thing I do after I unlock the door and lock it behind me is load my gun. Only then if there's anything still in the car do I go get it. I figure King'll bark if somebody tries to sneak up on the house once I'm inside."

"That's good, but I still don't like the idea of Grubbs stalking us. We better go talk to the cops."

• • •

Detective Lieutenant Dave Callahan was seated across the desk from them. A file folder was open on the desk in front of him. Tom recognized the message of pasted-up newspaper letters Judith had received.

"Mr. Borden, you're sure it was Harry Grubbs?"

"I haven't forgotten that face, Mr. Callahan."

"Did you by any chance get a license number?"

"Yeah, I did." He handed over a slip of paper. "I don't know how I thought of it, I was so worried about Judy. But somethin' told me to write it down."

"I'll have it checked. Even if it turns out the car is registered to Grubbs, though, remember he has a perfect right to drive on the streets of this city."

"But last time you said something about getting some kind of order . . . "

"A restraining order, yes. But do you think you can make a case? You've encountered him how many times?" He paged through the folder. "Once in a grocery store, and once tonight. That's not very often. It'd cost you money to go to court, and you'd probably not be successful."

"But do we have to put up with him stalking us? Isn't there something you can do?"

Callahan paused for a moment. "Look. I've got two years to go until I can retire. In my time on the force, I've been puked on by drunks and stoned by rioters. I spent six weeks with my leg in a cast because a holdup man ran me down when I tried to stop him. I've had over a dozen shoot-outs with armed crooks. I've had a partner shot dead right beside me. Then I had to explain to his widow why the crook who shot him was out on parole instead of behind bars.

"I've earned that retirement. I'm not going to throw it away by doing something that somebody could sue me for, like shadowing Grubbs when I've nothing to go on."

"Sounds to me," Tom said, an angry edge in his voice, "like you've already retired on the job. You knew the risks when you became a cop, just like I knew the risks when I became a machinist. I haven't quit cuttin' metal just because I might lose a finger."

"Sure, I knew the risks. But I figured I had a bargain with the public. I'd take the risks of protecting you, if you'd back me up. You're not keepin' your end of the bargain. You elect prosecutors who'd rather settle for a plea bargain than prosecute the charge the crook really deserves. You elect judges who give light sentences for serious crimes. You elect governors who appoint parole boards that let crooks out on the street even before they've finished what sentences they do get. You elect presidents who appoint Federal judges who are always finding more rights for criminals hidden somewhere in the Constitution.

"And now us cops are learning that crooks have all kinds of civil rights. When we finally catch some scumball, he may have a gun, he may have a knife, he may be on drugs, he may be drunk, or he may just be lookin' for a fight. We have to be ready for anything. We've had cops shot when they stopped somebody for a minor traffic violation. We have to make a split-second decision about how to handle the guy. Then the guy claims we violated his civil rights, and we go to court. When you people get on the jury, you have hours and days to second-guess what we did. And as often as not, you decide we did violate his civil rights. So the cop goes to jail, and the scumball becomes a media hero.

"As far as the law is concerned, Grubbs has paid his debt to society. He's free to come and go as he pleases. If we interfere with that, we're violating his civil rights. If he sues me and wins, I personally pay the fine, or go to jail. The Department won't do a thing for me. I'm not going to take that risk, and neither is any other cop.

"If you want us to do something about Grubbs, you have to give us more to go on than the fact you saw him in a store, and he followed you home."

"But what about that message he sent us?" Judith asked. "Isn't that a threat?"

Callahan carefully picked up the message by one corner. "I've had it checked for fingerprints. Only your prints show. No one else's. He'd deny he had anything to do with it. He might even claim you prepared it yourself, and sue you for libel or defamation of character. Do you really want to go through that?"

"Are you telling me there's nothing we can do?"

"You can continue to be careful. Watch to be sure you're not followed. Don't open the door for strangers. Don't walk through deserted areas of town. Keep out of dark alleys. And let us know if he does anything overt."

"Look," Tom protested, "the last time he attacked us, we didn't open the door. He smashed it open. We did all those things you said and he still got us. Why should I believe they'll work any better this time?"

"I'm sorry, Mr. Borden, but there are limits on what I can do. I've told you what those limits are. I can't do any more than that. Until Grubbs actually commits a crime, I can't touch him." He stood up, to dismiss them.

As Tom stood up, he said, "Are you telling me I'm on my own? That you can't defend me?"

"We can't be everywhere. You're responsible for taking precautions to make yourself less vulnerable. We can step in only when there's a direct and explicit threat to you. Call me if you have any more information."

Numbly, Tom walked toward the door. Judith followed him in silence. Almost by reflex, he checked the car, then held the door for Judith before getting in himself.

Tom put his key in the ignition, then hesitated. "Callahan couldn't have made it any plainer, could he? They're not going to help us. They'll be real sorry when one or both of us ends up dead, but until then they can't or won't touch Grubbs."

Judith sat silently for a moment, then spoke. "I can't go on like this, Tom. I'm going to start carrying my gun with me. And I don't care if it's illegal. I'd rather stand trial for a gun violation than let him get to me again."

Tom glanced at her, but said nothing.

*That sure is a change in Judy,* he thought. *Six months ago she'd never have said that.*

He started the car and began the trip home.

# TWENTY

The message had come two days ago, in another junk-mail envelope with a phony return address.

MAKE YOURSELF AVAILABLE ALL EVENING TWO DAYS FROM NOW. STAND BY FOR A WRONG-NUMBER PHONE MESSAGE THAT WILL GIVE YOU A PASSWORD AND DIRECT YOU TO ONE OF THE PAY PHONES NEAR YOU. YOU WILL THEN BE GIVEN FURTHER INSTRUCTIONS. YOUR COUNTERSIGN IS "BROTHER."

He had picked up a pizza on the way home, figuring they could re-heat it in the microwave if the call came during dinner. He and Judith had just sat down to eat when the phone rang.

"Hello."

"Good evening," a male voice said. "May I speak with Mr. Collins, please?"

"Sorry, you must have a wrong number."

"Is this 458-2204?"

"No, it's -2209."

"Sorry to have bothered you."

*Click!*

Tom thought, *The error in the last number must be their way of telling me to go to pay phone number four. That's a block up and around the corner. I'd better get started.*

"Who was it?"

"The Justice Cooperative. They want me to go to a pay phone for instructions. I'll be back as soon as I can."

He stopped to think. *Take my gun? No, I don't know where I'll be going, and I don't want to get caught with it. This is crazy. Any crook I'd meet would have a gun, but I can't have one to defend myself. What kind of a country is this, anyway, that disarms the victims while the crooks go around armed?*

He drove to the pay phone, parked nearby, and paced around the phone booth. The sun hung above the western horizon, a huge red ball. To the south of the sun, the top of a cumulus cloud towered upwards.

*I hope we don't get rain tonight. I don't want to be out in it.*

A woman came by, glanced at Tom, and spoke.

"Are you waiting to use the phone?"

Startled out of his reverie, he groped for an excuse to explain his standing there. "I keep gettin' a busy signal. Go ahead. I'll try again when you're done."

*She looks ordinary enough, but is she a cop in disguise? Are the cops watching to see who's waiting for a call at a pay phone? Could they spot me as working with the Justice Cooperative that way?*

Then another thought struck him. *Does belonging to a conspiracy like the Justice Cooperative make you paranoid, so you suspect everybody of being after you?*

The woman finished her call and walked away, leaving Tom's questions unanswered. After what seemed like forever, but which his watch told him was only five minutes, the phone rang.

"Hello."

"Is this Mr. Collins?"

*That's the name they used earlier. It must be the password.*

"No, this is his brother. Can I take a message?"

"Very well. Listen closely. There is a strip mall on Linden just a few blocks from where your street dead-ends on it. In that mall is a liquor store. Do you know it?"

"I know the mall, and I've seen the store."

"Good. You are looking for a heavy-set man, five feet ten inches tall, in his late thirties, slightly balding, brown hair. He was just seen leaving his apartment wearing gray slacks and a dark blue, short-sleeved shirt. He's driving a green Chevy Nova, two-door, license UEX-483. He is known to shop at that liquor store.

"Park away from the mall lot. Check the cars outside the store. If you see the car, call" and the voice gave a number, "using the pay phone in the mall parking lot. Identify yourself with the same countersign, and say, "the package has arrived." If you don't see the car, go inside the store and check. Call the same number to report whether he's there or not. If he's not there, wait to see if he arrives. If he does arrive, call and report it. If he's actually going somewhere else, you will be called on that phone to release you from watching."

There was an abrupt *click!*

*They don't waste words, do they?*

He wrote the license and phone numbers on the palm of his hand with a ball-point pen. He then got in his car, pulled a band-aid out of the first aid kit, and covered the phone number with it. He tucked a moist towelette pack in his pocket in case he needed to scrub the phone number off in a hurry. Then he drove toward the strip mall.

He found a parking place around the corner from the mall. As he walked around the corner, he spotted the liquor store. It was located between a greeting card shop and an auto parts store. He walked up slowly and located the pay phone, then scanned the cars parked near the liquor store. None of them was the car he was looking for.

He glanced at the sky. The cumulus cloud had moved closer. It now covered half the sky, blotting out the setting sun. He was about to head for the liquor store when a car pulled into the parking lot.

*That's it. The green Nova. And it's got the right license.*

The car pulled into a parking space. A man got out and walked toward the liquor store.

*That's him. He fits the description.*

Tom tried not to attract attention as he slowly ambled toward the phone, dropped in a coin, and punched in the numbers.

A voice said, "You've reached" and repeated the number Tom had dialed.

"This is Mr. Collins's brother. He said to let you know the package has arrived."

"Keep an eye on it. Let us know if it gets lost."

*Click!*

*Okay, so I'm supposed to watch, and let them know if he leaves. But then what?*

He casually strolled down the mall, looking in store windows while keeping an eye on the liquor store doorway. From time to time he glanced at the sky. It was getting darker, and he heard a faint rumble of thunder.

Then he turned and looked around the neighborhood. The street across from the mall was parked solid with cars. He noticed a decrepit-looking car parked directly opposite the mall, with someone sitting in it.

*That's strange. It's got temporary tags on it, like it had just been bought from a dealer. Who'd buy a junker like that?*

A dark-colored, nondescript van slowly came down the street. It too was wearing temporary tags. When it reached the end of the mall, the driver of the junker car started his engine and pulled away. The van pulled into the spot the junker had just vacated.

Tom started back towards the pay phone, to make sure he could get to it in a hurry when his quarry left the liquor store. He reached the phone, and leaned against the side of the booth. He kept looking around, trying not to stare at the liquor store doorway.

He felt something wet strike his cheek. A raindrop. He wiped it with the palm of his hand, then dried his hand on his trousers.

*Damn! I sure don't want to get caught in a thunderstorm. What's happening in that store?*

Then the door opened. The driver of the Nova came out, his left arm cradling two cylindrical brown paper bags against his chest, and his right hand holding a key ring.

Tom heard a muffled *pop* from somewhere behind him. Suddenly the man he was watching jerked. One of his brown bags exploded in a spray of glass and liquid. A look of surprise crossed the man's face. He swayed slightly, then the sounds came again. *Pop! Pop!* The man slumped to the ground.

Tom looked behind him. A fat black tube protruded from the partially-opened side door of the van. It disappeared and the door closed. The van rocked as though someone were climbing over a seat. Then the starter ground. The engine caught, and the van smoothly pulled away from the curb.

Tom's attention was jerked back by a sudden scream. A woman was standing in the doorway of the card shop.

"There's blood all over him. He's dead!"

*I guess I don't need to make any phone calls. It's time to get the Hell out of Dodge.*

It seemed that the woman's scream opened the sky. Thunder crashed and rain began to pour down. Tom left the phone and dashed for his car. Behind him he heard the wail of a siren.

*Somebody must have called the cops. They sure showed up quick.*

Once he rounded the corner, a reaction set in.

*My God! I've just seen a killing. I've been a part of it. I tipped off the killer. If the cops catch me, I'm an accessory.*

By the time he reached his car he was drenched. He opened the door and crawled in. He wiped the water off his face, flicked it to the ground, then slammed the door. He slumped behind the wheel.

*It happened so quick. That guy was coming out of the liquor store, thinking about nothing but his booze, and just like that, bang, he was dead. He never even saw the guy who shot him. I guess if you're going to kill somebody, though, that's the way to do it. Nail him from ambush, before he even knows you're around.*

Outside, the wind-driven rain lashed against the car and filled the gutters. An approaching car had its headlights on.

*I'd better get moving. The cops'll be questioning anybody they find around here. Even if they can't pin anything on me, I don't want to be on record as being here.*

He ground the starter, turned on the windshield wipers, and put on the headlights. He pulled into a driveway, backed out, and headed back the way he'd come.

*I hate to use some guy's driveway to turn around, but I don't want to drive past that mall. I don't even want to be seen around here.*

Back on the main street, he found the rain had slowed traffic to a crawl. He simply followed the car in front of him. His wet clothes began to chill him, and he turned on the heater.

The drive to the entrance to his street was a short one. The rain was already beginning to slack off as he made the turn. By the time he reached his house, the rain had stopped and the sky had started to clear. The setting sun, still barely above the horizon, produced a glorious rainbow off to the east.

He pulled into the driveway and opened the car door. He sat there, lacking the volition to move.

*Everything looks and smells so clean after the rain. How can the world look so good when somebody's just been killed? And what about me? I got soaked, but how come I don't feel like I was washed clean? Does killing somebody leave a bloodstain on you that never comes off?*

Finally he pushed himself out of the car and slammed the door. King ran from his doghouse to the fence, wagging his tail and barking joyously.

Tom reached over the fence and scratched King's ears. He then went into the house.

"What happened, Tom?"

He hesitated. "Right now I don't want to talk about it. Let's watch the eleven o'clock news when it comes on. By then maybe I'll feel like talking."

"Shall I warm up some pizza for you?"

"No. I think I'd choke on it if I tried to eat."

• • •

The news opened with stories on the Mid-East crisis, the famine in Africa, and the latest congressional scandal. Finally the local news came on.

The screen showed a shot of the rain-washed mall parking lot. In the center of the picture was a sodden bundle, surrounded by police. The reporter spoke.

"Police are again baffled by today's slaying in the Linden Avenue mall. The victim, Henry Clark, has a long history of arrests and convictions for assault and armed robbery. He was currently on parole from a conviction for robbing a convenience store and pistol-whipping the clerk."

The scene then shifted to the studio, where the anchorman took up the story.

"Police say they suspect the killing was motivated by a dispute over drug territory. The police ballistics laboratory has confirmed that the killer used a 30-caliber hunting rifle. However, no trace of the gun, or any empty cartridge cases, have been found. A police spokesperson declined to speculate whether this killing was connected to a series of recent killings of people with long criminal records.

"The mayor's office issued a statement claiming that violence in the city is being exaggerated by the news media. According to the mayor's spokesperson, the number of killings so far this year is only slightly above last year's at this time, and the number of assaults and robberies is down slightly.

"And for another local story, we go to . . ."

Tom punched the remote and killed the picture.

"That's him. That's the guy I helped kill. I was supposed to watch for him, and call in if I spotted him arriving at the liquor store. By the time he came out of the store, the killer was in place and ready to knock him off."

He related the incident of the junker car that pulled out just as the van arrived. "I'll bet he was part of it too. He was sitting there holding a parking space, just in case the guy with the gun needed to park there. They probably had spotters like me at all the places the dead guy might have been likely to go to, and maybe even other guys holding parking spaces that gave a good shot at the target."

Judith replied, "I'm really puzzled about the police. Surely this rash of killings ought to alert them that something's going on."

"But there's been only two killings."

"Only two that you know about. The Justice Cooperative may have done a lot more that you don't know about."

"Not if the mayor's right, and the number of killings isn't out of line with last year's."

"But wait, Tom. If you kill off a lot of career criminals, the number of murders, assaults, and robberies is going to go down. And that's just what's happened. The number of criminals killed by the Justice Cooperative would be offset by the number of ordinary people who weren't killed by those same criminals. That could explain the mayor's statistics."

"Maybe you're right. In any case, I don't feel so bad now about helping get rid of that guy. From what the reporter said, he should have been locked up and the door welded shut long ago. It's a crime that he was out of jail. Just like it's a crime that Harry Grubbs is out of jail."

Judith made no reply. The grim look on her face was sufficient answer. After a while she spoke.

"When they want you to kill somebody, are you going to do it?"

"I don't have much choice. It's either kill Harry Grubbs myself, or kill somebody else in exchange for somebody else killing Grubbs. Besides, I've been an accessory to two killings already. I'm in too deep to back out now. And if they want me to take out somebody with a record like that guy's," he gestured at the now-silent TV, "I'll figure he deserved it."

# TWENTY-ONE

As Tom rounded the bend in the street on his way home from work, his house came into view.

*What's that flashing blue light? There's two cop-cars in front of the house. Oh my God! If something's happened to Judy I'll go shoot Grubbs myself. I don't care if I do go to jail for it. He's got to be stopped, and the cops won't do it.*

Then another thought hit him. *Are they waiting to arrest me? Do they know about the Justice Cooperative?* He hit the brakes. *Maybe I better run while I can.*

He shook his head and took his foot off the brake. *No, I better go home. Running at the sight of cops is going to make me look guilty of something. And what if it is Judy? Oh God, please let her be okay.*

He whipped his car around one of the police cars and into the driveway. He ran across the lawn and through the opened doorway.

"Judy! Judy! Where are you?"

He got no answer. He ran through the house, calling her name. Still no answer. He ran out the open patio door. In the back yard he saw Judith standing with Lieutenant Callahan and a uniformed policeman. It was obvious she had been crying.

"Judy! Are you OK? What's happened?"

Mutely, she pointed to the ground at Callahan's feet.

"King! What happened to him?"

Callahan spoke. "He appears to have been poisoned. We have the police veterinarian on the way. He may give us a more definite diagnosis."

Judy flung herself into Tom's arms. Holding back the sobs, she spoke. "When I came home, I took a fresh dish of water out for him, like I always do. He didn't come when I called him. I thought maybe he'd found a way to get out of the yard, so I started looking around. Then I saw him lying there. I went up to him, but he didn't move. Then I saw his legs were all stiff and his lips were pulled back from his teeth. He looked just like one of our barn dogs that had gotten into some of Daddy's rat poison. Oh, poor King."

Tom yelled, "This has got to be Grubbs's doing. Are you ever going to take this seriously? Does it have to be one of us dead before you do something?"

Callahan spoke calmly. "Mr. Borden, we are taking it seriously. Ordinarily, we'd treat a dog poisoning as vandalism. Unless the animal was a valuable show dog, the charge would be something like criminal damaging. We'd ask around the neighborhood to see if any strangers had been through, and that would be it. Because of the past threats to you, though, we're making a more thorough investigation."

At that point a uniformed officer came through the gate into the back yard.

Callahan continued, "Here's Sergeant Henry, the veterinarian who takes care of our K-9 dogs. He may want to take the carcass back to his lab for a more thorough examination." He turned to the officer beside him. "Sergeant, would you give Doc Henry any help he needs, while I talk to Mr. and Mrs. Borden inside the house?"

He motioned them through the patio door. Tom took Judith's arm and led her to a sofa in the living room. He sat down beside her. Callahan pulled up a chair to face them.

"Have you seen any sign of Mr. Grubbs since you last talked to me?"

Tom answered. "No. None at all." He turned to Judith. "Anything you haven't told me?"

She choked back a sob and spoke. "No. I haven't seen him."

"We don't have much to go on. Doc Henry's examination should tell us what your dog died of. If he was poisoned, Doc should be able to identify the poison. If it's a common poison, though, we probably won't be able to trace it.

"We'll also ask the neighbors if they saw anything out of the ordinary. Anybody who doesn't belong in the neighborhood, any strange cars, or anything like that.

"For that matter, how do you get along with your neighbors? Are there any of them who are upset with you? Any who resent your dog's barking? Does your dog ever get out and mess up your neighbors' yards?"

"No," Tom replied. "King has never gotten out. He never barks without good reason. The Scotts have always been friendly."

Judith broke in. "And old Mrs. Tompkins, on the other side, told me one day that she felt safer having King outside during the day. No, we've never had trouble with our neighbors over King."

"Okay, so we can assume it wasn't one of the neighbors. That still doesn't mean it was Grubbs. Any incidents of vandalism or rowdyism in the neighborhood? Did any kids ever come by and tease your dog?"

"Not that I know of," Tom answered. "We didn't have him yet when the kids were going to school. If any kids did tease him, it would've been during the day when neither of us was home."

"Okay, that's one possibility we can't yet rule out. Some juvenile delinquents might have poisoned your dog out of some perverted notion of fun.

"Now, have you ever noticed any rats in your yard? Might your dog have eaten a rat one of your neighbors poisoned? Or for that matter, have you set out any poisoned rat bait in your house?"

Judith responded, "We haven't seen any sign of rats in the house. I suppose a rat could crawl through the opening at the gate, or burrow under the fence, but we've never seen any."

The veterinarian called from the back of the house. "Lieutenant Callahan?"

"In here, Doc. Find anything?"

The veterinarian was wiping his hands on a towel as he entered. "I did a hasty autopsy. There was a piece of partly-digested fresh meat in the dog's stomach." He turned to Tom and Judith. "What did you feed him today?"

"Dried dog ration, like I always do. He doesn't get fresh meat, not even table scraps."

"I'll take the carcass and the meat back to the lab and check it, but right now I'd say it's a safe bet that someone fed your dog some poisoned meat." He turned to leave.

"Let me know what you find out," Callahan called after him.

"I'll have something for you in an hour or so," came the reply.

"Thanks, Doc. Let me know if I can do something for you."

Callahan turned to Tom and Judith. "Assuming Doc is right, somebody came by and threw your dog some poisoned meat. Unless we can find witnesses, though, we'll never be able to identify who did it."

"What do you mean!" Tom burst out. "This has to be Harry Grubbs's work. He's been taunting us, driving us crazy with worry. Now he's getting ready to close in. He knocked out one of our lines of defense. We won't get any warning until he actually breaks in and sets off the burglar alarm. By then it'll be too late. I already know how fast he can move once he gets inside. You've got to do something."

"What do you suggest I do, Mr. Borden? Arrest Mr. Grubbs? On what evidence? He'd sue for false arrest, and win. His lawyer would probably tell the jury you poisoned the dog yourself, to cast suspicion on Grubbs. Do you want a civil suit on your hands?"

"Lieutenant, you always seem to have lots of reasons why you can't do anything to help us. What are you waiting for? A couple of dead bodies? What does it take to get you to do something?"

Callahan responded in a tired voice. "This isn't a police state, Mr. Borden. We can't go jailing people because we think they might have committed a crime, or because we think they're likely to commit a crime, or just because they're politically unpopular. Getting a warrant to arrest someone requires that I convince a judge there's probable cause to believe someone has actually committed a crime, or that two people are conspiring to commit a crime. Without evidence, without testimony of a witness, without anything to go on, I'd never be able to convince a judge to issue a warrant."

"Well, can't you keep an eye on him?"

"We don't begin to have enough police to keep an eye on every potential criminal. Moreover, the courts have held that you don't have a right to police protection. You're responsible for your own protection. We can come into the picture only after something actually happens."

"Something has happened," Tom said, bitterness evident in his voice. "My dog was poisoned."

"And we're doing everything we can about that. Even more than we'd do in most cases." He stood up to leave. "I'll let you know what Doc Henry finds out."

Judith asked, "What will he do with King's body once he's finished with it?"

"Turn it over to the dog warden for disposal. That's what we do with dead K-9 dogs."

"*No!*" she shouted. Then she continued in a calmer voice. "No. Call us and we'll come and get him. I'm going to bury him in the back yard. On the farm we always buried our dogs when they died, and I'm going to do the same for King."

"Yeah," Tom added. "In a way King died for us. I'm not going to see him tossed onto the city dump."

"Very well, I'll let you know when Doc Henry is finished with the body."

• • •

Lieutenant Callahan had done better than just let them know. He had called personally to report the results of the examination.

"The dog definitely died of poisoning. However, it's a common rat poison. There's no way we can trace it."

Then he had sent a policeman, going off duty, to deliver King's body back to them.

Judith held a flashlight while Tom dug a hole in a part of the flowerbed that hadn't been planted yet.

"That looks big enough, Tom."

"Okay. I wanted to be sure it was deep enough that rats or whatever wouldn't get at him."

He carefully laid King's body, still wrapped in the cloth that had covered it when the policeman brought it, into the grave. He then began shoveling dirt back into the hole.

Tom looked up at Judith. "Should we get another dog?"

Judith bit her lip. In the dim light of a crescent moon, he could just make out the frown on her face.

"We need the protection the dog would give. But I'm afraid another dog would just be poisoned too. I don't want that."

"Yeah. Though that sounds like we're protectin' the dog more than the dog's protectin' us."

"It does, but I can't think of a dog as just a furry burglar alarm. It's alive. It has a personality. Getting another dog isn't like sticking a new battery into a burglar alarm."

"Yeah, you're right. King was really pleased to see me come home at night. I liked havin' him jump up to the fence at me. I'll miss that. No point in gettin' another dog that'll just be poisoned right away. It isn't fair to the dog."

He finished filling the hole, smoothed the dirt with the shovel, then hoisted the shovel on his shoulder as he followed Judith toward the house.

# TWENTY-TWO

As Tom walked back from the tool crib with a set of freshly- sharpened cutting heads, a thought struck him.

*I haven't seen the foreman all day. I wonder if he's sick or something.*

He walked toward the foreman's office, a glassed-in cubicle in the center of the shop floor.

*What's that? Sven Gunderson's name is the only one on the sign. What happened to the foreman?*

Gunderson was seated at his desk. Tom poked his head in the doorway. "What happened to the boss? His name's gone from the sign. Is he sick?"

Gunderson looked up from his paperwork and leaned back in his chair.

"He's been promoted. He'll be production manager now. He starts Monday. Today he's gettin' a briefing from the guy who's retiring."

"Who'll be foreman? They decided yet?"

"Yep. I'm gettin' the job."

"Well, congratulations, Sven. That's great. When is it official?"

"It'll be announced tomorrow. Officially I start Monday. Actually I started today."

"Any word on who your replacement'll be?"

"Yep. He recommended you for the job. But you ain't s'posed to know that yet. It still has to be approved, so don't go spendin' your pay raise."

Tom's first reaction was elation.

*Hey! They've noticed that I've been doing a good job. That feels good. And with the extra money, maybe Judy won't have to work any more.*

Gunderson's next words came like a dash of cold water.

"Now that I'm foreman, I won't have to put in so much overtime. My ol' lady'll be glad to see me home on time more often. When we get a job here that has to be pushed out the door at night, you can see to it."

*Oh, God! With King poisoned yesterday, I really need to be at home with Judy. Grubbs is closing in on us. The promotion is great, but why NOW of all times.*

Gunderson picked up a sheet of paper from the desk. "You can start tonight. We got an order from Honda that has to be on their truck by eight."

"It's not on the schedule for my cell."

"That's right. It needs broaching, and your cell can't do that. It's scheduled for Harshman's cell. You make sure the castings get out of the foundry on time, and that Harshman gets 'em done. Then make sure they get through final inspection. Have Harshman rework 'em if you have to. But get 'em on that truck on time."

*This is impossible. Should I tell him I don't want the promotion? I do want it. I've worked hard for it. It'll be years before there's another chance like this. Besides, I'm in the same fix Judy was when they offered her a promotion. If I don't take it now, it'll go to somebody else when there's another opening.*

*Can I beg off for tonight? I can't leave Judy alone at home. She's already upset as it is.*

*But getting out of overtime tonight doesn't help. I'll have to start staying late after Monday anyway, every time we have an overtime job. Damn! Why couldn't the promotion have held off until Grubbs was taken care of?*

He sighed. "Okay, I'll get 'em out. Don't worry about it. When are the castings due out of the foundry?"

Gunderson checked the schedule. "About another hour."

Tom looked at the clock and started ticking off activities on his fingers. "Okay, coming out of quench they ought to be cool already. Then I want 'em to be inspected for hidden flaws before Harshman gets 'em. And I want his cell set up to take 'em as soon as they're out of inspection. Yeah. We can make it, if nothing goes wrong."

"That's your job, to see that nothin' does go wrong. Or to see it gets fixed if it does."

Tom walked slowly back to his machining cell.

*I better call Judy and let her know I'll be late getting home. Then I better check with the foundry to make sure those parts are on schedule. Let's see. Then I better make sure Quality Control is ready to inspect them, and that Harshman's ready to start the setup on his machines so he can tackle the parts as soon as they're out of QC. Then QC'll have to be ready for final inspection.*

*Wonder if I can get a forklift driver to take the parts to QC a few at a time, as soon as Harshman gets them done, instead of batching them and taking them all at once. That way QC can be checking some while Harshman is finishing the rest.*

He reached his cell, checked that the machines were running smoothly, and put the cutting heads in the proper racks. He then went to the cell's computer terminal and brought up the schedule on the screen.

*Good. No changes. This batch of parts will be finished on time. I sure don't want my own cell fouling up when I'm supposed to be acting as assistant foreman.*

As he watched his helpers, another thought came to him.

*Wonder if they'll pick one of these guys to replace me at this cell? In case they ask me, I better have a recommendation. Anderson? No. Too relaxed. He follows orders fine, but he won't push. Miller? Could be. He's got a feel for the machines. Farrell? He's got more experience than Miller. I don't know if he's got the drive to follow through. I guess I better start finding out.*

He called to Miller. "Jim."

Miller straightened up from where he was watching a machining operation.

"What is it, Tom?"

"Gunderson gave me an errand to run over in the foundry. I may be gone a while. See to it that these parts get batched and over to QC as soon as they're done. Don't let 'em sit around. Get a forklift driver over here right away."

"Okay. Shouldn't have any problems with 'em in QC, though. I been gaugin' the parts as they go. Everything's right on the money here."

"Good. Stop the machines and fix 'em if the parts start gettin' out of tolerance."

He walked to the pay phone, left a message for Judith at her office, then headed for the foundry.

He stuck his head in the foundry foreman's office. "Hi, Mike. I'm checkin' on this set of parts." He handed over a copy of the routing form.

"What happened to Gunderson?"

"He can't stay overtime today. He gave me the job of gettin' these things out on time. Accordin' to the schedule, you're supposed to have 'em out in thirty minutes."

"Well, we're a bit behind schedule now. We're short a man today, so they didn't come out of the furnace on time. They're going through quenching now. As soon as they're done, we'll get 'em to you."

"Look, Mike, that puts me in a bind. I got to have these things on the loading dock by eight tonight."

"Tom, I feel for you, but I can't quite reach you. There's just no way I can speed up the quench."

"Okay, how about breakin' up the batch. Each time you get some out of the quench bath, send 'em to QC. They can be checkin' some of 'em while you're workin' on the rest."

"That ain't the way it's supposed to go, Tom." The foundry foreman waved the sheet of paper. "This traveler is supposed to go with the whole batch."

"If you do it that way, we won't make the delivery. Honda'll be unhappy. Then the production manager'll be unhappy. Then there'll be some questions asked. And I'm goin' to give straight answers."

"Well, maybe I could bend the rules a bit for you, Tom, but I don't have a forklift driver to keep shuttlin' between quench and QC."

"I'll find a forklift driver. You get those parts ready."

He returned to Gunderson's office and explained the problem.

"That'll work, Tom. We got two forklift drivers on today. I'll ask one of 'em to stay on and keep those parts movin' for you. Pete's been lookin' for some overtime anyway."

With that problem solved, Tom headed for Quality Control.

"Ed, I got to have some parts out on time tonight. I'm goin' to have the foundry send 'em straight to you soon's they come out of quench, a few at a time. That way you can be checkin' some of 'em while they're finishin' the rest. Then I'll start sendin' 'em back to you as quick as they come out of machining."

"That doubles my workload, Tom. That way I got to check 'em before you get 'em, then check 'em again after you're done."

"Look, Ed, I don't want my guys workin' on parts that already have flaws. Besides, it won't double your work. You just check 'em for internal flaws when they come out of quench. We won't add any internal flaws. When they come back, all you got to check 'em for is the machining."

"Okay. I guess I can do that. But it ain't accordin' to the rules."

*Hang the rules, he thought, as he walked to Harshman's cell. Dammit, those guys in QC think their job is to find bad parts, when they really ought to be helping us to keep from making bad parts. Wonder if I can do anything about that after I get promoted? If I get promoted, that is.*

Harshman was watching one of his helpers gauge a part as it came out of the final machining step.

Tom held out the routing sheet. "Bill, Gunderson tells me you've got this run of parts for Honda."

"That's right. What's the problem?"

"No problem. Sven can't stay overtime tonight, and he told me to see they get out on time. I've arranged for the foundry to send 'em to QC a few at a time, as they come out of quench, and for QC to check 'em for internal flaws." He looked at his watch. "The first castings ought to be reaching you in about an hour. Can you be set up to start workin' on 'em as soon as they get here?"

Harshman looked at the parts still going through his cell.

"Yeah, easy. This batch'll be out in thirty minutes. I'll start the setup on the first machines as soon as they're clear. If I have to, I can finish the setup on the last machines while the parts are already started through."

"Good. I'll check back with you as soon as the parts are out of QC."

He headed back to his own cell. "Jim, how're things going?"

"We finished that batch on schedule. As soon as the first machines were clear, I started the setup for the next job on the schedule."

"Good. How's it look?"

"We'll have it done before quittin' time."

"Okay. Treat any extra time you have as scheduled down-time, and take care of any maintenance that's due on the machines. If there's any extra time after that, check the cutting heads and exchange any that need sharpening. I'll be at Harshman's cell if you need me."

*Well, looks like Miller can follow through. Tomorrow I'll have to give Farrell a chance to take over the cell, to see if he can handle it. But it's good to know at least one of 'em can take over for me. If I get promoted, that is.*

He returned to Quality Control. "How're my parts comin', Ed?"

"Your driver brought four of 'em, then went back to wait for more. The first two had bad flaws. We're still checkin' the others."

Tom checked the schedule sheet. "I'm supposed to get two dozen castings, and Honda needs only twenty finished parts. I guess I'm okay so far."

*Yeah, if nothing else goes wrong. I just don't need a big screw-up when I'm trying to show I can handle the assistant foreman's job.*

One of the QC technicians handed Ed a slip of paper. He looked at it, then spoke.

"The last two are okay. As soon as your driver gets back, you can have 'em."

Tom looked toward the foundry. "Here he comes now. Get started checkin' this load, and I'll have him take the two good ones away."

Tom followed the forklift to Harshman's cell. "Here's the first castings, Bill. You can start as soon as your setup's completed."

"It'll be about another ten minutes. Then we'll start the first one through."

Tom glanced at the wall clock. *That's not too bad. By breaking the batch coming out of the foundry, we've made up the time they lost in making the castings. We're just about back on the original schedule. I should be able to get home to Judy before nine.*

He headed back for his own cell. "Any problems, Jim?"

"Nope. We'll have the parts through on schedule. I checked on the maintenance. A couple of filters in the hydraulic lines are due to be replaced about now. I sent Anderson to get replacements."

"Good."

*Well, Miller seems to be taking hold. That means we can move either him or Farrell up and hire a new helper. We won't need to bring in some senior guy to take over the cell.*

He returned to Harshman's cell. The machines were idle.

"What's the problem? How come you're not workin'?"

"We finished those two parts. We're waiting for more."

He looked at the clock. *Damn! Nearly all the time I saved by breaking the batch is lost because some castings were bad and Harshman has nothing to work on.*

He headed for Quality Control. "Where's my parts, Ed?"

"Sorry, Tom. Two more bad ones. Evidently the foundry had a problem with their molds on the first part of the batch. However, we got two good ones for you."

"But that leaves me with no safety margin. If there's any more bad castings, I can't finish the order."

"I don't break 'em, Tom, I just find the breaks."

"Yeah, I know. You can't inspect quality into a part, it has to be built in. But there has to be a better way than finding the flaws after it's too late to do anything about 'em."

He looked at the clock. *More time lost because Harshman doesn't have anything to work on. It'll be a tight squeeze to get the parts on the loading dock by eight.*

*And Judy! She'll be sitting home alone, wondering if Grubbs is lurking around somewhere. Hell of a note. She's locked up in the house while a slimeball like Grubbs is free to go anywhere he wants.*

He headed back for Harshman's cell. The next two castings were going through the machines.

"You sent the parts you finished back to QC?"

"Yeah. Pete took 'em when he brought these two."

"How'd they look?"

"They should pass. They checked out okay here."

The forklift arrived with another pallet full of castings.

"How many you got, Pete?"

"Four of 'em. It's the same four I delivered to QC on my last run from the foundry, so they must all be good."

"Good. I hope whatever mold problem they had got fixed."

Again Tom looked at the clock, willing it to slow down, while the machines ran fast.

*I not only got to get these parts out, I got to get home to Judy. She shouldn't be alone like this. If this's going to happen every night, maybe I don't want this promotion.*

*But I do want it. I earned it. Besides, we need the extra money.*

*Dammit, why should I have to give up a promotion so I can be home to protect my wife? That's what we're supposed to have cops and judges and jails for. That's what I'm paying taxes for. But everyone seems to be more worried about protecting the rights of slimeballs like Grubbs than they are about people like me. How much taxes does Grubbs pay? How much extra work does he make for the cops? He's probably committing crimes right and left now. He just hasn't been caught.*

He followed the forklift to Quality Control.

"How're the finished parts, Ed?"

"The first two you sent back were good. We'll get these two checked right away."

Time dragged by for Tom in a seemingly endless round of trudging from the machining cell to Quality Control to the foundry and back. The pile of finished parts grew slowly at the exit to Quality Control. Two workers were strapping them down to pallets.

Tom noticed that Pete was sitting idle, waiting for the next batch of castings.

"Pete, why don't you take these pallets of finished parts to the loading dock, while you're waiting for more work?"

Pete leaned forward to put the forklift in gear. "Good idea. That'll save time later."

*Right. And the more time we save, the quicker I can get home to Judy.*

Another thought struck him. *I better not say anything about saving time, though. Most of these guys want as much overtime as they can get, just like I used to. They probably want to run right up to eight o'clock. I better just keep talking about the deadline, not about how much I want to get home.*

Finally the last castings came from the foundry and passed inspection. Tom followed them to the machining cell.

"This is it," he said to Harshman. "We got exactly twenty good castings, and we need to turn out twenty finished parts. Don't let anything go wrong here. I'm going to check my own cell."

He found that the new hydraulic line filters had been installed, and the records updated. The tool racks held several freshly-sharpened cutting heads.

*Okay, Miller has shown he can cut the mustard. Tomorrow I better give Farrell a chance to show his stuff. After all, he's senior to Miller. I just don't think he's as good with the machines.*

He walked past Quality Control. The fully-loaded pallets were gone. Another one was being loaded. The four bad castings were set to one side, to be returned to the foundry.

"How are they doing, Ed?"

"All good parts so far, Tom. Don't spoil any, and you'll make it."

He gave the clock a glance. *Looks like we'll make it with time to spare. Good! That's less time for Judy to be alone.*

As he approached Harshman's cell, he heard a shout.

"Stop the machine! The cutting head broke!"

He quickened his pace. He found Harshman examining the last of the castings, as it rested on the broaching machine's work platform.

"What's wrong?" Tom asked.

"A piece of the cutting head snapped off," Harshman replied, "right inside this hole we're broaching through the casting. The rough spot on the head gouged the work piece."

"Can you polish out the gouge?"

Harshman fiddled with a gauge for a moment. "No. It's too deep. If we grind it out, the hole will be out of tolerance. We were doing the final polishing of the interior when the tool snapped."

*Oh, my God. Now what? I can't rework this part, and there aren't any more good castings. And this was supposed to be my chance to show I could handle the assistant foreman's job.*

*But dammit, it's not my fault the foundry turned out lousy castings. It's not my fault the tool broke. They can't expect miracles out of me.*

*Maybe it's not my fault, but they'll remember it happened on my watch. From now on, even if I do get promoted, I'll be remembered as the guy who botched an order on his first time in charge. I've got to do something. But what?*

He covered his eyes with his hands, and took a deep breath.

"What do you want me to do?" Harshman asked. "Grind it out anyway?"

"That won't help. We can't send out a part that's out of tolerance. Let me check on something."

He returned to Quality Control. "Ed, where are the flaws in those bad castings?"

Ed reached into the wastebasket and pulled out some sonograms. He smoothed them out on his desk.

"This one's got a big crack right here," he pointed.

"No good. No way we can use that one."

"This one's got a void in the center here."

"No good either. Looks like they didn't pour that one right."

"Probably not. That's why we usually get voids in that spot."

Tom's frustration reached fever pitch. *Then why don't you tell them to fix the problem? There's no point in them pouring bad castings.* However, he held his tongue.

"This one has an inclusion right here in this flange around the base."

"Wait a minute," Tom said. He unrolled the blueprint for the part and compared it with the sonogram.

"That may be okay. We need to drill a hole right there anyway. If we can get through the inclusion without breaking the bit or cracking the casting, we're in business. Can you take another shot of that, and focus on the inclusion, so I can see exactly what we're up against?"

"Sure. It'll be a few minutes."

Ed's crew brought the casting back inside, and ran another sonogram.

"Here's the result, Tom. We sharpened up the picture a bit right around the inclusion. Good enough?"

"Yeah, that's fine. Thanks a lot, Ed."

He leaned out the door and waved to Pete. "Get this casting to Harshman right away."

Tom showed the sonogram to Harshman and compared it with the blueprint.

"It looks like the inclusion is completely within the hole you're supposed to drill. What you got to do is drill the hole without breaking anything. Can you do that?"

"Yeah. I'll drill until we reach the inclusion, then grind through it. Even if I break a grinding head, it won't hurt anything. But Tom, it looks as though the inclusion runs right up to the edge of where the hole is supposed to be."

"Well, make the hole a bit out-of-round. Stretch it in the direction of the inclusion. Just don't go outside the maximum tolerance on that side."

"Okay. I think I can do that."

Tom headed back for Quality Control.

*I don't want to watch. It would just about kill me if Harshman screws it up. Besides, it would make me nervous if my boss were watching me run a critical operation. I don't want to do that to Harshman.*

"Ed, how're the finished parts coming?"

"Everything fine so far, Tom. Your driver just brought numbers eighteen and nineteen. We're checkin' 'em now."

"Good." He looked at the clock.

*It's going to be close, but we ought to get that last part on the loading dock by eight.*

He forced himself to get a cup of coffee from the vending machine. He stood by the machine as he drank it, forcing himself to sip it slowly. Then he ambled toward Harshman's cell.

"Everything's fine, Tom. We got the hole drilled and ground with no problems. It's a couple of ten-thousandths off center and out of round, but it's still within tolerance everywhere."

"Not the kind of work we like to do, is it?" Tom said "But it's better than sending a short shipment. How's the rest of the job coming?"

"We're doing final polishing now. It'll be ready in less than five minutes."

Tom followed the forklift to Quality Control. He stood with

his hands in his pockets, shifting his weight from one foot to the other, as he waited for the inspection to be completed.

"It's a good one, Tom."

*Thank God for small favors!* He let out a breath he hadn't realized he'd been holding.

"Pete! Let's get this last batch out to the loading dock. Honda's truck is due any minute."

He followed Pete to the dock, counted the parts one last time "just to make sure," then returned to Harshman's cell.

"Thank your guys for me for gettin' that job out on time. They shouldn't've had to make up for the foundry's problems, but they did."

He checked his own cell. It was properly cleaned up and closed down. He headed for his locker, changed clothes, grabbed his lunch pail, and clocked out.

*Better be careful. Grubbs just might be hanging around here instead of around our house.*

However, there was no sign of Grubbs in the parking lot. He left for home.

*Traffic's light tonight. The trip home ought to go fast. Even so, I'll take the short route. I don't want Judy home alone any longer than she has to be.*

Shortly he pulled into his driveway, behind Judith's car.

*This twilight must be playing tricks on me. I thought for a minute I saw King coming around the corner of the garage, like he always did. What kind of a no-good would poison a dog, anyway? But Grubbs has done a lot worse than poison a dog. He's got to be stopped.*

As he started to unlock the door, he saw the burglar alarm was set. He disarmed that first, then opened the door.

"Judy! I'm home."

Judith's voice sounded distant. "I'm upstairs."

He started up the stairs, but came to a halt just before the top, as she came into view. She was seated in a folding chair in the hallway outside the bedroom door, reading a book. Beside her was a TV table holding her gun.

She stuffed a bookmark into the book, slammed it shut,

dropped it on the table, and ran to him.

"Am I ever glad you're home."

"What's going on?"

"Grubbs followed me home again."

"All the way to the house?"

"No. He kept going straight when I turned off the boulevard."

"I guess he doesn't need to follow you. He already knows where you live. He's just letting you know he hasn't forgotten you."

"How much longer do we have to put up with this?

He made no reply as he held her, but his thoughts were bitter. *What kind of a country is this where the honest people lock themselves up and the crooks run loose? That isn't the way it was supposed to be.*

# TWENTY-THREE

It wasn't until Tom got home that the day turned sour. Until then he'd felt on top of the world.

As the starting whistle blew, Tom had been watching Farrell direct the other helpers set up the cell for the first job of the day. Gunderson approached him.

"Tom, I heard about how you pulled the fat out of the fire last night. You did one helluva good job in getting that shipment off to Honda on time."

"Thanks, Sven. But you don't know how close I came to giving up when it looked like there was no way to manage it."

"But you didn't give up. That's what counts. By the way, what would you've done if the defect hadn't been in a part of the flange you were going to drill away anyhow?"

"I thought about that while I was driving home. I decided I'd have cut off the bad section of the flange, cut a good section off another of the bad castings, and had the welding shop put 'em together."

"Yeah, that's the way I did it once. That'd work fine. Anyhow, I'll make sure the production manager knows how you saved his hide."

"Thanks, Sven."

The rest of the day had gone equally well. The scheduled work had gone out on time, all the work was well within tolerance, and Tom had received an "attaboy" from the production manager. By quitting time he was feeling good.

He walked in his front door in a good mood.

"Tom, here's something for you. It must be from the Justice Cooperative. The return address is a phony."

Instead of the usual letter, this was a bulky package. He placed it on the kitchen table and opened it. Out came a stack of photocopies of newspaper articles, and copies of police and court records. They all concerned someone named Tim Bartlett. Tom scanned them slowly.

"My God! This guy must be one of the most rotten creeps ever born. Look at this! Rape, plea bargained down to Gross Sexual Imposition. Sentenced to time already served. Assault and battery, plea bargained down to simple assault. Sentenced to 30 days and six months probation. Jail time reduced to time already served. Armed robbery, plea bargained down so the gun charge didn't stick. Murder, plea bargained down to manslaughter. Served one year before parole. It just goes on and on like that. Since he was in his 'teens, this guy has robbed, beaten, and killed right and left, yet he's served less than two years in jail for all of it. And now he's out free."

"Why are they sending you this information?"

Tom reached the bottom of the stack, found a letter typed on the familiar faded dot matrix printer, and started reading it.

"This is the guy they want me to execute. I've got to let them know if I'll do it."

"NO, TOM. YOU MUSTN'T DO IT."

"What d'you mean? If I don't execute this guy, I'll have to execute Grubbs myself. It's one or the other."

"That's just it, Tom. If Grubbs comes in here, you're justified in killing him. The prosecutor might not even press charges."

"But I don't want him in here. I want him killed before he comes after us again."

"That's just the point. If you went out and killed him before he came after us, I'd agree it'd be right, even if it would be against the law. The way he's stalking us, you could probably even convince a jury it was right.

"But this really scares me. Look, Tom, it's all well and good to say we have no choice. But we do have a choice. This Bartlett never did us any harm. You can't just go out and kill someone who's no threat to us. That's just plain wrong."

"Hangmen kill people who aren't threatening them. How is this different?"

"That's because the government sentenced someone to death. The hangman is carrying out the sentence. He knows what the criminal did. Here you don't even know this man."

"What's knowing him got to do with it? Soldiers kill people they don't even know. I don't have to know this guy personally to execute him. In fact I'd rather I didn't."

"But a soldier only kills people who threaten him and his country."

"When your father went to Vietnam, he killed people who were no threat to us here at home. They were a threat to him only because he was sent there. If he'd stayed home, they wouldn't have been a threat to him either."

"They were a threat to the South Vietnamese people. I've heard him tell about the terrible things the North Vietnamese and the Viet Cong did."

"Your dad didn't know any of those people he was defending. They were total strangers, just like the ones he killed."

"He didn't have to know them. The government sent him there to help our friends. The enemy there was a threat to our allies."

"Then what's wrong with my helping someone I don't know, through the Justice Cooperative?"

"The Justice Cooperative isn't the government."

"The government! The government!" He was shouting now. "What's all this about the government? Look, dammit! The government isn't doing its job. I can't put it in fancy words like your lawyer friends could, but what's a government anyway but people getting together to defend themselves? You don't lose your right to defend yourself just because there's a government. When the government doesn't do its job, we don't have to sit here and take it. We have a right to defend ourselves."

"But this is lynch law. You might make a mistake. The Justice Cooperative might make a mistake. The reason for having a government is to have laws and courts. If you accuse someone of some crime, your story is heard by people who aren't involved, and who can look at the facts without being prejudiced for either side."

Tom paused a moment, then continued in a calmer voice. "This guy was tried in court. He was turned loose again, time after time. That's not justice. And when we can't get justice from the government, we have a right to get it for ourselves. We have a right to get together with other people to defend ourselves. I'd be simply helping out a neighbor who's in trouble. Helping out a neighbor is just as American as a barn-raising. You ought to understand that."

Judith waited a long moment, then continued in a low voice. "Tom, let's move. Let's get away from here and from Harry Grubbs. Then you won't have to kill this Bartlett person."

"Where would we go? Your father said crime was going up even in your home town. There's no way to get away from it. We'd just be going from crooks we know about to crooks we don't know about.

"And if we moved, what kind of a job could I get? I've worked hard to get the promotion I just got. If we move, I'll have to start all over at the bottom. Maybe even in a different kind of job."

"That would be a lot better than being convicted of murder. That's what'd happen if they caught you."

"No, Judy. No. This is my home town. I grew up here. My folks are buried here. I'm not going to let some crook chase me out of here.

"Besides, what's to say that if we move, Grubbs won't just come after us? He's made up his mind to get us. We'd be giving up everything we have, and still not escaping him. We don't need to run away, we need to get justice. And since the government won't give me justice, I'll get it for myself, and I'll take the help of anyone who'll help me.

"Look, Judy. Do you think I like the idea of killing somebody? I don't even like the idea of killing Harry Grubbs. I'd do it just like I'd kill a mad dog, to keep him from hurting somebody else. I'm doing this because I don't have any choice. And I'm doing it as much for you as for me. I'm not going to have you thinking I can't protect you, and I'm not going to have your father thinking I'm not a good husband for you.

"Now, are you going to support me, or am I on my own?"

She started to speak, then bit her lip. She turned away and walked to the stairs. He heard the *slap-slap-slap* of her sandals as she climbed the stairs. There was a long moment of silence, then he heard their bedroom door slam.

He stood silently, hands balled into fists at his side. Finally he slammed a fist into an open palm, then strode to the kitchen table. He pulled out two pictures of Bartlett, burned the rest of the papers, and flushed the ashes down the garbage disposal.

He pulled on a light jacket, stuck his gun in his pocket, and opened the front door. He hesitated briefly as he looked at the stairway, then closed the door and set the burglar alarm.

He walked to a pay phone and called the number in the message, then gave the password.

"I'm ready to take on the job."

"What tools do you want to use?"

The code for rifle was "chainsaw;" for a handgun it was "hammer."

"I think I'd prefer to use a hammer."

"Do you want us to provide you with a birdhouse, or will you make one?"

That was the code word for a silencer. He'd decided he could make one. It would be cheaper than having them provide one. They were charging him enough for the gun as it was.

"I'll make it myself."

"Very well, we will send you the plans along with the tools. You will receive instructions by parcel delivery."

There was a *click* as the speaker hung up. Glumly, Tom headed back for his house.

He disarmed the alarm, unlocked the door, and stepped inside.

*Now what? Do I sleep on the couch? No, dammit. Not unless she tells me to. Sharing a bed with her isn't like it's supposed to be, but at least we can touch each other. I don't want for us to end up just living in the same house like a couple of strangers who're only sharing expenses.*

He took off his shoes and tiptoed up the steps. One of the steps squeaked under his foot.

*Damn. I forgot about that squeaky step. I've got to get that fixed. I wonder if the noise woke her.*

He hesitated outside the bedroom door, then turned the knob. He slid his feet to avoid tripping over anything as he groped his way into the pitch-black room.

"I'm awake, Tom. You can turn the light on."

He reached behind him and flipped the switch. He saw she was lying on her back, arms under her head. Apparently she'd been staring at the ceiling in the dark.

"I couldn't sleep, Tom. Not after walking away from you like that.

"Look, Tom. I know you're doing this for me. But I'm scared. I'm scared of what'll happen if you don't go ahead with it, and I'm scared of what'll happen if you do. But I'll support you whatever you do. It just isn't right that we should have to make a choice like this."

"Thanks, Judy. I told 'em I'd go ahead with it. But I'd sure hate to lose you over something I did mostly for you."

"Tom, please hold me. That's all. Just hold me. I need to know you're there."

He quickly got into his pajamas and crawled under the covers. She nestled in his arms. She kissed him lightly on the cheek, then laid her head on his shoulder. Soon her breathing became steady, and she dropped off to sleep. After a while he gently untangled himself from her.

*How come these country music singers are always singing about holding somebody in their arms all night long? I can't do it. My arm goes to sleep. Maybe they know something I don't, but I think they're just full of it.*

# TWENTY-FOUR

The instructions from the Justice Cooperative had come a few days after Tom's call to them. He was to obtain a specified amount of money in cash, and place it behind a loose brick in a decorative wall in a park downtown. He had worried that something would go wrong, and the money would end up in the hands of some kid, or some park worker. He couldn't possibly claim it, and he'd have to draw out more money from an already meager bank account. However, things must have gone right. Yesterday a delivery truck had pulled up to the house and left a package. The return address on the package was phony. Judith had checked.

Inside the package was an envelope marked OPEN ME FIRST. It had contained instructions. The first item on the list was to obtain some plastic gloves at a paint store, and to wear these every time he touched anything in the package. After that, he was to open the remaining parcels inside the package. Now he was following the instructions.

He put on the plastic gloves. They were a bit tight. He made a mental note to put cornstarch into the next pair he used.

He started with the parcel labeled #1, which was something

wrapped in newspaper. He unwrapped it carefully. It was a gun.

It was nothing fancy. Nothing a gun collector would take a second look at. It had a black matte finish, plastic grips, and fixed black sights.

*Well, it doesn't have to be fancy. It just has to work once. After that I'll get rid of it anyway.*

He picked it up, and turned it over several times as he examined it. There was a manufacturer's name on it, and the name of a city in Spain. Obviously imported. No, more likely smuggled. He had no doubt the Justice Cooperative had brought it into the country without telling the Feds or paying duty on it. So he'd not only bought a gun illegally, the gun itself was illegal too.

He frowned. *What do the gun-grabbers think they're doing? Can they really believe that gun registration, waiting periods, and outright gun bans will keep guns out of the hands of crooks? Drug smugglers bring tons of cocaine into the country every day. Guns could be smuggled just as easily as drugs.*

*No,* he thought, *so long as there are criminals who want guns, there'll be a market for smuggled guns. Even if the gun-grabbers could confiscate every single gun in the whole United States, the very next day some crooks'd be smuggling them in to sell to other crooks.*

*No,* he told himself, *the gun grabbers can't be honest in saying they want to ban guns in order to stop crime. They aren't stupid. If even I can see that banning guns will only make gun- running more profitable, they have to see it too. Which means they have other reasons for wanting to ban guns, reasons they aren't willing to admit.*

*But what could it be? Suppose they could succeed in disarming all the honest people, never mind the crooks. What happens when the government has all the guns? If guns in the hands of the people are the last-ditch defense of the Constitution against a dictatorship, how will we defend the Constitution if the gun-grabbers have their way? Is that what they really want, to keep us helpless while they take away our rights?*

*And what happens then? Do those college professors and TV news people and the people who write anti-gun editorials in the papers really think that once the government has all the guns, they'll be safe? Do they really think that once the government has all the guns, they'll still be allowed to teach and say and write whatever they want? If they think that, maybe they are stupid.*

He carefully re-wrapped the gun, and opened the other parcels in sequence. One contained a magazine for the gun. Another held enough cartridges to fill the magazine. The explanation with them stated that they were subsonic, so they wouldn't make any sound after they left the gun muzzle. He noted the bullets were hollow-points. Even in 9-millimeter, they should have a high probability of a one-shot stop. Then another thought struck him.

*I'm not trying just to stop this guy. I have to make sure he's dead, even if it means pumping the whole magazine into him.*

The final parcel was a rolled-up set of plans for a silencer. He studied them with a machinist's eye. Some of the parts he could get at a hardware store, like the rubber washers. Others he'd have to make at the plant. Most of those were some identical metal holders for the washers. They and the washers were to be stacked up, and the stack held together with a couple of long machine screws. Making that up would be a snap. He could do that some evening when his former cell was idle and he was pushing the work out of some other cell.

He'd also have to take the barrel of the gun in to the plant and thread it so the silencer could be screwed onto it. That would be the tricky part.

*I can't afford to let anyone see me do that. I'll have to do that right the first time, too. If I botch it, there's no way to get another barrel.*

With that he carefully repacked the box, hid it under some old newspapers, and stripped the gloves off his hands.

# TWENTY-FIVE

The next evening, as Tom had hoped, there was a job scheduled that required overtime work. Fortunately for his plans, the job required machining operations that couldn't be done in his former cell. He'd delivered the news to Miller, hiding his own pleasure that the cell, now Miller's, would be idle.

"Sorry, Jim, the overtime has to go to Harshman's cell tonight. These parts for Chrysler need broaching. I'll do my best to send some overtime your way soon."

*But,* he told himself, *I can't afford to let it look like I'm playing favorites. I've got to give everybody an equal shot at overtime, or I'll have guys mad at me. Then they won't deliver for me when I really need them. But I'm sure glad I can sneak some work on my old cell tonight.*

What he hadn't expected was that Gunderson would stick around.

"I got some paperwork to get out, Tom. Quarterly reports on machine use. I hate it, but it's part of bein' foreman. I'll be lookin' around the floor, but you keep on top of that Chrysler job."

"Okay, Sven. I'll see that it gets out on time. Don't worry

about it."

*Now how am I going to explain what I'm doing, running an unscheduled job? If I'm lucky, he won't notice it.*

At the scheduled time he stuck his head in the door of the office he now shared with Gunderson.

"Sven, the Chrysler parts ought to be comin' out of QC now. I'm going to check on them."

"Okay, Tom. By the way, I got word today that the Suggestion Committee approved your idea to run all castings through QC before they come here for machining, and to send the sonograms back to the foundry when they spot a problem. The foundry people really liked the idea. They said they'd been wantin' more feedback on problems, so's they could fix 'em."

"I'm glad they liked the idea. I think it'll help us get stuff out quicker if we don't have so many defects before we even get our hands on the work."

*And the bonus for the idea will be nice too. There ought to be some real bucks saved if the foundry puts out fewer bad castings. Judy and I can use the money.*

First he headed for Harshman's cell.

"Bill, how soon'll you be ready for this Chrysler job?"

"The last parts on this job've already cleared the first machine. I can start the setup now. I'll be ready in about twenty minutes. I'll start the setup on each machine as soon as it's finished on this job."

"Okay. That'll mean some of the Chrysler parts'll be waitin' for you to finish a setup, but there's no way around that. How long before the whole job's finished?" Harshman stepped to his computer terminal and called up the scheduling program. "If nothin' goes wrong, we'll have the whole job done in two hours."

"Okay, good. We'll make the schedule with no sweat."

*That means I got to get my own job finished before then. That won't give me much time.*

He next went to the foreman's office in QC.

"Ed, how're my parts coming?"

"We got 'em from the foundry all at once. We're checking

'em as fast as we can. Does that make any problems for you?"

"No, we couldn't've taken 'em any sooner anyway. We had another job to get out on the same cell. I'll send a forklift right away."

He tracked down the forklift driver.

"Pete, I need about two hours of overtime on your 'lift. Can you do it?"

"You bet. I'll call home and let the ol' lady know I'll be late."

The quitting time whistle blew just as the first pallet of parts arrived from QC. Within minutes the shop was empty. The only sounds came from Harshman's cell. With the first of the Chrysler parts being machined, Tom headed for the locker room. He removed the gun barrel from his lunch pail, and stuck it in his pocket. Then he headed for his former cell.

*First I've got to get the barrel threaded. Cutting the metal should take only a couple of minutes, but I got to get it right the first time.*

He first turned down the end of a scrap rod until it was the same diameter as the gun barrel, then set up a machine to thread the test piece. When it was finished, he examined the threads carefully.

*Looks good. I can do the barrel now. But I better check on Harshman's job first. I don't want to feel rushed while I'm doing this.*

The job was running smoothly at Harshman's cell. Another pallet of castings arrived from QC as he watched. He headed for QC to check on the rest of the batch.

"About three-quarters done, Tom. We'll have the last of 'em to you in less'n half an hour."

"That's good enough, Ed. It'll take us longer'n that to get started on the parts we have now. Findin' many defects?"

"Only one so far. Some porosity in one end of the casting. Evidently they didn't get all the bubbles out of the mold. I sent the sonogram on that one to the foundry. They'll see it tomorrow."

"Okay, thanks. We'll start gettin' the finished parts to you for final inspection in a few minutes."

With that he returned to his former cell. Carefully he clamped the gun barrel in the chuck and started the program running. He watched nervously as the tool began cutting threads on the muzzle end of the barrel.

*Looks good. Three-eighths of an inch of thread. The threads're clean.*

Quickly he removed the barrel from the chuck and headed for the locker room. He slipped the barrel back into his lunch pail, then walked past the office. Gunderson was still poring over his sheets of paper.

"How's it going, Sven?"

"For doin' these reports the first time, not bad. After this they ought to go faster."

Another check at Harshman's cell.

"No problems here, Tom. Setup is finished on all the machines, and the first finished part is out. They'll come out at one every two minutes from here on."

Tom did a quick mental calculation. *One every two minutes. Yeah, we'll make it easy. Just so's nothing goes wrong. But I got to hurry on my own job.*

With the barrel threaded, the tricky part was over. The rest was tedious, but not critical. If he spoiled a part, he could make another one.

Quickly he punched the dimensions for the first piece into the controller. It would be a cup-shaped piece, with two ears for the screws that would hold the whole assembly together, and a nipple threaded to mate with the end of the barrel.

He placed a block of metal in the feed tray. The robot arm picked it up and started it through the first machine. While it was being machined, he started entering the dimensions for the matching piece that would go at the other end of the assembly. As soon as the first machine was clear, he put another block of metal in the feed tray, and switched the program to the second part.

Within minutes both parts were finished. He held them in his hand for a moment, then headed for the locker room.

He checked that no one else was in the room, then opened

his lunch pail. He carefully threaded the barrel into its mating part.

*Okay. Couldn't ask for a better fit. No one but me'll ever see it, but I still don't want to do a lousy job.*

He placed the second piece against the first. *Yeah, the screw holes line up right. If I just copy the dimensions for the rest of the parts, everything ought to fit okay.*

Suddenly the door opened. The janitor stepped in.

"Hi, Tom. What's up?"

Tom stuffed the parts into his lunch pail and slammed it shut, then turned. "Nothin'. I just needed a snack. It's been a long time since lunch."

"Yeah, it has been for me too. And I'll be goin' home later than you will." He started pushing a broom up and down between the rows of lockers.

Tom closed his locker and started to leave.

*Oh, God, I hope he doesn't think I'm stealing something. That's all I'd need, is for the gate guard to check my lunch pail. Why'd he have to come in right now?*

He went back to Harshman's cell.

"Keep your fingers crossed, Tom. We're over half way done and not a single problem."

"You send any finished parts to QC?"

"Yeah, when Pete brought me some more castings, I sent back everything I've finished so far."

He walked past the office. Gunderson was still at work with his report forms. He hurried to his former cell and started setting it up to make a run of identical items. He had bought several packages of rubber washers at a hardware store, checked them with a micrometer, and selected enough washers of the same thickness to make up the silencer. The cuts in the metal rings that held the washers would be slightly shallower than the washer thickness, so the washers would be held tightly when the silencer was assembled. He placed a thick metal rod in the feed tray. It would be sliced into disks. The disks would then be shaped into flanged rings. He started the parts through, watched the first disk as it went through all the stations, then headed for Harshman's cell.

"Just about done, Tom. Four more castings to go."

Tom glanced at the wall clock, and did another mental calculation.

*Okay, we're right on schedule. I better check with QC.*

"Ed, what's the story on the Chrysler parts?"

"We sent the last of the castings to your shop, Tom. There're five extras here, just in case you run into some kind of problem. I figured I'd hold 'em here unless you needed 'em. No point in sendin' 'em to you and then havin' you send 'em right back."

"Okay, thanks. I don't think we'll need 'em. But don't send 'em back to the foundry until we finish the job. How're the finished parts?"

"All checked out okay so far."

"They ought to. Give us good material to work with, and we don't spoil it." He headed back to where his personal job was running. He reached the cell and stopped short.

*Oh, no. Gunderson's here. Now what'll I do?*

"Tom, there's nothin' scheduled on this cell. What's goin' on?"

He raced for an answer. "I'm makin' some things my wife needs for a crafts project. I used scrap materials for it."

Sven nodded his head. "Yeah, my wife got into crafts once. Ceramics. We ended up with a house full of coffee mugs, vases, and ashtrays. Good thing she got tired of it when she did. The house was startin' to look like a china shop."

"I don't think this'll get that bad. What with her job and all, Judy doesn't have enough time for it to get out of hand."

"That's good." He paused. "How's the Chrysler job comin'?"

"I just came from QC. We got all the castings we need. Harshman wasn't havin' any problems last time I checked. I was just goin' to check on him again."

"Good. I got the reports finished. I'm leavin'. Just be sure that job gets to the loading dock on schedule."

"I will. Good night."

"'Night."

As Gunderson turned to leave, Tom did his best to avoid

showing his relief. He leaned on a machine frame, to counter the sudden weakness in his knees.

*That was a close one. I better let Judy know what excuse I used, just in case anyone ever asks. Trying to keep my stories straight is getting tougher and tougher.*

He stood beside Harshman as the last part dropped into the receiving tray. The robot arm then stacked it on the pallet.

"Take 'em away, Pete. Let's get 'em to QC right away."

He followed the forklift out of the shop, and stood shifting his weight from one foot to the other as the QC technicians gauged the parts.

"That's it, Tom. They're all within tolerance." Ed signed the routing sheet and dropped it in his OUT basket.

"Okay, Pete, take 'em to the loading dock, so the packing crew can tie 'em down."

He followed the forklift to the loading dock, watched as the parts were tied down to pallets, and then returned to the machine shop. The Chrysler parts weren't his problem any longer.

He returned to his former cell. All the parts he needed were stacked in the finished parts tray. He put them in a paper bag and headed for the locker room. Minutes later he walked out the door and headed for his car. As was his custom now, he flipped a quarter to decide on a route home, then drove off.

• • •

After dinner he went to the basement, donned a pair of plastic gloves, and retrieved the pistol from its hiding place. He reinserted the barrel, then began putting the silencer together. Finally he held the completed assembly in his hand. He paused for a moment.

*Okay, only one way to tell if it works.*

He filled a box with sand, loaded a cartridge into the magazine, inserted it into the magazine well, and racked the slide. He pointed the gun at the box of sand, hesitated briefly, then squeezed the trigger.

*Pop!*

The sound was barely noticeable, even within the confines of the basement. He disassembled the silencer, checked that all the parts were still in good condition, then reassembled it.

*No point in cleaning the gun. It's going to be used only once more, and that one shot isn't going to gum it up.*

He hid the gun and the silencer separately, stripped off the gloves, then dug the bullet out of the sand. The hollowpoint had expanded correctly, mushrooming to half again its original diameter.

*Yeah, the Justice Cooperative sent me good stuff. I guess they know what they're doing.*

He took the bullet to the garage, hammered it into a shapeless mass, and tossed it in the garbage can.

*No way anyone's going to match the marks on that bullet with anything else now.* He entered the house. Judith looked at him, but said nothing. Somehow he didn't feel like saying anything either. He tried to watch the news, but his attention kept wandering. Finally he gave up and got ready for bed. Neither he nor Judith said anything. He turned out the light, and after a long time, finally fell asleep.

# TWENTY-SIX

The message from the Justice Cooperative was almost anticlimactic when it came.

THE BEST TIME FOR YOUR ACTION APPEARS TO BE THIS COMING FRIDAY. ARRANGE TO BE OUT OF THE CITY BUT NEARBY. YOU WILL BE PROVIDED WITH A CAR TO RETURN TO THE CITY. CALL THE NUMBER BELOW ON WEDNESDAY EVENING BETWEEN 7 AND 7:15 PM WITH THE NAME OF THE MOTEL WHERE YOU WILL BE STAYING. YOU WILL BE CONTACTED THERE AFTER YOUR ARRIVAL.

Judith seemed reluctant but offered no argument. She opened the evening paper and leafed through the entertainment section.

"Here's an ad for a country music concert next Saturday at a campground north of town. The map shows it's about 40 miles away. We can get tickets at the gate."

"Yeah. Looks like a good lineup of performers. Some of the top names'll be there." *Wonder if I'll be able to enjoy it.*

He made several calls and finally found a motel near the campground that still had a room available.

• • •

Friday evening was frantic. Tom felt as though he had no time to think. He and Judith arrived home about the same time. They grabbed the suitcases they'd packed the night before, and headed out of town on the northbound Interstate. An hour later they were at the motel, having stopped only to pick up some hamburgers at a McDonald's. Judith started to eat hers. Tom was intentionally holding his for later.

Shortly after they reached the motel, the phone in their room rang. The caller was short and to the point.

"I have a message for Mr. Collins's brother. There is a car at the end of the motel building, with temporary tags." He gave the license number. "The key is under the floor mat. Be at telephone number ten by eight PM. Call this number for additional instructions." Frantically, Tom pawed through the drawer in the nightstand, found a pad of paper and a pencil, and wrote down the number. The caller continued. "In any case, have the car back to your motel by three AM. Leave the key where you found it." There was a *click* as the caller hung up.

*Eight PM! That's just over an hour from now. I'll have to burn up the road to get there. It took almost that long to get here.*

He found the car with no problem. His heart sank as he walked around it and looked at it. *It's a junker. Looks like it won't even make the trip back to the city. The only thing that looks good on it is the tires. How do they expect me to get there in an hour in this thing?*

He packed the gun, the silencer, and a kit of tools he'd prepared, under the front seat. He put the hamburgers on the seat beside him.

To his surprise, the car's appearance belied its behavior.

*Hey! The engine runs as smooth as one of my machines at the plant. And the brakes work fine, with no squealing.* He drove over a speed bump in the motel parking lot. *And the shocks're in good shape. Somebody must've jacked up the body and put a whole new car under it.*

• • •

Telephone number ten was a pay phone in a strip mall in a quiet neighborhood across town from his house. He checked in on arrival.

"This is Mr. Collins's brother. I was told to call this number."

"Your party is still at home. He regularly goes to location number three on Friday evenings. If he follows his usual pattern, he will be leaving within the next fifteen minutes. Stand by for further instructions."

Tom turned on the map light in the car and scanned the computer printout. It was printed on onionskin paper, and was difficult to read under the best of circumstances. In the dim light he could hardly make it out. Finally he found what he was looking for.

*Location number three. That's the Sunset Bar and Grill.*

He checked the location on a city map, and plotted a route from where he was.

*Should take me about five minutes to get there.*

He had hardly finished locating the spot when the phone rang.

"Hello."

"I have a message for Mr. Collins's brother. Your party has just left his house. Stand by for further information."

Tom paced in front of the phone, then decided that might attract attention, and returned to the car to wait. After what seemed line an eternity, the phone rang again.

"Your party has definitely arrived at location number three. He is driving a gray Ford Escort with license plates BJ4291. You can meet him there in the parking lot as he leaves."

Tom drove to the Sunset Bar and Grill. The neon sign in front made it easy to spot. He cruised the parking lot until he found Bartlett's car. He then pulled into a parking place in a darkened area that gave him a view of both Bartlett's car and the front door.

He slipped on plastic gloves, and pulled his equipment out from under the front seat. He unwrapped the gun, inserted the loaded magazine in the magazine well, racked the slide once, pulled it back slightly to verify there was a round in the chamber, then flipped on the safety. He then screwed the silencer to the front of the barrel. The whole thing went back under the seat. A police scanner he'd bought at Radio Shack went on the seat beside him. He then slouched down in the seat and prepared to wait.

*Damn! The smell of those hamburgers is making me hungry. But I can't eat them now. I'll need them later. No telling how long Bartlett'll be in there. This place doesn't close until one. I might be here until then.*

The luminous numbers on the car clock advanced slowly, tediously, almost hypnotic in their regularity.

Suddenly his head snapped erect. *Damn! I started to nod off to sleep. Can't have that. I'd miss him and have to do this all over. Wonder if listening to the radio would help. No, that might attract attention to the car. I got to make it look like the car's empty.*

Nine o'clock came and went. So did ten o'clock. Tom rolled down the car window, hoping the cool evening air would help him stay awake.

*Boy, if I had to do this in winter, it'd be miserable. Even in warm clothes I'd be freezing to death. Wonder how they manage it then?*

Pressure in his bladder reminded him it had been a long time since he'd emptied it.

*Oh-oh! I didn't think about that. Now what do I do? I sure can't go inside and use the men's room. I can't be seen here, not when I'm supposed to be forty miles north of town. And I can't take a leak right here in the parking lot. That's gross. Just have to hold it, I guess. Maybe it'll help keep me awake.* Eleven o'clock slowly came and passed. Each time the front door opened, he carefully scanned the faces of those leaving. None of them matched the photos he'd memorized.

*He sure must have a lot of beer-drinkin' buddies in there, he's taking so long. Hey! What if he comes out with somebody? That'd mean witnesses. I can't very well shoot them just to keep them quiet. I guess that means letting him go and trying again.* Two men came out. Neither was Bartlett. Tom tracked them to their cars with his eyes, verifying that both left the parking lot.

A group of men came out, laughing and talking. It was hard to see their faces, but he finally verified that Bartlett wasn't among them.

*They're sure taking their time about leaving. What'll I do if he comes out while they're still in the parking lot?*

But they left individually, one car at a time.

The door opened. A man stood in the doorway, leaned on the doorframe, and then slowly, deliberately, started walking across the parking lot.

*That's him! That's Bartlett!*

Tom started the engine, but left the lights off. He was about to pull out of the parking space when a thought hit him.

*Wait a minute! When I was thinking about this before, it was easy enough to say I didn't have any choice — it was either kill Grubbs myself or kill some other crook in exchange for somebody else killing Grubbs. But I do have a choice. I can go shoot him, or I can just drive out of here and go home. No one's forcing me to go pull the trigger on him.*

*After all, I don't even know this guy. He's never done me any harm.*

*But if I do just drive away, I haven't solved my problem. Then I have to go after Grubbs, or wait for him to come after me. Or after Judy. Yeah, I have several choices. But none of them is any good. Killing this guy is a bad choice, but all the others are even worse.*

*Besides, I already know this guy deserves to be killed. It's a dirty shame that he was ever let out of jail.*

He eased the car forward, then went down one row of cars and started back up another.

*Got to get him on my side of the car. And I want to get to his car about the same time he does. But I don't want to attract his attention.*

Bartlett swayed slightly as he walked between two rows of cars. He seemed to pay no attention to Tom's car as it crept forward.

Bartlett reached his car, leaned on the roof with his left hand, and fumbled at the door with his right. Tom pulled abreast of him, stopped, and rolled down the window.

Bartlett looked at Tom, turned to face him, and waved his arm.

"Hey, buddy. I dropped m'keys 'n' can't fin' 'em. C'n y' gimme some light?"

Through a dry throat, Tom croaked out "Sure."

He brought up the gun and pointed it out the window, making sure the ejection port was still inside the car.

Bartlett's eyes suddenly widened. He thrust out his left hand, as though to stave off the bullet. His mouth opened, as though he was going to say something. Tom pulled the trigger.

*Pop! Pop!*

Two dark splotches appeared on Bartlett's shirt. He swayed, then leaned against his car. His mouth worked, but no words came.

In his mind, Tom screamed silently, *Die, damn you! Die!*

He pulled the trigger again.

*Pop!*

Bartlett slowly slumped to the ground, dragging his right hand down the side of the car.

*He's stopped. Baron said I'm not justified in shooting once he's stopped. But this isn't an intruder in my house. I'm executing a vicious criminal. I've got to be sure he's dead, not just out of the fight.*

He raised the gun and carefully aimed it Bartlett's head.

*Pop! Pop!*

In the dim light from the neon sign, two holes were visible in the back of Bartlett's skull.

*There! That does it. Now I got to get out of here.*

He looked around. Two men were coming out the door of the bar.

*Got to get away without attracting their attention.*

He laid the gun on the seat and eased the car forward. As he reached the exit from the parking lot he turned on the headlights. A car was coming down the street from his left. He reached across the seat and switched on the police scanner.

". . Car thirty-four. Proceed to . . ." Hissss! There was a burst of noise that blotted out the dispatcher's voice. ". . report of a domestic disturbance. . ."

As the oncoming car passed, he made a left turn and headed for the downtown McDonald's.

# TWENTY-SEVEN

He pulled into the McDonald's, bypassed the take-out window, and pulled into a parking space.

*There. The hamburgers in the bag ought to make anybody think I was here, not someplace across town in a bar and grill parking lot.*

The police scanner squawked. ". . . Car Twenty-nine. Proceed to . . ."

He unscrewed the silencer from the gun.

*Got to take that apart first. Even having one without a license will put me in jail.*

He pulled out the two screws and let the assembly collapse onto a spread-out newspaper. One after another he pulled the washers out of the retaining rings. The rings went in one stack, the washers in another. He wrapped each stack separately in a sheet of newspaper. Each end-piece was wrapped separately, then the screws.

The scanner squawked. ". . This is car Sixteen. Requesting backup. Subject appears to be armed. . ."

*Now for the gun. Having an unloaded gun in a car isn't illegal, but I've got to make sure it can't be traced to those bullets I used.*

He carefully unloaded the gun, stripped it as though for cleaning, then picked up a rat-tail file and dragged it through the barrel a few times. For good measure, he used the file on the chamber and on the ejector.

*There. They'll never match the marks on that gun to anything. But the file marks on the barrel may be incriminating themselves. Got to get rid of the gun quick, too.*

". . .Cars Seventeen and Twenty. Proceed . . " Hisss! . ." Sunset Bar and Grill. Report of a man found dead in the parking lot. . ." Hisss!

*Oh, God! Somebody's found him. Got to get rid of this stuff right away.* He reassembled the gun and stuffed it under the seat.

He then felt around for the empty cartridge cases.

*That's five of 'em. How many times did I shoot? Was it six? Did I miss any empty cases?*

He emptied the magazine and counted the unused rounds.

*Okay, that's all of 'em accounted for. Now to get moving.*

He repacked the food in the sack, dumped the package of washers in a nearby trash barrel, and drove out of the parking lot.

*Okay, now to find some dumpsters where I can get rid of this stuff, one batch at a time, without anyone noticing me.*

He drove slowly down the street. Ahead there was another fast food restaurant.

*That's probably a good place. Cars go in and out all the time, and no one thinks anything if they see you putting something in the trash.*

The scanner crackled again, and a voice came through the static. ". . . This is car Seventeen. Man found shot to death, next to a locked car. Keys on the ground beside him. No sign of a struggle. No empty brass. Driver of the adjacent car says he found the victim but touched nothing. Send a forensic team and the ambulance. . ."

*I don't have much time. They'll have those bullets examined soon.*

The retaining rings went into the trash at that restaurant. As he pulled out of the parking lot, a police car turned the corner, lights flashing and siren howling.

*They've spotted me. Now what do I do?*

But the car swept by, weaving through the traffic that made way for it. Tom clutched the wheel with nerveless fingers as he watched the police car disappear.

*Honk!*

He looked behind him. A car full of teenagers was waiting for him to leave.

*Okay, okay, guys, take it easy.*

He took a deep breath, swallowed, then eased the car into the street.

*Better not put everything in the same area. Spread it around, so they'll have to search more places.*

He drove to another section of town and disposed of the remains of the silencer.

*Get rid of the empty brass next.*

That went into a dumpster behind a grocery store.

*What about the unused bullets? Can't throw them in the trash. That might hurt somebody. They'd better go in the river. Save them until last. They're not marked by the gun anyhow.*

Next the gun came apart. First the mutilated barrel went into a dumpster.

*Got to get rid of the rest of the gun quick. Having a gun without a barrel would look kind of fishy, even if it is legal to have it in the car.*

The slide went in one dumpster, the frame in another.

*Okay, now get down to Front Street. There's several places where I can get close to the river.*

He wound his way through streets that appeared seedier and seedier. He reached Front Street, and turned to follow the river.

*Now what? This place really looks bad at night. I've got to get out of the car to give these bullets a real toss. If I go where there's light, somebody might see me. If I stop in a dark spot, no telling who's waiting there to get me.*

He cruised down the street, looking for something, he wasn't sure exactly what. Finally he spotted a stretch of road with a guardrail right above the river.

*The berm's wide enough there that I can pull off the road, and I can see anybody coming either way.*

He slowed to let a car pass him, waited for an oncoming car to get by, then stopped and pulled off the road. He stepped around the car, flung one handful of cartridges into the river, then flung the rest.

He got back into the car and stripped off the plastic gloves. His hands were damp with sweat despite the cool evening.

*Finally I'm clean. There's nothing here in the car that can connect me with the bullets they'll take out of Bartlett's corpse. Now I've got to get back to Judy without attracting attention.*

He switched off the police scanner, then turned at the next intersection, taking a street that would lead back to the center of town.

*Maybe I better find a place to eat. These hamburgers're cold already. Don't want them to get soggy. If I can find a shopping mall, I can park there and eat.*

He drove to one he knew was nearby. A police car, its blue light blinking, was standing in the parking lot.

*Oh-oh. They're waiting for me already. But they can't be. They don't even know who I am, let alone that I'd come here.*

Nevertheless, he went on by and found another mall. He entered, pulled into a parking space in a well-lighted area, and opened the bag of hamburgers. He took out a package of fries, put the milkshake in the cup-holder, and started to unwrap a hamburger.

He held the sandwich for a long moment and stared at it. The smell of the cooked meat made his gorge rise.

*There's no way I could eat that thing. I'd choke on it. I may as well get rid of it.*

He re-wrapped the food, got out of the car, and tossed everything into a dumpster. The wadded-up plastic gloves followed.

As he walked back to his car, he was suddenly reminded of the need to empty his bladder.

*I can't wait any longer. I better use the men's room in the shopping mall.*

He entered the building, and went directly to the men's room.

He opened the door, checked to see if anyone was inside, and then entered.

*Don't want anyone to see me here. I'm supposed to be out of town this weekend, and have all kinds of receipts to prove it.*

As he left the building, he suddenly noticed that the parking lot was nearly empty. There had been several dozen cars parked in it when he arrived. As he reached his car, a police cruiser, its blue light flashing, pulled up beside him.

*Oh, God. They've got me. After everything I did to get away clean, they've got me.*

He slumped against the side of the car, waiting for the inevitable challenge.

A policeman leaned out the window of the cruiser. "Sir, we have a hostage situation in that bar over there. We're clearing the parking lot. Please move your car out of here."

He gulped and found his voice. "Okay, officer, I was just leaving."

The cruiser drove towards another one parked in front of the bar the policeman had indicated.

He got in the car, closed the door, and slumped down for a long moment. He forced himself into motion. He fumbled several times before he could get the key in the ignition, and finally cranked the engine. Numbly, he headed for the nearest on-ramp for the northbound Interstate.

# TWENTY-EIGHT

Tom rapped "shave and a haircut" on the motel door, then put his key in the lock. As he swung the door open, he saw Judith in the far corner of the room, gun at the chest-ready position.

"Thank God you're back, honey. I was getting worried." She stopped, shocked, as she saw his face.

"Tom! You look terrible! Is everything okay?"

He shut and bolted the door behind him, then looked in the mirror over the dressing table. His face was drawn and gray. He hadn't realized he looked as bad as he felt.

He turned to face her, tried to speak, then finally found his voice.

"I did it, honey. I killed him. And I got away."

She came to him, and touched his cheek.

He continued, "It was hard to do, honey. I didn't know how hard it was going to be. I kept thinking, I don't even know this guy. Why should I kill him? I had to remind myself what he'd done and why he deserved to be dead, and what Grubbs had done and why it had to be me who killed this guy.

"Then when I started shooting, he wouldn't *die*. He just stood

[ 225 ]

there. Finally he dropped, and I finished him off with two shots to the head.

"Then every mile of the way back, I felt like I had a big neon sign on my car that said 'killer.' Every car that came up behind me, I thought sure was the cops after me."

"You've got the post-shooting trauma Mr. Baron told us about."

"Yeah. And I can't go to a shrink for help. He'd have to turn me in. I can't go to our pastor, either. He'd tell me to turn myself in. There's nobody I can go to for help."

She reached out, took his arm, and led him to the bed. She started unbuttoning her blouse.

"Here, honey. Let me help you forget."

He sat on the edge of the bed and stared at her with empty eyes. "No, thanks, Judy. It wouldn't be any good. It hasn't been any good since . . . since . . ."

She sat down beside him, her hands clasped in her lap. "I know. Ever since then I've felt so — so *dirty*. I couldn't bring myself to offer you something dirty."

Tom responded, "And all I can think of is him hurting you, and that I'm reminding you of what he did."

They sat silently for a long moment, then he stood abruptly. "I'd better take a shower. Then let's get some sleep. Maybe we can enjoy things tomorrow."

# TWENTY-NINE

The next morning they ate breakfast in silence, then checked out of the motel and headed for the concert.

Judith said, "We've got an hour before the concert starts, but we need time to buy tickets and get parked." She picked up the map the motel clerk had given them. "The map says follow this road west three miles to an intersection, then turn north. The campground entrance is on the left about two miles north of the intersection."

They had gone a little over a mile when they rounded a bend and found a line of cars halted in the road. The line stretched ahead and out of sight around another bend.

"Wonder if there's been an accident?" Tom said.

"This might be concert traffic."

"If it is, we're in for a long wait."

The cars inched ahead, finally reaching the intersection shown on the map. Then the problem became obvious. Traffic was converging on the intersection from three directions, and the road leading north was full of stopped traffic.

"This thing must be backed up all the way from the campground gate. We'll never get there for the first act."

Judith opened the program she'd picked up at the motel. "It's a local group. 'Red Clay and the Firebricks.' Probably a warm-up act. I guess we won't miss much. But I'm surprised they don't have a traffic policeman at this intersection. The way cars block it, traffic isn't moving as fast as it could."

*Right now I don't think I want to see a cop,* Tom thought, *even to clean up this traffic mess.*

He had no sooner completed the thought than he heard a siren. The rear-view mirror showed a police car driving the wrong way in the left-hand lane, lights flashing, and coming at high speed.

*They can't possibly be after me. Can they?*

They weren't. Behind the police car came a huge bus. The police car slowed as it reached the intersection, then led the bus north toward the campground, using the southbound lane to go around the backed-up cars.

"That must be one of the performers," Judith said. "They're giving him a police escort through all this traffic."

Tom made no reply. He was deep in thought. *Wonder if I'll ever get over jumping every time I see a cop. And if I don't get over it, what happens to me? I wonder how many crooks give themselves up just to put an end to the suspense. Am I going to do that? I can't. I've got to get hold of myself.*

They finally reached the intersection and made the turn north. Traffic seemed to pick up a little speed. They soon reached the campground entrance. Here there was a traffic officer alternately admitting cars coming from the north and the south.

*Having a cop here is a good idea. That's how an honest man should react. And that's what I am. I'm an honest man who had to get justice for myself because the government wouldn't give it to me. I've got to quit thinking like a crook who's escaping the cops.*

They followed a long line of cars, campers, pickup trucks, and even a few motorcycles, to a row of ticket booths. Tom paid for concert tickets for each of them and bought a parking pass for the car. He then followed the signals of boys waving huge, orange-painted paddles who directed the cars to an open field.

"They sure have this thing well organized," Tom said, "once you get inside the gate."

Judith gestured with the program. "I think they have this concert every year. They probably have it down to a routine by now."

"Wish they could do something about the traffic outside the gate."

"That's the local government's doing, not the concert managers'."

"That explains it. The government's screwed up again."

He parked the car. They pulled lawn chairs out of the trunk, and followed the crowd toward the music.

They reached a fence with another gate. Beside it was a sign with a list of prohibitions.

Tom pointed at the sign. "I can understand them not wanting glass bottles inside. But what are 'pressure sprayers'?"

"I don't know. Maybe if you need to ask, it doesn't apply to you anyway."

They showed their tickets, and entered. They found themselves at the top of a hill that formed a natural amphitheater. At the bottom there was a stage. Next to it was a tower covered with loudspeakers, and next to that a huge TV screen showing the performers. On either side of the seating area there were rows of tents with signs advertising food and souvenirs. Behind the tents there were rows of portable toilets. At the top of the hill there was a motor home set up as a mobile sheriff's office. Beside it were several all-terrain vehicles marked "SHERIFF." Next to the sheriff's camper was a first aid tent.

Judith said, "It looks like we don't have to get close to the stage. We can sit as far back as we want and still see and hear the music."

Tom nodded toward the sheriff's camper and replied in a low voice, "Yeah, but let's not get too close to the cops here."

Judith's face took on a concerned look, but she said nothing. They walked along the hilltop to a point about midway between the two rows of concession tents, and set up their chairs.

The first act was just ending. As the musicians left the stage, the TV screen showed a series of advertisements for the food available at the concessions, and for what must have been local merchants.

Tom gestured toward the screen, which was extolling the virtues of an agricultural weed-killer. "Maybe we could use some of that on the back yard. Replace it with green-painted blacktop, and I wouldn't have to mow it."

"Please, Tom, don't take me any farther from green grass than you have to."

"Just kidding, honey."

She flashed him a smile. She was glad he was able to kid around with her. She hoped that meant he was pulling himself out of the previous night's depression. Grubbs's attack had put up a barrier between them that she hadn't been able to cross.

She stood up. "While we're waiting for the next act, why don't we look at the souvenir tents?"

"Okay, good idea. It beats sitting here in the sun."

They strolled down the row of tents. Most seemed to be selling T-shirts and baseball caps. Rebel flag T-shirts seemed to be popular. Many others bore names and pictures of rock or country bands, sports teams, or military services. Some bore rude slogans. Tom pointed at one of the latter.

"I can't imagine anyone having the nerve to wear that. Nobody at the plant would even think of it."

"Somebody must buy them, or they wouldn't be on sale."

"None of this stuff is special to this concert. Looks like these people sell the same stuff no matter where they set up. Rock concert, country concert, all the same stuff. Maybe that junk does sell at other events, but I don't see people around here wearing them."

As they turned to go back to their seats, Tom felt a drop of water on his face. He looked to the side, and saw a boy walking down the rows of lawn chairs, methodically squirting people with a water pistol. Some of the people were squirting back with water guns of all sizes. He grabbed Judith's arm.

"Let's go. We're getting caught in the cross-fire here."

"Why move? The water feels good in this heat." She moved closer to the water-fight, spread her arms, and slowly spun around as people turned their squirt guns on her. Then she came back to where he stood.

"There. I feel a lot cooler now. If I had a squirt-gun, I'd use it on myself."

"Maybe that's what that sign was about. People don't mind getting squirted with an ordinary water gun, but no one wants to get zapped with some kind of high-pressure sprayer."

As they returned to their chairs, a disk jockey from a local country music station came on stage to introduce the next act. The performers came on stage, to a roar of welcome from the crowd.

Just then, out of the corner of his eye, Tom saw one of the Sheriff's ATVs heading his way. His heart pounded and he gripped the arms of his chair. He relaxed only when he saw two Emergency Medical Technicians from the first aid tent running behind the deputy.

*I've got to quit reacting like I'm guilty of something. Dammit, I'm not guilty of anything. I did what the government should have done long ago. If they'd done what they're supposed to do, Judy and I wouldn't be in the mess we're in, and a lot of other people would be better off too.*

A few minutes later, the tractor returned. A stretcher had been laid across the back, and one of the EMTs was walking beside it, holding the head of a man strapped to the stretcher.

"Wonder what happened to him," Judith said, as she nodded toward the tractor.

"The way his face looks, I'd guess he had heat stroke. I've seen guys at the foundry look like that when it's a hot day and they haven't taken enough salt tablets."

"Maybe we ought to be drinking lots of liquids, and eating some salty things."

"Yeah. Why don't we head down to a food stand? I could use some pop and some pretzels. We can hear the music just as well there, and there'll be less of a line than during intermission."

A short time later they were back at their seats, each with a six-pack of Coke and a bag of pretzels.

Tom ripped open a bag of pretzels and turned the open end toward Judith. "This ought to hold us until it's time for lunch."

During the intermission before the next act, Tom heard one of the Sheriff's tractors start up again. He took a deep breath, let it out slowly, and forced himself to relax.

*If I keep jumping, they're going to think I am guilty of something, and start asking questions. I've got to act like any ordinary person would act when something happens.*

He put on a slightly bemused smile, and followed the deputy with his eyes as the tractor wove through the crowd. Near the bottom of the hill, he lost sight of the tractor. A few minutes later it emerged from the crowd. Two teen-aged boys were following it. As the tractor passed near him, he could see a six-pack of beer perched on the back.

"Oh-oh." He nudged Judith. "Underage drinking. Wonder what the cops'll do with them?"

The deputy opened each beer can and emptied it on the ground. Then he led the boys to the side of the camper, where he took a digital photo of each. He then turned them loose.

Judith nodded her head approvingly. "That seems to be a good way to handle it. He's stopped them from drinking, and he doesn't really need to do anything more."

"Yeah, and he's got the pictures as evidence of the first violation if they're caught with more beer. Turning them loose with a warning may be the best way to handle it."

*But is it? What's this going to teach them? Will they learn they can break the law and get away with nothing but a warning? What happens when they do something worse? Will they still get turned loose with only a warning?. Look at Grubbs and Bartlett. Both of 'em have long histories of getting away with things. Plea bargains. Reduced sentences. Early release from jail. The system did a good job of teaching them they really could get away with murder. Not to mention rape and assault. I finally stopped Bartlett, and if the Jus-*

*tice Cooperative holds up its end of the deal, somebody else will stop Grubbs. But Bartlett'd still be alive today if the system had taught him long ago that crime doesn't pay. Instead it taught him just the opposite.*

*Maybe those kids ought to get more than just a warning. The cops may not be doing them any favors by turning them loose. Sure, it saves a hassle for the cops. But maybe that's part of what's wrong with the system. It's just too much of a hassle for the cops and the prosecutors to give the crooks what they deserve. So the crooks never do learn anything.*

Tom's thoughts were interrupted by a young couple who carried chairs into the open space in front of him and Judith.

"Are we blocking your view?" The man asked.

"No," Judith replied, "we can see just fine."

The new arrivals placed a cooler on the ground, set up their chairs on each side of it, then removed their outer clothing. The man was wearing swimming trunks; the woman was wearing a two-piece bathing suit. They then proceeded to apply suntan lotion to each other. Once they were thoroughly lubricated externally, the man took the top off the cooler and each pulled out a can of beer.

Judith leaned towards Tom and said in a low voice, "Looks like a couple of sun-worshippers."

"Yeah. Hope they don't get burned to a crisp. This sun is hot."

"It might be worse than that. Dad had to have a skin cancer removed from his face. The doctor told him it was probably from working in the sun so many years. After that he always wore a hat and a long-sleeved shirt when he worked in the field."

"Well, it's their problem, not mine. I'm glad you suggested we both stay covered up. I don't want to be laid up with a sunburn. I want to save my sick leave for when I really need it, not use it up because I did something stupid."

Judith laughed and pointed. "There's someone who's keeping the sun off his head." Tom looked where she pointed, to see a man wandering by with an empty Coors 12-pack box pulled down over his ears.

"Yeah. I just hope he didn't finish that whole thing by himself."

"And look over there," Judith pointed. "What's that he's wearing on his hat?"

"Looks like a couple of deer antlers stuck on a hard hat."

"And look over there," she pointed. "That man's wearing half a watermelon on his head, cut like a football helmet."

A thoughtful look came on Judith's face. "You know, this is probably the biggest collection of individualists either of us has ever seen. Look at all the rebel flags, the crazy hats, and the opinionated T-shirts."

"Yeah. Thank God there are still some people like this around." He chuckled. "Can you imagine what some liberal newspaper reporter would think if he came out here? He'd just about have a heart attack."

Towards the end of the next act, Tom turned to Judith. "Let's go get some pizza for lunch. If we go get it now, we can beat the line."

"Sounds like a good idea."

"What should we do with our pop?" He pointed at the partially emptied six-packs.

She waved her hand to take in the chairs around them. "People seem to be leaving their stuff unguarded. No one seems to be worried about having their things stolen. Besides, these lawn chairs cost more than a six-pack of Coke, and we wouldn't carry them with us everywhere."

"Yeah, I guess you're right."

When the intermission came, they were back in their chairs. Tom put the box of pizza on his lap, and opened the top.

He nodded toward the couple in front of them. "If we'd thought to bring a cooler, we'd have a place to put this pizza."

"This concert apparently happens every year. If we come back, we'll know to bring a cooler." She paused, then added "And a couple of squirt-guns."

A Sheriff's tractor drove past them. This time Tom was able

to watch it calmly.

*Maybe I am getting over my jumpiness. But I think it's going to take a long time to get over it completely. Maybe I'll always be scared that somehow the cops'll connect me with that killing.*

A gaggle of small boys ran by. Each had a squirt gun, and they were all spraying each other, laughing as they went. As the crossfire sprayed other people in the crowd, they retaliated with their own squirt guns. Soon there was a pitched water-gun fight going on a few yards away. Tom was getting drenched. He put the slice of pizza he was eating back in the box and closed the lid.

*I know those kids are just having fun, and don't mean any harm. But do any of them ever think about what it'd be like to point a real gun at somebody and pull the trigger? Have they been trained to take guns seriously? Do they know the difference between a toy and a real gun? When Judy and I have our kids, I'm going to make damn sure they know the difference. Sure, they'll play cops and robbers, or cowboys and Indians, or Galactic Patrol and Aliens, or whatever shoot-'em-up games the kids play nowadays. But they'll know the difference between play and the real thing.* Then he added bitterly to himself, *If we ever have any kids. Even if Grubbs is killed, can we forget the past and get on with our lives?*

The fight moved away, and he opened the box again. Soon it was empty. He started to look around. Judith pointed. "There's a trash barrel. Why don't you get rid of these empty pop cans at the same time?"

"Sure." He gathered up the debris and threw it in the trash. The next act was being introduced as he returned to his chair.

By mid-afternoon the pop and the pretzels were gone. Tom held up the empty pretzel bag.

"Think we could use some more pretzels?"

"And some more pop. I don't want to get dried out."

The pop, the pretzels, and the last act were finished at the same time. Tom gathered up the debris around their chairs, and dropped it in a trash can near the exit. They then headed for the car.

Judith turned to Tom. "This has been a nice day, honey. I'm

glad we came. I just wish we'd had some other reason for doing it than what we did."

"Right, Judy. It was a nice day. A really normal, ordinary day."

"We ought to come back next year."

"Yeah, let's do that."

*Sure, let's do that. If I'm not in jail, or they haven't put me in the gas chamber. Or if Grubbs doesn't get us before the Justice Cooperative gets him. Next year is too far off to think about. But she's right. It was a nice day. First one I've had in a long, long, time. I ought to be grateful for it.*

With that he straightened up and began to hum the final tune of the last act.

# THIRTY

Judith opened the screen door and found an envelope Scotch taped over the main door lock. She pulled it off, disarmed the alarm, and opened the door.

Tom carried their suitcases into the house. As usual, his first move was to load his gun.

He then went back to the mailbox and picked up the mail. Judith handed him the envelope she had taken from the door.

"Here. This was taped to the door. It might be something important."

He flipped it over to look at both sides. "It's addressed to me, but there's no return address." He opened it.

The letter inside was on the letterhead of the police department, and addressed to him.

MR. TOM BORDEN: PLEASE CALL THE POLICE DIS-PATCHER AT . . .

He sat down in dismay and held his head.

"Oh, my God! They know! They know! Somehow they know!"

Judith took the letter and read it. "No, Tom. If they knew they'd be waiting here for you. They wouldn't be asking you to call them."

*Okay, what would an honest man do? One who knew he hadn't done anything wrong? He'd be puzzled, but he'd call the dispatcher.*

He punched in the number.

"This is Tom Borden." He gave his address. "I'm replying to a message left on my door."

"Yes, Mr. Borden. Just a moment. I'll have to check the log book." There was a pause. "Here it is. Your burglar alarm went off last night. The responding officer found the back door ajar and jimmy marks around the lock. He entered the house but found no one. He was able to relock the door. This morning we obtained the alarm key you left with your neighbor, Mrs. Tompkins, and reset the alarm. Please check to see if anything is missing."

Judith's voice came on the line. Tom realized she must be using the upstairs phone. "This is Mrs. Borden. What time did this happen?"

"According to the record, just past two AM. That's why we didn't try to obtain the key from Mrs. Tompkins at that time."

"Is Detective Callahan on duty tonight?" she asked.

"Yes, he is."

"Please tell him we're going to inspect the house, then we're coming to see him."

"Very well."

"Good-bye."

Tom hung up without saying anything. He turned to Judith as she came down the stairs.

"What's this about seeing Callahan?"

"This might not have been an attempted burglary, Tom. This might have been Grubbs. Get your gun. We're going to inspect every room and every closet in this house, then we're going down to the police station to talk to Lt. Callahan."

They started at their bedroom at the end of the upstairs hall. One of them covered a door as the other opened it. They found no one. Nothing seemed to be missing. They worked their way through the rooms down the hall, went down the stairs, then inspected the first floor.

Judith said, "If there's anyone still hiding in the house, they have to be in the basement."

"Okay, I guess I'll have to go down there."

He opened the basement door, switched on the light, and started to step down.

*Wait a minute. If I go down there slowly, anybody down there can see me before I can see them. I'd better run down those steps, head for the near corner, turn around, and scan the basement.*

He took the steps in three bounds, had his back into the corner in two long strides, and scanned the basement over the sights of his gun.

"Nobody in sight"

"Okay, I'm coming down."

"Take it slowly. No point in breaking a leg."

Shortly she stood beside him. Then they prowled the basement. They found nothing.

"Okay, Judy, that's it. The house is secure. I couldn't see anything missing. Now let's go see Callahan."

• • •

Lt. Callahan seemed unconcerned about their report. "What's the problem, folks? A burglar tried to break in. He set off your burglar alarm. That scared him off. According to the records, the responding officer reached your house within three minutes. He happened to be patrolling your neighborhood when the dispatcher called him, and did even better than our standard response time. He found nothing, and you found no one hiding in the house and nothing missing.

"Seems to me everything worked just like it was supposed to. That burglar won't be back. He'll try to hit a place that isn't so well protected. I wish every householder would take the precautions you folks have."

Judith spoke in a sharp voice. "That's if it was a burglar, Lieutenant."

"What else could it have been."

"I think it was Harry Grubbs."

"That doesn't fit. Even if Grubbs were trying to get you, you weren't home. He'd be wasting his time. Since the house was empty, it's more likely it was a burglar. With over half the homes in America having guns, burglars would much rather hit an empty house than one with somebody home. I've talked to lots of burglars. They tell me that they're afraid to hit a house with somebody home, because they might get shot. They're more afraid of meeting an armed householder than they are of the police."

Tom thought, *If burglars are really that scared of people with guns, why are you cops so eager to take away our guns?* But he kept that thought to himself. Instead, he followed Judith's lead.

"Maybe he didn't know the house was empty. Part of our burglar alarm system switches lights and the TV on and off when there's nobody home in the evening, just to make it look like there are people around. The house wouldn't have looked empty."

"Besides," Judith added, "my car was still in the garage. Only Tom's car was gone. Unless he had seen both of us drive off together, he'd logically expect that I was home alone. The lights would make it look like I was moving from room to room, and watching the TV, until I went to bed. Since we both have to get to work in the morning, we usually get to bed around eleven. That's when the automatic lights are set to go out. He could reasonably expect that I'd be asleep by two AM. Then he could surprise me."

"But as soon as he opened the door, the alarm would alert you. He'd have known he couldn't get away with it."

"Only if he knew we had a burglar alarm. He might not have known we have one. He may have thought that once he poisoned our dog, we had no protection."

"Please, Mrs. Borden. You have no proof he was the one who poisoned your dog. All of this is pure speculation."

"It may be speculation, but it fits all the facts. Including the fact that he made a threat to get us, and the fact that he's been stalking us. I think my speculation is pretty solidly grounded."

"Even if it is, we have no evidence we can use to arrest him. Without that evidence, I can't do anything."

"Can't you find out whether he has an alibi for last night?" Tom asked.

"It doesn't matter whether he has one or not. He doesn't have to prove he *wasn't* there. You have to prove he *was* there. In the absence of any evidence he was there, his lack of an alibi would be irrelevant.

"I still think it was an ordinary burglar," Callahan continued. "That theory fits the immediate facts. However, if it was Mr. Grubbs, he'll be back. A burglar would be discouraged; Grubbs would not. I strongly suggest you take precautions. If it was Mr. Grubbs and he does come back, we'll respond as promptly as we can.

"Finally, Mrs. Borden, I don't want to sound insensitive about this, but your preoccupation with Mr. Grubbs could be interpreted by someone less charitable than I am as paranoia. I strongly suggest you refrain from saying anything more about him until you have some evidence. Otherwise you're likely to turn off the very people whose help you'll need if it does turn out to be Mr. Grubbs."

He stood up, dismissing them.

They slowly walked to their car. Once inside, Tom exploded.

"Paranoid! What the Hell does he think this is, anyway. We know that sonuvabitch Grubbs has been after us. We're not imagining things. Dammit, even paranoids have enemies, and Grubbs is sure our enemy."

"Easy, Tom. You're right, but blowing your stack isn't going to help. We need to stay calm and think."

"Okay. Maybe the Justice Cooperative will solve the problem for us. I've carried out my end of the bargain."

"Yes, and you've paid a terrible price for it last night and today."

"Okay, it's their turn to carry out their end of the bargain."

Just as they entered the house, they heard the phone ring. Tom grabbed it. Judith heard him say, "Sorry, you must have a wrong number."

He hung up, then turned to her.

"That was the Justice Cooperative, with another wrong number. I've got to get to the pay phone on Willow. It's three blocks away. I'd better hurry."

"That means leaving me in the house alone."

"And it means my going to the phone alone."

"Then we'd better both go. That way there's two of us to his one."

"And we'd both better have our guns. I'll take the car instead of walking."

He drove to the phone, parked next to it, and waited. When it rang, he was out of the car and had the phone off the hook before the second ring.

"Hello."

A voice said, "I'm calling for Mr. Collins.

"This is his brother. I'll take a message."

"Be able to account for every minute of the coming week. This is the last message you will receive. You will have no further contact with us. Good-bye." *Click!*

"But . . . But . . . Hey, wait a minute!"

But the phone was dead. Tom finally hung it up.

He related the message to Judith, then added, "It sounds like they're going to make their move this week. I hope they make it before Grubbs makes his next move."

# THIRTY-ONE

om watched the forklift taking a pallet of parts to the loading dock, where the truck from Honda would pick them up.

Miller turned to him and spoke.

"It's a shame we got only an hour of overtime tonight. I could use the extra money."

"Well, that's the way the schedule worked out. You got started on the parts early enough that they're done by now. One of these days the suits're going to figure out a way to schedule these rush jobs during regular working hours. Then nobody'll get any overtime."

"The guys won't like that. A lot of them count on the overtime to meet expenses."

"I know. I like overtime too. But the company doesn't."

He returned to the shop, clocked out, and headed for the locker room.

*The time on my time card will account for this much of the evening. Judy and I'll have to do something to account for the rest of it. Maybe we ought to go out to eat.*

A flip of a quarter sent him home by the short route. Nevertheless, he watched carefully as he entered his street. There was no sign of anyone lurking near the entrance. All the way to the dead end, the cars looked familiar.

He parked in his driveway behind Judith's car and scanned the neighborhood carefully.

*In another month it'll be almost dark when I'm getting home. That's going to make it tougher to keep an eye on things.*

He pulled his gun out from under the seat, draped his jacket over it, picked up his lunch pail, headed for the door, and checked the alarm.

*I figured right. Judy did have the alarm set. No point in dropping our guard just because it's still daylight. Grubbs could attack us any time.*

He opened the door, and reset the alarm as soon as he was inside.

"Judy, let's eat out tonight."

"Where do you want to go. Taco King?"

"Not Taco King. Someplace fancy, where I can pay with a credit card. That way we'll have a record to account for our time."

"You'll have to wear a coat and tie."

"Not that fancy. There's got to be some family place that I don't have to dress up for."

She checked the yellow pages. "Here're several that look good." She pointed at the page. "How about this one? It's not too far away."

"Sutters? Yeah. I've heard some of the guys at the shop talk about it. They thought it was pretty good. Give me ten minutes to get cleaned up."

When they were ready to leave, Tom opened the door carefully, scanned the neighborhood, and then stepped outside. He kept watch as Judith locked the door behind him and set the alarm. They walked to the car, with Tom scanning ahead and Judith scanning behind them. He unlocked the passenger-side door, locked it behind Judith, then unlocked his own door. He backed out of the driveway and headed for the restaurant.

He parked in a lighted area near the door, but found it impossible to get a table from which he could watch the car.

"I didn't think about this," Tom said. "This place isn't like a McDonald's. You don't have glass all around you, so you can see out."

"You wanted a fancier place. This is it. Let's enjoy the meal, not stew about whether you can see the car."

"Okay, but I'm going to give the car a good check when I go out."

"You ought to do that anyway," Judith replied. "I always do after work, even though I park in a lot with an attendant."

"Yeah. I check mine at the plant, too. You know, I wonder if we'll ever get back to living like ordinary people?"

"Remember what Lieutenant Callahan said last night. He wished other people would take the precautions we do. It's the ordinary people who don't take the precautions we do who get mugged and burgled."

"Yeah, but that's not the answer. Ordinary people shouldn't have to live like this. There's something wrong when the crooks go around without a worry, and the honest people lock themselves in."

"There is something wrong," she said. "We already knew that. Mr. Baron warned us that the laws are stacked in favor of the criminal."

Just then their salads arrived. Tom sprinkled his with oil and vinegar from the cruets on the table, and took a forkful. He munched thoughtfully for a moment, then spoke.

"You know, I wonder if the crooks are as afraid as we are? Do crooks recognize other crooks, and leave them alone? Or do crooks get mugged, and have their houses broken into, just like honest people?"

"They probably don't have signals to identify each other, like lodge brothers. The cops would learn the signals too. But probably some of them know each other. So they probably don't bother the ones they know."

Suddenly she smiled. "If a lawyer falls into shark-infested waters, do you know why the sharks let him alone?"

"No, why?"

"Professional courtesy."

He laughed. "You'd better not let your bosses hear you talk like that."

"Mr. Abernathy told me that one. I hear lots of lawyer jokes at the office. The lawyers seem to enjoy telling them."

"Well, I hope they get as much fun out of telling them as the people do who hate lawyers. But while sharks may let lawyers alone, I can't imagine crooks leaving each other alone out of professional courtesy."

Their meals arrived then. For the next few moments they shuffled salad plates, silverware, and the breadbasket to make room.

Judith spoke again. "Do you remember that night we were at the police station and Lieutenant Callahan had to take time to handle the drug dealer who'd been shot?"

"Yeah."

"Well, there was a case of one crook going after another. No professional courtesy there."

He made a dismissive gesture. "Yeah, but that was a turf thing. One was cutting into the other one's sales."

"Maybe muggers defend their alleys just like drug dealers defend their street corners."

"Could be. But housebreakers? I doubt it. And how about the guys who hold up gas stations and convenience stores? Would one of 'em avoid hitting a particular gas station because he thought it was in some other crook's territory? Doesn't make sense to me."

She laughed. "I don't know. Maybe some college professor has studied it. But I don't think I'll bother looking it up."

"Yeah." His face turned glum. "Even knowing that wouldn't help us, would it? Even if the crooks don't steal from each other, we still have to watch out."

They finished their meals, then ordered dessert. When it came, Judith spoke. "This is one nice thing about eating out. We don't have to have the same dessert. I don't go for lemon meringue pie the way you do, so I can have a cherry pie."

"I like cherry pie too, but Mom always made lemon meringue for special occasions. It's my favorite." He fell silent and looked thoughtful.

"It still bothers you, doesn't it?"

"Yeah. I always knew I'd lose them some day. But I figured it'd be after an illness or something. Not like that, anyway. Both wiped out, just like that, by some drunk who shouldn't've even been on the road."

She hesitated a moment, then asked, "Do you think the Justice Cooperative is the right way to make this country safe for decent people again?"

It was his turn to hesitate. Then he spoke. "No. No, it isn't. From the beginning, I went along only because I figured I had no choice. You needed to be defended, and the government wasn't doing the job.

"I remembered how it was when we went along with the system after Grubbs attacked us. The government gave us a hard time before the trial, and Grubbs's lawyer gave you a hard time at the trial. Then after all we went through to help them put Grubbs away, they turned him loose again.

"Since they weren't going to help us, I had to take help where I could get it. But I sure wish it hadn't been necessary.

"I'm not sorry Bartlett's dead. He was nothing but a wolf that needed to be killed to protect decent people. But I don't think I'll ever forget the sight of him lying there. I don't see how hangmen stand it."

"Maybe they do it like soldiers do," Judith said. "I remember Dad always spoke of North Vietnamese as 'dinks.' I didn't dare say anything when I was growing up, but after I left home I'd sometimes try to remind him they were human beings too.

"Now I think I see why he did it. If he ever let himself think of them as human beings, he'd be in the same fix you are."

"Yeah, Dad always referred to the North Koreans as 'gooks,' too," Tom replied. "But anyway, the Justice Cooperative isn't the way it should be done. It's just that it's better than letting the crooks run loose."

They finished their desserts, and got up from the table.

Judith remarked, "This is another reason I like eating out. I can get up and walk away from a table of dirty dishes."

He gave a chuckle. "You want to use paper plates at home?"

"No, I like eating off good plates. It's just that once in a while it's nice to let somebody else clean them up."

Tom paid the bill with his credit card, and they walked out the door. Tom first looked the parking lot over carefully, then headed straight for the car. With both of them inside and the doors locked, he felt he could relax a little.

As he drove home, he kept watching traffic, for any sign they were being followed, or that someone in a gray car was waiting for them.

He pulled into the driveway, and stopped the car. He started to get out, then spoke.

"Do you suppose we ought to carry our guns in the open? If Grubbs is watching, that ought to discourage him."

"NO!" Judith continued in a calmer voice. "Absolutely not. Remember what happened to the Browns. If Grubbs saw us walking in with our guns, all he'd have to do is make an anonymous call to the police, and we'd be arrested for breaking the law against having a loaded gun in a moving car.

"Even if a lawyer could get us out of trouble, it'd take a long time and cost us a lot of money." A hard look appeared on her face. "Let's keep the guns as a surprise for Mr. Grubbs if he walks in on us again."

# THIRTY-TWO

"Want to eat out again, like we did last night?" Tom asked.

"Yes, but not at a place like Sutter's. That gets expensive."

"Got any other ideas?"

"Why don't we eat at Taco King," she replied, "then go to the shooting range? Together they won't cost any more than Sutters, and we haven't been shooting in a while. I don't want to get out of practice."

Tom thought, *I don't want you out of practice, either. Not with Grubbs so close after us. And I'd better keep in practice, too.*

• • •

Once they were seated in the fast food place, Tom looked around. "I feel more comfortable here, where I can see the car. I've been uncomfortable about leaving our cars unprotected."

"Why?"

"Because Grubbs might mess with them. Our burglar alarm doesn't protect them. He could get at our cars at night when we're asleep. King would have given us warning, but we don't have him now."

Judith's face took on a thoughtful look. "Maybe we ought to get another dog, even if we know he's going to be poisoned. At least that might convince Lieutenant Callahan that it was more than coincidence."

"JUDY! YOU COULDN'T!"

"Tom, I think I could. I think I could deliberately sacrifice a dog to get Grubbs."

That was a change in Judith that Tom didn't like. But he saw no point in arguing over it. "Well, let's think about it. Besides, the problem isn't only at home. Grubbs could get at our cars while we're at work, or while we're out like this. That's why I want to keep an eye on the car now."

"What could he do?"

"Lots of things. Like cut a brake line. The first few times we used the brakes, we'd lose brake fluid. Then we'd have no brakes at all. Or he could monkey with the steering. Or he could do something really nasty, like connecting a bomb to the starter."

"I never thought about him tampering with the cars. Maybe we'd better lock them in the garage every time we come home. That would mean we could go directly into the house through the door from the garage, too."

"I've thought of that," Tom replied, "but I didn't like the idea. Using the garage is okay in winter, when we want to keep snow and ice off the cars. That's why we got a house with a garage. But locking the cars up in summer seemed to me like crawling just that much deeper into a bunker. I'm tired of hiding out from Grubbs."

"I am too. But if protecting the cars is one of the precautions we have to take, we should do it."

When their orders arrived, they ate without further conversation, and left for the firing range.

• • •

When they entered the firing range, Tom stepped up to the cashier's window to register.

"We're using our own guns, but I'd like a box of 9- millimeter hardball."

"That won't last you long."

"Probably not, but I'll buy more when that runs out."

He paid the fee with a credit card, making sure that the time and date were printed on the receipt. He and Judith donned their ear protectors, then went to their assigned station, near the right end of the firing line.

He pulled the target carrier to him, hung a silhouette target on it, and started it back downrange. He turned to Judith.

"How far away do you want it?"

"Make it ten yards."

He stopped the carrier at the ten-yard mark.

"You want to go first?" he asked.

"Okay. I'll probably use up the whole box."

"That's okay. I'll keep buying one box at a time, so we have a good record of how long we spent here."

Tom sat down on a bench while Judith took her place at the firing line. A couple of stations down, a boy who looked to be about ten or twelve was firing. He was using a gun that looked far too big for him. Even so, he was handling the recoil well. There was surprisingly little muzzle flip.

Tom got up, strolled over, and stood well behind the boy. He was firing at a silhouette target. The shots were tightly grouped, about a hand-span wide, in the middle of the chest.

He spoke to the man who seemed to be with the boy. "Your son?"

"Yep. I'm making sure he knows how to handle a gun."

"He's doing pretty well, isn't he?"

"Yeah, especially for that gun."

"What is it?"

"A Desert Eagle. It's a .44 Magnum. I thought it would be too much gun for him, but he insisted, so I let him try it. Usually he shoots a .45 Government Model."

"Looks like he's going to be a good shot."

"I'm proud of him. By the time he gets out of high school, he ought to be ready to try out for the Olympic team."

The man suddenly extended his hand. "By the way, I'm Jeff Carter."

Tom returned a firm grip. "Tom Borden. Pleased to meet

you, Jeff. That's my wife Judy over there." He nodded his head in Judith's direction.

Jeff glanced quickly at Judith, then took a long look at her target. "She's not doing so bad either. She been shooting long?"

"We just took it up early this summer. I was kind of worried that she wouldn't like it, but she does. She's better at it than I am."

"Say, you live in town here? What d'you think of this guy Carling, who's running for city council? He says if he's elected, he'll introduce an ordinance to ban any gun that'll hold more than six shots."

"Guess I hadn't given it much thought. I don't think I've even changed my voting registration since we moved to our new place two years ago. But if he passes that law, both Judy's and my guns'll be banned."

"Well, you better think about it. I'm sure going to work hard to defeat him. I'm getting all the gun-owners I know to work for his opponent."

"What's he hope to gain by banning my guns? He can't be stupid enough to think that crooks won't get guns anyway."

"He's not stupid. He knows what he's doin'. Politicians have been trying to disarm us citizens as long as we've had a country. The American Revolution started over gun control."

"What?" Tom exclaimed. "I thought it started with the Boston Tea Party."

"There wasn't any shooting at the Boston Tea Party. The first shooting was at Concord, where the British troops were on a gun-control mission. They'd been sent to capture supplies of gunpowder. The Minutemen stopped 'em, and chased 'em back to Boston. After that, the war was on."

"I recall my history book said the British were trying to get the colonists' gunpowder, but I'd never heard anyone call it a gun-control mission."

"That's 'cause most history-book writers are on the side of the gun-grabbers. They can't hide the facts completely, but they sure try to disguise 'em."

Just then a man who had been standing nearby came up and spoke. "Hello. I'm Isaac Greenberg. I couldn't help overhearing what you were talking about. Gun control came a lot closer to me than 1776.

"My grandfather escaped from Germany in 1938. His parents and his brothers weren't so lucky. They disappeared into Dachau.

"He told me that it was the Weapons Law of 1938 that convinced him he'd better get out. Already in 1933 the Nazis had seized all the guns owned by Jews, gypsies, and others they didn't like. In the 1938 law, Jews were forbidden to take part in any business involving guns, either making or selling them. Later, after my grandfather left Germany, his father wrote him that the law was amended to prohibit Jews from owning any weapons, even knives and clubs.

"With the Jews disarmed, it was easy for the Nazis to round them up. They couldn't fight back."

"How'd the Nazis know which Jews had guns?" Tom asked. "How'd they know where to go?"

A one-sided smile crossed Greenberg's face. "That was easy. Back in 1928, the Weimar government passed a gun registration law. All gun owners had to register their guns. The permits had to be renewed every year. The law was supposed to stop the street fighting between Nazis and Communists." He snorted. "All it did was disarm the decent people.

"Anyway, when the Nazis won the elections in 1933, they inherited all those lists of gun owners. All they had to do was refuse to renew a permit, and the gun owner had to turn in his guns or be jailed for breaking the gun registration law. It was all very nice and legal on the part of the Nazi government. The Nazis had no problem finding out who had a gun."

"I hadn't known those details," Carter replied. "But yeah, I knew the Nazis were real big on gun control. They wanted to be sure they had all the guns."

"Right," Greenberg responded. "Under that 1938 Weapons Law, only the police and the Army could have guns. And the

Nazis, of course. Everybody else was disarmed."

"That's the definition of a police state, isn't it?" Jeff said. "Where only the police have guns?"

"I think of what happened to the Jews in Germany," Greenberg continued, "every time I hear somebody say they want to register guns only to keep them out of the hands of criminals. Most of the people who say that are lying through their teeth. And even if they're sincere, they set things up for the next Hitler who wants to seize power without opposition. In the final analysis, your ultimate protection against tyranny is your gun."

They were interrupted by Jeff's boy, who came back carrying his target, a wide grin on his face.

"Look, Dad! How'd I do?"

Jeff put his arm around the boy's shoulder. "You did fine, Danny. Here, show your target to Mr. Borden and Mr. Greenberg."

The two men made appreciative noises over the target.

"Your Dad says you might be an Olympic shooter some day," Tom said.

"I sure hope to. I'm going to keep practicing so I can make it."

"Say," Jeff spoke. "Either of you ever been to Colonial Williamsburg?"

"No, never been."

"Me neither."

"Me and the wife took the kids down there last summer. They got a movie there they show you about the history of the place. There's this one part where the British governor sends troops to Williamsburg on another gun-control mission.

"The night watchman spots 'em comin', and starts banging on the metal triangle he uses for an alarm. All the while, he's yellin' 'They're stealing the powder!'

"My kids sure were impressed by that. All the rest of last summer, they played they were the colonists at Williamsburg. I could hear 'em out in the back yard, yellin' 'They're stealing the powder!'

"Yeah, even before we had a country here, the politicians were tryin' to take away our guns. Carling is just runnin' true to form."

"Anyway, I was glad to have the kids see that movie. They need to know that we won our independence with guns. The schools sure don't teach them that."

He turned to his son. "Got any more ammo left, Danny?"

"Nope. I used it all. That gun isn't too big for me, Dad. Can I shoot it some more?"

"The gun may not be too big for you, but the ammo is too big for my pocketbook. That's all for tonight. And the next time, you'll have to shoot a .22. I can't afford to feed a Desert Eagle every time."

He turned back to Tom and Greenberg.

"Nice talkin' to you guys. Don't forget, register to vote, and vote against Carling if you want to keep your guns. The people at Williamsburg and at Concord fought for your right to own a gun. Don't you let 'em down by not votin'."

"You can bet I'll register and vote," Tom said. "Nice meeting you. And goodnight, Danny. Keep up the shooting."

"Let me assure you I'm going to vote against Carling, and I'll advise all my friends to do the same," Greenberg said. He turned to leave.

"Good idea, Isaac" Tom said, "and be sure to tell 'em about your grandfather."

Tom returned to their station as Judith walked back from the firing line.

"I finished the box. You want to shoot now?"

"Yeah. Sorry I missed seeing how you did, but I wanted to see how that boy was shooting. He's going to be a crack shot if he keeps it up. But let me take a look at your target."

Judith's target wasn't nearly as good as Danny's had been, but it was good enough.

"Not bad at all, Judy. Ten yards is longer than any distance inside our house, and still you've got a pretty good group in the torso." He scanned the entire target. "Only two fliers. Not much danger to the neighbors. You're going to be a holy terror if you keep that up. I'm proud of you."

He bought another box of ammunition, put it on his credit card, and returned to the firing line. He decided he might as well put the target at the same range Judith had used.

*There's no hurry,* he thought, as he fired slowly. *Part of the reason for doing this is to create an alibi anyway.*

He emptied the box, then brought the target back.

"You're doing pretty well too, Tom. You've definitely improved since that gun training course."

"Yeah, this practice helps."

But the thought that came to his mind wasn't of the target he'd just fired. Instead he pictured a man lying in a puddle of blood in a parking lot, with two holes neatly punched in the back of his skull.

*Yeah, I'm gettin' so I can shoot pretty good. I just hope nobody ever finds out just how good I've done.*

He shook his head to clear it of the unpleasant image, then looked at his watch. "This is late enough. We'd better get home."

They gathered up their gear, packed it in their range bags, and left.

# THIRTY-THREE

Tom pulled into the drive and stopped behind Judith's car.

"Let me check your car over, then let's put both of them in the garage."

"Okay. I'll stay here and cover you."

He disarmed the alarm and opened the garage door. He plugged in a trouble light on an extension cord. He tugged at the hood of Judith's car, to make sure it was still latched. He unlocked the car door, unlatched the hood, and checked under it. Nothing seemed to be out of order. He spread a drop-cloth under the car, crawled under, and checked everything he could think of. Nothing seemed to be loose or out of order. Nothing was there that shouldn't be.

"Okay, it looks like it hasn't been messed with. Let's get the cars inside."

With the cars inside and the garage door locked, they entered the house. "You know," Judith said, "I never really thought about it, but one of the advantages of a burglar alarm is that when you come back to the house, you can be sure nobody has broken in. There's nobody inside waiting for you. To get in, they'd've had to trigger the alarm."

"Yeah, you're right. That's worth a lot. Especially when we know somebody's after us."

While Judith cleaned her gun, Tom thumbed through the newspaper. An item caught his eye and he folded the paper so he could read it more easily.

### MAN TAKES LAW INTO OWN HANDS

Manuel Garcia, of Austin, Texas, and his family had for the past three years been sleeping on the floor of their house, which had frequently been shot up by a street gang. Last night, Garcia awoke to the familiar sounds of bullets hitting his house. "I finally had enough," he said. He grabbed a carbine, loaded it, and fired at the car in the street from which the bullets were coming. The car then drove off.

The police came at Garcia's call. They later found the car. Two of its occupants had been wounded by Garcia's fire. Police confiscated Garcia's carbine. A spokesperson from the prosecutor's office said Garcia would face prosecution, but the charges had not yet been determined.

*Boy, what a rotten deal,* Tom thought. *The cops must have known all along who was in that street gang, but they never did anything in all the years that poor guy was being shot at. As soon as he defends himself, they want to charge him with some crime or other. And what's he going to do when the rest of that gang comes back? He doesn't have a gun any more. He'd better get out of town.*

When he finished the paper, he turned on the TV and hopped from one channel to another.

*Boy, what lousy programs. Stupid sitcoms, brainless game shows, travel shows about places I wouldn't want to go to, and couldn't afford even if I did want to go. No wonder Judy doesn't watch TV. Maybe I ought to read some books, like she does. But not a murder mystery. Right now I don't think I could take that.*

Judith finished assembling her gun, slipped a magazine into the well, racked the slide, and flipped on the safety.

"Okay, Tom, I'm finished. You can clean yours now."

With an emphatic gesture, he thumbed the OFF button on the remote.

He took the seat at the card table they'd set up on the middle of the living room, disassembled his gun, and started the cleaning process. He turned to Judith, who was seated on the couch.

"Judy, what's that book you're reading?"

She held it up. "A biography. Thomas Jefferson."

"Interesting?"

"Yes, it is. It has a lot about his work on the Constitution and the Bill of Rights. After what Judge Leahy told us about the Second Amendment at the gun-training course, it's really fascinating. I'm finding there's a lot here I didn't know about. The people who wrote the Constitution were worried about the government getting out of control and being a threat to our lives and our liberties. That's one of the reasons why some of them insisted on protecting their rights with the Second Amendment. They figured that as long as we had guns, the government couldn't become tyrannical."

She turned to a page she'd marked with a slip of paper. "Here's a quote from Jefferson himself, about gun control laws. He said they, 'disarm only those who are neither inclined nor determined to commit crime'. And here's more, about that kind of law. 'Such laws make things worse for the assaulted and better for the assailants; they serve rather to encourage than to prevent homicides for an unarmed man may be attacked with greater confidence than an armed man.'"

"He was sure right about that," Tom said. "Why can't our politicians see that now? They aren't stupid. Even to get elected to office they have to be pretty smart. They're lying to us for some reason or other. I've got some pretty good guesses about why they're lying, too.

"Let me have a look at that book when you're done, okay?"

"Sure. I'll probably have it finished by tomorrow night. It's not due back at the library for another week."

He wiped the solvent off his gun, oiled the slide and trigger, then put it back together.

"It's gettin' pretty late. Maybe we ought to get to bed."

"You're right. I'll finish this chapter, then come upstairs."

# THIRTY-FOUR

Tom awoke with a start as Judith shook his arm.

"Shhh!" she whispered. "I heard a noise. Like a window breaking."

He whispered back. "But the burglar alarm didn't go off." He looked toward the clock-radio. "Hey! There's no light. The power must be off." He looked out the back window. "But there's street lights on across the alley. It must be just us."

He picked up the phone from the night-stand. "Phone's dead, too. No alarm, and we can't call the cops."

There was a noise from downstairs, like someone had bumped a chair.

Judith clutched his arm. "Grubbs is back!"

"Maybe if we fired some shots out the back window it would scare him off."

"I don't want him scared off," she replied. "I want to get this settled!"

He grabbed his gun from the nightstand and rolled out of bed. He crouched and duckwalked to the bedroom door. The hallway was black. The only light came through the doorway across the hall, from a street light out front.

He groped his way to the bed, where Judith was adjusting the covers. "Can't use our plan. The stairwell light is out." The plan had been to use the hall as a fatal funnel, with the intruder silhouetted by the stairwell light.

"What'll we do?"

"Shoot him as he comes through the doorway. The street light'll backlight him. You get behind the dresser on the hallway wall. I'll get behind the dresser on the side wall. Don't move from there, and shoot only towards the door."

He groped his way to the dresser, found the jar of sugar he'd placed there, and removed the lid. He hastened to the doorway, and scattered the sugar down the hallway toward the stairs. Then he crouched behind the dresser.

He listened intently. There was no sound from outside. His ears were filled with the roar of his own blood. His breathing seemed to wheeze like a steam locomotive.

*Creak!*

*Thank God I never had that squeaky step fixed. He's coming up the stairs.*

Moments later there was a faint *crunch* from the hallway.

*It's working. He's stepping on the sugar.*

Silence for a long moment.

*Crunch.*

*Crunch.*

*Crunch.*

Tom held his breath. *He's coming down the hallway. Got to spot him as he gets to the door.*

He tried to breathe slowly and shallowly as he stared at the faintly lighted rectangle that was the doorway. Suddenly a darker shadow loomed in the doorway.

A beam of light stabbed through the darkness towards their bed. In his mind's eye Tom saw a flashlight taped to the barrel of a long gun, with a cardboard tube taped to the flashlight to give a narrow beam.

*BLAM! BLAM!*

The shotgun blasts left his ears ringing. The muzzle flash

blinded him. As he shook his head to clear it he heard shots from across the room, and saw muzzle flashes from Judith's gun.

The figure in the doorway swung sideways, and the light beam searched around the dresser, probing for Judith.

*Please God, NO!*

Fighting the afterimages, he lined up the luminous dots of his sights with the figure's head and fired three shots as fast as he could get the sights back on target and trigger them.

For a long heartbeat, nothing happened. Then the shotgun crashed to the floor and the figure slumped down. Tom waited, then cautiously stepped around the dresser, holding his gun ahead of him. He approached the figure, then kicked the shotgun around so the still-shining light fell on the figure lying on the floor. Two holes in the side of his head made it clear he wasn't going to give any more trouble.

Judith came to Tom's side. "I don't know what went wrong. I swear I had my sights right on him."

"Where were you aiming?"

"The torso, like Mr. Baron told us."

"That's what I figured. And when he didn't drop, I figured he must be wearing body armor. That's why I went for a head shot."

Tom pushed at the figure's ribs with his bare foot. "Yeah. He's wearing a flak jacket. You probably hit him square, but it didn't do any good."

He stepped toward the bed, grabbed the flashlight they kept on the headboard, and returned.

"Okay, now let's see what Mr. Grubbs looks like with a couple of holes in his head."

He glanced at the exit wounds, swallowed hard to keep from retching, then grabbed the figure's hair, pulled the head up, and shined the light square in its face.

"That's not Grubbs!" Judith gasped.

"You're right. I never saw him before."

"But he can't be just your ordinary burglar. He came right to our bedroom intending to kill us."

He dropped the head, allowing it to *thump* on the floor, then turned the light toward the bed. "What're those lumps under the covers?"

"While you were sugaring the hallway, I fluffed up the covers and stuffed the pillows under them, to make it look like we were still in bed."

"Good thinking. It worked."

From outside there came the wail of a siren.

"Police? One of our neighbors must have heard the shots and called them."

Moments later there was an insistent pounding at the front door.

"Power's off," Tom said. "Can't use the intercom. We better open the door before they bust it down, like the drug Gestapo did at the Browns."

Judith took the flashlight. "I'll get it. You back me up from the stairs." She went to the closet and pulled out a housecoat.

He heard the *slap-slap* of her slippers as she went out the door. He found his own slippers, then returned to the corpse and searched it quickly, using the flashlight on the shotgun for illumination.

As he came down the stairs, he heard Judith's voice.

"Hello, officer. My name is Judith Borden. My husband and I live here. An intruder came into the house tonight. He fired a shotgun at our bed. You will find him on the floor in our bedroom upstairs. I'll have more to say about the incident once I've been able to consult with my attorney. I'll call him now, if one of you will escort me to the pay phone down the block. Our phone is out."

As Tom stepped up behind Judith, he saw a policemen come around the side of the house.

"She's right, Sarge. The phone line's been cut, and the seal on the electric meter's been broken and the power shut off."

"Okay, I'll send someone with you. Better call the power company and the phone company while you're at it."

# THIRTY-FIVE

he technician from the power company arrived promptly. Just as the power came on, Mr. Cohen, from Judith's law office, pulled in the drive. Tom turned on some lights in the living room, while Judith led Cohen to the kitchen. Additional police officers soon arrived. Tom led them to the bedroom and turned on the lights. He then went to the kitchen. As he entered, the refrigerator was humming, recovering from the loss of power.

Judith repeated for Mr. Cohen the statement she'd made to the police.

"You handled that well, Mrs. Borden. However, you'll have to tell them more. Especially after they've had a chance to examine the body.

"Now the thing you have to remember is that ninety-five percent of the people the police have to deal with are guilty as Hell, and are lying about it. Moreover, in the vast majority of cases where the police deal with a fresh corpse, it's murder or manslaughter, not self-defense. Subconsciously, they'll just take it for granted this is the same kind of situation — it's murder, and you're lying about it. Their mindset is to look for evidence that will convict you, not for evidence that will exonerate you.

We'll have to point out to them any evidence in your favor that we'll want to use later, just to make sure they collect it and recognize its importance.

"They'll also try to play mind games with you, to get you to say something incriminating. A common trick is to try to trap you into saying that you weren't really in danger, but fired anyway. Another trick is to suggest that maybe the gun just went off by accident, that you really didn't intend to shoot. If you agree with that, you've just confessed to manslaughter. Your story is that you feared for your lives, and you intentionally fired in self-defense. Just stick to that.

"Now tell me exactly what happened, as quickly as you can. I'll get my video camera from the car, and try to record everything that we might need to have later."

Judith and Tom related their stories while Cohen recorded them on a pocket recorder.

Finally, he asked, "Anything more you can think of, either of you?"

"No," Judith replied. Tom simply shook his head in the negative.

"Very well, let's go make a statement to the police. Remember, you must make it clear you feared for your lives. Don't say anything that might be misinterpreted to imply you were waiting to lure the intruder into an ambush."

They returned to the living room, which had filled up with police officers, including Lieutenant Callahan.

"Hello, folks," Callahan greeted them. "Sorry to have to meet you again under such unpleasant circumstances. We'll get the body out shortly. Now if you'll just tell me what happened, we can get this over with quickly."

"Excuse me, Lieutenant," Cohen interrupted. "Do you know these people?"

"Why, yes. I've dealt with them before, when they were threatened by a dangerous criminal."

"So you know them. Are you using that acquaintance to play the 'good cop' in a 'good cop, bad cop' routine?"

"Why counselor, I'm just doing my job."

"That's right. You're paid by the government to put people in jail. My job is to keep innocent people out of jail, and I intend to do just that.

"Now, if these people were career criminals, your first words would have been to read them their Miranda rights. Have you done so for them?"

"No. I haven't. They're not suspected of anything, so I didn't see any need to."

"What if their statements to you lead you to suspect them of something?"

"Why, then I'd read them their rights before questioning them further."

"What you mean is you'd read them their rights after you tricked them into saying something you could use against them. Why not read them their rights now?"

Callahan shrugged, took a laminated card out of his pocket, and read the formula.

Cohen turned to Tom and Judith. "You have just been warned by an agent of the government that you have the right to keep quiet before you say something you'll regret later. Any career criminal with an ounce of brains would shut up completely after that warning.

"However, since you acted in self-defense, I encourage you to make a statement. Before you do, however," he turned to Callahan, "what have you learned about the deceased?"

With evident reluctance, Callahan replied, "We've identified him. He was a professional hit man. He had been serving a term for murder, and was released on parole just a couple of weeks ago."

*Didn't take him long to get his old job back, did it?,* Tom thought. *Guys we've had to lay off down at the plant don't get their jobs back that quick.*

Cohen excused himself, and returned quickly with a video camera. "Very well. Let's start from the beginning. Mrs. Borden?"

"I was awakened by a sound which I thought was glass breaking."

Cohen held up his hand to interrupt her. He turned to Callahan. "Have you found where the intruder entered the house?"

Callahan looked around. One of the police officers spoke. "Yes. He used a ladder to get in a kitchen window."

"Very well, let me get that on tape." The officer led them out the back door and to the window where the ladder was still in place.

"It looks brand new," Tom observed. "No dirt on the steps."

"Probably bought specifically for the occasion," Cohen remarked. "It would have been abandoned when the intruder left, probably through a door. That's consistent with the intruder being a professional killer."

He carefully panned the camera up and down the ladder, around its base, and around the window.

"Now, let's look at the inside."

Enough of the glass had been broken out to allow the intruder to reach the catch and open the window.

Judith pointed to a chair by the dining room table. "That's out of place. I know I pushed it in as I was straightening up the downstairs before I went to bed."

"Yeah," Tom added. "That must be the noise we heard. He bumped that as he was going by."

Tom then led the group up the stairway, pointing out the squeaky step as he went.

In the hallway, something crunched under Callahan's shoe. He bent down and rubbed his finger through the dusting of white powder on the floor.

"What's this?" He nodded to one of the police. "Get a sample. We'll have the lab check it. It might be cocaine."

Tom said, "Don't bother. It's probably sugar. I must have spilled some the last time I brought some coffee up here."

Callahan gestured to the officer to take a sample anyway, then followed Tom down the hallway.

In the bedroom, Tom pointed to the holes shredded in the bedclothes, then to the dressers where he and Judith had hidden themselves. He briefly recounted the events following the intruder's appearance at the bedroom door.

Callahan asked, "You didn't make any attempt to scare him away?"

"Like what? Go downstairs after him? I didn't know who it was, or what he wanted. Protecting our silverware or the TV set wasn't worth the risk of getting shot."

"Why didn't you yell, or fire a warning shot?"

"In our gun training course, we were told never to fire unless we knew where the bullet was going to go. Absolutely no warning shots. As for yelling, I guess I was hoping that if we didn't bother him, he'd just take what he wanted and go away."

"And if he didn't just go away?"

"That was different. We'd have to defend ourselves. When he came upstairs without taking time to loot the downstairs, I figured he was after us for sure. I was right. He came in here and just opened fire. He didn't ask for our money or anything. And when Judy's shots didn't stop him, he was about to kill her. I was lucky to stop him in time."

"Did you touch the body?"

"Yeah. I got my flashlight and looked at his face. I wanted to see who it was. But if you're asking did I move the body, no, I didn't."

While Tom was speaking, Cohen was videotaping the layout of the room, and the body. Then he spoke.

"Lieutenant, you can see the pool of blood around the head. Clearly the body hasn't been moved. Across the hallway, you can see two bloody splashes, and a third bullet hole. Clearly the intruder was already inside this room at the time he was shot. My clients were definitely in danger of their lives, and the intruder fired first."

"That's the way it looks, counselor. But I'm still puzzled about the motive. Why should a professional hit man come in here and try to knock off a couple of people who never saw him before? I wouldn't be surprised but what there's drugs or something involved here."

Judith opened her mouth as if to speak, then clamped it shut and seemed to shrink backwards. If Callahan noticed the movement, he gave no sign.

Callahan turned, looked again at the body, then spoke to the sergeant beside him.

"Need anything else from here?"

"No, I think we have everything. We even dug the bullets out of the front wall."

"Okay, let's wrap up the body and get back to the station house." He turned to Tom and Judith. "Let me have your guns. We'll need them as evidence."

Cohen spoke softly. "Do you plan to give them a 24-hour police guard, Lieutenant?"

A pause. "No. There's no way we can do that."

"Then why do you want their guns?"

"Why, it's routine. Surely if Mr. and Mrs. Cohen were acting in self-defense, they'd be willing to cooperate."

Cohen continued. "It's clear that my clients need their guns for protection. Somebody sent this hit man after them. That somebody may send another one. With the waiting period law, they can't just go down to the store and replace their guns tomorrow, even if they could afford it. You'd better allow them to defend themselves, Lieutenant. Under the circumstances, I'm confident I could get a court to grant an injunction prohibiting you from taking their guns."

Callahan stood silently for a moment, a look of frustration on his face. Finally he turned to the officers around the body.

"Okay, snap it up, guys. Let's get out of here."

In a few minutes, the police were gone, leaving Tom, Judith and Cohen standing in the living room.

Tom spoke. "I can't believe this. Here we are, lucky enough to stop a professional killer before he got us, and the cops take it for granted we're involved in some kind of drug ring or something, and want to take away our guns. It's crazy."

"But remember, Tom," Judith said, "that's just how Mr. Baron and Judge Leahy told us it would be. The laws are stacked in favor of the criminals."

"Yeah, I remember. I guess I didn't really see it clearly then, but it's sure clear now."

Tom turned to Cohen. "What next? Will we have to go to a trial?"

"Probably not," was the reply. "I doubt the prosecutor could get an indictment, considering the facts of the case. He'll probably decide not to prosecute.

"The important thing is not to let them scare you. Don't let them bully you into pleading guilty to some lesser charge, just to avoid a trial for murder. If it came to a trial for murder, I feel confident the jury would acquit you. But I really don't think it will come to that.

"However, let me talk to the prosecutor about that. In the meantime, I have a couple of recommendations. First, get out of this house for a few days. Make yourselves scarce, just in case another hit man comes after you. Make it hard for anyone to find you. Second, get some professional counseling. You've been through a life-or-death experience. It's bound to affect you.

"Next, if I'm going to defend you, you have to level with me. Why would a professional killer come after you? What have you been doing?"

Judith responded. "I think I can answer that, Mr. Cohen. When I first asked you if you'd defend us, we were already being stalked by a criminal who went to jail because of Tom's and my testimony. I have a strong feeling he's the one who sent this killer after us. I assure you we're not dealing drugs or anything like that."

"Well, if that's the case, then you'd better hide for a while."

"That's easy to say," Tom responded, "but there's no way we can do it. We both have jobs, and we need the money. We can't just quit and become hermits."

"Then be very careful. Now, goodnight. I need to get this videotape copied, and the copy notarized. Will you be at work in the morning, Mrs. Borden?"

"I suppose so, even though I'll probably be sleepy all day. I may as well be at work as here."

"Very well, I'll see you tomorrow."

# THIRTY-SIX

As the door closed after Cohen, Tom burst out laughing.

"My God, Tom. What's so funny?"

"Get counseling, he told us. The counseling I need, I can't get. But for this guy, I don't think I'll need any counseling. He deserved what he got, and I'm not in the least bit sorry about blowing him away."

"Maybe not, but now that it's over, I'm scared to death to think about how close he came to killing us. And we may have to deal with another one."

"Maybe we will, and maybe we won't," Tom said grimly. "Come look at something."

He led the way upstairs to their bedroom. He opened the bottom drawer of his dresser and pulled out a gun in a peculiarly-shaped holster.

"I found this on the body while you were going downstairs to let the cops in. I've never seen anything like it. He had this holster inside his pants. This stiff round leather thing keeps the outline of the gun from showing through the cloth. I took the gun, the holster, and the spare magazine he was carrying. I wanted to make sure I got everything, so the cops wouldn't realize anything was missing."

"Why'd you take it?"

"I wanted a gun that couldn't be traced to me."

"But why?"

His voice was flat, almost challenging. "Because I'm going to kill Harry Grubbs myself. And if I can, I'm going to do it before he sends another killer after us."

She paused a moment, a thoughtful look on her face. "That's probably what you should have done in the first place. He's a threat to us, and we have to stop him."

A faraway look came to her eyes. "Once when I was a little girl, Daddy and I found a rattlesnake at the edge of the wood-lot. He killed it with a hoe he was carrying. He told me there used to be lots of rattlesnakes around there. He said the pioneers in this area had a saying, 'Every settler has to kill his own snake.'"

"They were right. We have to get rid of our own snake."

"We do. And this time I'm going to do it right. But that's for tomorrow. Let's get some sleep."

"Yes, if we can sleep after all this."

. . .

As Judith poured Tom's coffee the next morning, she wore a concerned expression. "Last night you said you were going to go after Grubbs yourself. But can you do it?"

"Yes!" he replied emphatically. "The Justice Cooperative taught me a lot of things I didn't know before. I learned how to track somebody down, how to study his habits, what to look for, how to ambush him. I learned how to make a silencer. Yeah, they taught me a lot.

"I have a few days vacation saved up now, and I'm going to take them, one at a time, to take care of Harry Grubbs. I'll watch him, find out his habits, and ambush him, just like I did that guy for the Justice Cooperative. And I have no doubt I'll be able to pull the trigger when I get him in my sights."

Judith stood silently as questions ran unbidden through her

mind. Does it get easier each time you kill someone? What had happened to Tom, that he could so easily consider killing someone? What had happened to her, that she'd approve of it? What had happened to the two of them, that they'd talk calmly about killing someone? Why did a couple of ordinary people who just wanted to live ordinary lives have to become killers? She shook her head. There were no answers. There would be no answers.

Tom spoke. "What about the bedclothes and the mattress? I don't want to spend another night on a bed with shotgun holes in it."

"I'll call Sears today and order new things."

"Okay. And I'll call the alarm people and ask if they can't do something about protecting us even when the power goes off."

# THIRTY-SEVEN

"You're sure drinkin' a lot of coffee today, Tom," Gunderson said.

"Yeah. I'm tryin' to stay awake. I don't think I got more than two hours sleep last night."

"Be glad you woke up. You might'a been put to sleep for good."

"Yeah. You can say that again. I'm damn lucky to be alive. If Judy hadn't heard that noise, he'd have caught us asleep in bed"

The phone on Gunderson's desk rang. He picked it up.

"Machine shop, this is Gunderson."

He listened a moment, then held it towards Tom.

"It's your wife."

Tom took the phone. "Hi, honey. How d'you feel"

"Rotten," came the reply. "But I have good news. Mr. Cohen says the prosecutor decided to call it self-defense. He won't prosecute."

"Thank God for small favors!"

"And you remember Jenetta and Sam Brown?"

"Sure."

"They offered to take us out to dinner tonight, and then to

see the latest BATMAN movie. They wanted to show their thanks for your help in getting their house secured."

"That's nice of them. What time?"

"Oh, that's another thing. Sears promised to deliver the new bedding about 5:30. I told the Browns we'd call them as soon as the bedding was delivered."

"Okay, good. The schedule here looks pretty clear today. I should be home about the time Sears gets there. See you then."

"I'll tell the Browns we'll do it. Love you. 'Bye."

"Love you. 'Bye."

He handed the phone back to Gunderson. "Good news. The prosecutor's willing to admit we were defending ourselves."

Gunderson shook his head. "It's a crazy country we live in. Used to be you'd be a hero for killing some skunk like that. Now you're violatin' his civil rights."

"Yeah, it is crazy. But there's nothin' I can do about it. I just have to live with it. You can't fight City Hall, and all that."

He turned to the computer terminal behind him, and brought up the schedule for the next day.

"Looks like tomorrow's schedule is light, too. I've got some errands I need to run. Mind if I take tomorrow off?"

"Nah," Gunderson replied, "go ahead. I can handle what little's on the schedule."

"Okay, thanks."

*Good. Now I can get started tracking down Harry Grubbs.*

Tom got up from his chair.

"I'll take a swing around the shop floor and check on how things're going."

*And also get rid of some used coffee, before my back teeth float away.*

"Good idea. And while you're at it, check on those castings for the Chrysler order. Make sure the foundry's on schedule."

"Okay. I'll go over there right away. And I'll check on QC, too, to make sure they're ready to inspect the parts as soon as we finish 'em."

• • •

The toss of the coin had sent him home the long way. He arrived at his house just as the Sears truck was pulling away. Judith met him at the door.

"Hi, honey," he said. "I saw the Sears truck leave. Did they put the stuff on the bed for you?"

"They hauled the mattress upstairs and put it on the bed. I have to make up the bed yet."

"What'd you do with the old stuff? Do I need to drag it downstairs?"

"They agreed to haul it away. I didn't know what else to do with it."

"Yeah. Couldn't even give it to Goodwill, with all those holes in it. Okay, call the Browns while I clean up."

• • •

They walked out of the theater, into the cool evening air.

Tom held up his hand and then spoke. "Feel that breeze. Summer's over, I guess."

"Yep," Sam replied. "Once Labor Day came, it cooled off in a hurry. Don't know where summer went. 'Course, I spent most of it fixin' up the damage the drug Gestapo done to my house. Now I got it fixed up the way you said. Nobody's gonna bust in like that again."

"Hell of a note when honest people have to worry more about the cops smashin' things up than they do about crooks," Tom said.

"Too bad we ain't got Batman here to fix things," Sam replied with a chuckle. "He sure finished off the Joker tonight."

"Yeah. I wonder what they'll do for the next movie. They can't keep revivin' the Joker every time."

"Oh, sure they can. You ever seen the ol' Frankenstein movies on late night TV? They kep' revivin' that poor ol' monster no matter how many times the mob of peasants burned the castle down."

"You know," Tom said, "one thing bothered me about the movie tonight. They tried to make out that Batman was just as nutty as the Joker, only it just happened that the law was on his side. It's like they're tryin' to say there's no difference between crooks and honest people, it's just which side the law is on. Like if the crooks was writin' the laws, we'd be the crooks."

"What d'you mean, IF the crooks was writin' the laws? You seen what happened to me. You know what happened to you'n Judy. You think the crooks ain't writin' the laws? You think honest people'd write laws that hurt honest people?"

"Maybe you're right. I just never thought about it that way."

Jenetta broke in. "You folks want to get some coffee before you go home? We can stop in at a diner."

Tom looked inquiringly at Judith. She paused a moment, then spoke. "We need to get some sleep. But somehow I really don't want to go back to the house. I'm not sure I'll ever sleep peacefully there again."

Jenetta pointed ahead. "There's a Starbucks up there. That okay?"

"Sounds good to me," Tom replied.

Once they were seated inside the restaurant, Tom turned to Judith.

"You said you couldn't sleep peacefully in our house. Do you want to move again? Go somewhere else?"

"No. It isn't like it was in our old apartment. I couldn't stay there. Everything there reminded me of . . . of what happened.

"No, this is different. No matter where we went I think I'd still be anxious. I'd still feel that I might wake up and find someone in the house. Or never wake up at all. No matter where we went, I don't think I'd ever feel completely safe again."

"I know what you mean," Jenetta said. "I still jump every time I hear somebody knock at the door. I'll probably never get over havin' those drug goons bust in, knock us down on the floor, and shove their guns at us."

"Maybe none of us'll ever get over it," Sam said. "My Dad was with the Rangers in Vietnam. Spent a lot of time in what he called 'Indian Country.' Enemy territory. He tol' me once that he still slep' with one eye open. Couldn't get over havin' to be alert all the time."

"Lord, I hope we can get over it," Tom said with a sigh. "I don't want to be jumpy the rest of my life."

"I hope so too," Judith said, "but after the burglar alarm failed us, I don't think I'll have any faith in it again. I can't count on being awakened before someone gets to the bedroom."

"We can get a dog again," Tom said. "That would give us some warning, even if an intruder cuts off the power and the phone again."

"Yes, I do want to get a dog. But I'm afraid I can't any longer think of a dog the way I did when I was growing up. Then a dog was practically part of the family. We let them in the house. We played with them." A smile crossed her face. "We kids even fed them under the dinner table. We had to do it when my parents weren't looking."

Her face grew serious again. "But after Grubbs poisoned King, I have to think of a dog like . . . like a fuse in a fuse box. Something that blows out to let you know something's wrong. The dog would be there to get killed before the killer reached us. I wouldn't want to make him part of the family, because he's there to be sacrificed."

"Once we have kids, they'll want to play with the dog," Tom said. "They'll want to make it part of the family."

"I know. And we can't stop that. I don't want them growing up thinking that dogs are expendable. But I don't think I can ever get back to the way I was. Not after all that's happened to us."

The waitress brought them the coffee they'd ordered. Tom sipped at his.

"Hey, this is pretty good stuff. A lot better than what I get out of the coffee machine at the plant."

"Is it better than what I make?" Judith asked, with a wicked glint in her eye.

"Better not answer that, Tom," Sam said with a grin. "No matter what you say, you're in trouble."

At that they all laughed.

Sam spoke up again. "I seen the piece in the police news

'bout what happen' to you folks las' night. Paper says neither of you was hurt."

"No bullet holes in either of us," Judith replied. "But the psychological scars are there. Even if we get over jumping at every noise in the night, we'll never be the same."

"Nor will my parents." She turned to Tom. "Dad called while you were still on your way home."

"You didn't tell me that."

"Everything was in such a rush when you got home that I forgot. Anyway, he'd seen something about the shooting on TV, recognized our house even though they didn't use our names, and called me."

"He's worried about us?"

"Of course he is. After all that's happened, do you blame him? I tried to reassure him we'd be okay here, but I'm not sure he believed me. I didn't really believe it myself."

Tom shook his head in disgust. "We tried to tell the cops. We tried to get it through their heads that we were in danger. They didn't want to listen. And if they'd taken away our guns, like they wanted to do, we'd be helpless the next time some crook showed up."

"Worse 'n' that," Sam said. "They want to take your guns away *before* the crooks come bustin' in."

"Yeah, you're right. 'Victim disarmament,' I heard somebody at the Deer Hunters call it."

"You got that right. I seen in the paper a couple weeks ago where the police chief wants to limit bullet sales. Says it's needed for officer safety."

"Officer safety!" Tom spat out. "He ought to be worried about *our* safety. That ought to be his top priority. He could get complete officer safety by just puttin' all the rest of us in jail.

"I sure don't envy the cops their jobs. They take a lot of risks. But their safety isn't the most important thing. Our safety is. That's why we have cops, to keep *us* safe. But they can't be around all the time, so we need to be able to protect ourselves. Sacrificing our safety to increase the safety of the cops has things tail-end-to."

"Tha's right. They can't protect us anyhow. Their job is mos'ly to draw the chalk line around the body on the sidewalk and write up the report. We got to be able to protect ourselves."

"Besides," Tom went on, "rationing ammo doesn't stop the crooks. I doubt if a crook uses up a whole box of ammo in his entire life. Judy and I each shoot up two or three boxes every time we go to the range. Rationing ammo hurts us, not the crooks."

Judith turned to Sam and asked, "Speaking of shooting, did you ever get your rifles back from the drug Gestapo?"

"No. Miz Stryker say she's still workin' on it, but I figure I ain't never gonna see them guns again."

"Did you get some more guns?"

Sam paused, then spoke. "I ain't tol' nobody 'til now, but I got some. Buddy o' mine knew a guy who could sell me some pistols, an' who wouldn't ask me no questions."

"I hope they weren't stolen somewhere along the line."

"No, he says they come from some widow woman who was gettin' rid of some of her husband's guns. They're legal, but no records. Private sales. I got 'em the nex' day. No waitin' period."

"Hell of a note when honest citizens have to go around the law so they can protect themselves," Tom said. "Something's really wrong with this country."

Sam shook his head. "That ain't no news, Tom. We already knowed that. An' nobody'll do anything about it. You hear any politicians tryin' to fix it? They talk an' talk, but the only thing that'll work is puttin' the crooks in jail. But they got all kinds of excuses for lettin' 'em off.

"You see that thing in the paper the other day? Guy who shot the Seven-Eleven clerk?"

"Yeah, I remember that one."

"You see where he was gonna get a light sentence 'cause it was a first offense? 'Til somebody leaked his juvenile court records?"

"Right. He was already a big-time crook before he was eighteen years old. Drug dealing. Armed robbery. But we weren't supposed to know that. The paper was full of mush about how he'd been in foster homes and all that. How he'd had an unhappy childhood. As though that justified shootin' a clerk.

"And the editorials. How it was all the fault of the gun. If we had more gun control, he wouldn't have tried to hold up the store. They didn't say a word about gun control after his record came out. Once they couldn't blame it on the gun, they shut up."

Judith stifled a yawn. "I don't think I can keep going much longer. We'd better get home and get some sleep."

"Yeah," Tom added. I don't want to fall asleep at the wheel on our way home."

As they left the restaurant, Tom turned to the Browns and said, "We really appreciate your taking us out tonight. We needed some company to help us get over last night."

"Glad to do it," Sam responded. We owed you somethin', and we figured this'd help you take your mind off last night."

•  •  •

Tom had hardly shut the door behind him when the doorbell rang. He keyed the intercom.

"Who is it?"

"Police. Lieutenant Callahan. We'd like to talk to you."

"Oh, God!" He looked at Judy. "Do you suppose it's about that guy Bartlett? Maybe I better head out the back door."

She put her hand on his arm. "If it were, they'd have been more forceful than that. Besides, running would only make you look guilty. Anyway, if they are after you for killing Bartlett, they'll have a cop out back waiting for you." She went to open the door.

"Good evening, Mrs. Borden. And Mr. Borden." Lieutenant Callahan and a police sergeant entered the room.

He went on without any preliminaries. "Harry Grubbs was killed this evening. Do you folks know anything about it?"

A puzzled look on his face, Tom responded, "Was it on TV? We didn't see it." He looked at the wall clock. "No, it's not eleven yet. It couldn't have been on TV yet. No, we hadn't heard anything about it."

"Would you mind telling me where you were this evening?"

Judith responded calmly, "We went to dinner and a movie with friends."

"Mind if I check with them?"

"Why should I mind?" She gave him the Browns' phone number, and pointed at the wall phone by the kitchen door.

Callahan punched in the number, then spoke.

"Hello. I'm Police Lieutenant Callahan. We had a report of a disturbance in your neighborhood this evening. However, when the officers arrived, they couldn't find anything. We're calling everyone on the block to see if we can get more information."

He paused a moment, evidently to let the other party answer.

"It was reported about 8:30, so we assume that's when it took place."

Another pause.

"You were out at that time? Was it with some of your neighbors?"

Pause again.

"With the Bordens? No, I don't need to check with them. If you'd been out with some neighbors, I could cross their names off my list of people to call. I'll keep calling your neighbors until I can find out more about that reported disturbance. Thank you for your cooperation."

He hung up the phone and turned to Tom and Judith. "Okay, they back up your story."

"Why shouldn't they?" Tom demanded. "It sounds awful funny to me that you had nothing but excuses when we asked you for help against Grubbs, but when he's killed, you're all worked up about it. Why should we know anything about his death?"

"Well, for one thing, we found the car your intruder used last night. It had been stolen earlier in the day, and was left just around the corner from your house. Your intruder evidently intended to go back to it, but you took care of that.

"We found a letter in the car that implies Grubbs hired your intruder to kill you. Evidently the letter was left in the car to make sure Grubbs was implicated if anything went wrong.

"We went to Grubbs's apartment to pick him up. He was

out. We waited, until we got a call that he'd been found dead at the back entrance to a pool hall. Somebody evidently knew he was a regular patron there, and that he usually went in and out the back door. When we got there, we found he'd been shot twice from what had to be close range, but no one around there heard anything.

"Since you were doubly connected with Grubbs, I figured you might know something."

"I'm not sorry he's dead, but this is the first I knew of it," Tom said.

Judith added, in a low voice, "I hope you're willing to admit now that it wasn't paranoia when I thought Grubbs was the one who broke in while we were gone. Whether it was actually Grubbs himself or his hired killer instead, he was the one behind it.

"I hope the next time some crime victim comes to you asking for help, you'll be more willing to listen, instead of writing them off as paranoid."

"I can understand your anger, Mrs. Borden," Callahan replied, "but you have to recognize that the police can work only on the basis of evidence that'll stand up in court. You'd be unhappy if I arrested you simply because I knew you wanted Grubbs dead. Even if I did arrest you, it'd never go to trial since you have an alibi. And if you sued me for false arrest, you'd win. But without solid evidence, I couldn't have made a case against Grubbs stick, and he could have sued me successfully for false arrest. That's the way the Constitution is written."

"Too bad it protects the crooks more than it does the honest folks," Tom said bitterly.

"Sometimes it seems that way, doesn't it?" Callahan replied. "Well, thank you, folks. I've got to try to find someone who does know something abut the demise of Harry Grubbs. Goodnight."

He turned and opened the door. The police officer preceded him out, and he closed the door gently behind him.

# THIRTY-EIGHT

Tom lay awake, staring into the darkness. He turned to look at Judith. In the dim light cast by the clock-radio on the headboard, he could just barely make out her face. She seemed completely relaxed. She'd fallen asleep right after they'd made love.

He thought, *This was the first time it's been any good since this whole mess started.*

The shattered door on their former apartment had been fixed the next day. Their shattered lives were only now being put back together.

Knowing that Grubbs was dead took an enormous load off him. He knew the load it had taken off Judith was even greater. They would still have to take precautions against crime, but they no longer had to worry that they were being stalked.

In other ways things were definitely looking up for them as well. With his promotion, he was making enough money that she could quit work. They could finally start the family they'd been wanting. A smile crossed his face. *If tonight was any indication, that won't take long. Her old enthusiasm has come back. And maybe that'll keep her mother off our backs.*

Nor were he and Judith alone in their relief. The man (woman? child?) he'd avenged in the parking lot at the Sunset Bar and Grill must have shed a big load, too. He hoped the man (woman?) who'd avenged him and Judith likewise got relieved of his burden when he in turn was avenged.

But somehow his relief wasn't complete. His thoughts returned to his conversation with Judith after Lieutenant Callahan had left.

"I hope it's not blasphemy," Judith had said, "but I say thank God Grubbs is dead."

"Yeah. And I suppose I ought to be saying, thank God for the Justice Cooperative."

"Aren't you?"

"No. I can't."

"They saved you from having to kill Grubbs, like you were going to do."

"Yeah. But somehow, it isn't right. It just isn't right that people should have to go around avenging themselves when they'd been done an injustice. It isn't right that the government doesn't carry out justice. It isn't right that criminals should be turned loose to roam the streets. It isn't right that honest people should have to hide behind locked doors. The Justice Cooperative shouldn't be necessary."

"You're right," she said, "but the world isn't perfect. Be glad the Justice Cooperative was there when we needed it."

"But Judy, what do we know about the Justice Cooperative? I never met any other members. I don't know who the leaders are. Is the Justice Cooperative really a Death Squad run by cops who can't get crooks off the streets any other way, so they get ordinary folks to knock them off? Is it run by the Mafia, who use ordinary folks to knock off their rivals? Or is it run by ordinary folks who are so fed up with the way the laws favor the crooks over the honest people that they've turned vigilante?"

"That's a good question," she'd replied. "And even if it wasn't run by rogue cops or the Mafia, even if it was just ordinary people who got fed up, how long can they be trusted to go after only the crooks who really deserve it? How long before they started using it to settle personal scores?"

"Yeah, I didn't think about that. And even if the Justice Cooperative doesn't get corrupted, how about other people? Will they start taking the law into their own hands? Will professional hit men start executing criminals for hire, when honest folks feel threatened? Will lynch mobs start hanging the criminals the law wouldn't touch? We don't want to live in a country where that happens. But how do we get back to a country where the laws protect the honest folks against the crooks?"

They'd come to no conclusions, but he couldn't stop thinking about the problem.

Going through Grubbs's trial had been really tough on him and even tougher on Judith. But at least both sides had gotten a fair hearing, before an impartial jury. There had been a judge to see that the law was followed. Both sides had their own lawyers to present their case. The Justice Cooperative didn't have any of those things to make sure no mistakes were made. They could say all they wanted to about reclaiming your right to get justice; it was still a damned poor second to holding a fair trial.

Worse yet, when you went outside the law to get justice, you risked becoming like the crooks. Look at Judith, ready to sacrifice a dog just to get Grubbs. And deciding she'd rather shoot an intruder than scare him off. Look at him, ready to stalk and kill Grubbs just like the hit man Grubbs had hired to kill him and Judith. Yeah, he told himself, he was on the right side, but by using their methods he came awfully close to being like them. That's one big reason why the government owed the honest people justice, so they wouldn't have to become like the crooks.

And that was the real problem. After Grubbs had been found guilty in a fair trial, the cops and the courts had failed to do justice. They'd failed in what they were supposed to do. The only way he and Judith could get justice was to get it for themselves. But there was something rotten when people who had been wronged had to carry out justice for themselves, then had to go sneaking around in constant fear of the cops.

Dammit, he told himself, he was one of the people who made this country work. One of the people who did the hard, dirty, tiring jobs in the mines, the mills, and the farms. The people who paid their bills, who paid their taxes, who stopped at stop signs even at two in the morning. And who worked hard to raise decent kids.

And what did they get for it? The government treated them as nothing but tax cows. The politicians milked them to buy the votes of the people who didn't work, who didn't pay taxes, who didn't obey the laws, and whose kids would grow up to be tax-eating leeches just like their parents. The crooks looked on the honest people as sheep to be sheared, and to be killed if they objected. And the crooks' allies, in the capitols and in the courts, made it impossible for the ordinary working-man to get justice.

He thought of George, the young black man who'd been at the gun training course. He'd been trying to climb out of the pit he'd been born at the bottom of. The crooks were trying to kick him back in. And would the government help him? No. It sent him to a school that didn't even teach him to read. And if the crooks stole all the money that guy had, the government's attitude would be, it's only money, and not very much at that. Not worth bothering about. The government wouldn't defend him against the crooks. It wouldn't even allow him to defend himself. The only thing the government would do was corrode his soul by paying some woman to have his kids, so long as he didn't marry her.

He thought of the Browns. They too were trying to climb out of the pit they were born in. They were both working and paying taxes. They were restoring a house somebody had let run down. And what did the government do? It wouldn't stop the crooks who were ruining the very neighborhood the Browns and their neighbors were trying to rebuild. Instead, it tore up their house and undid all their work.

No, it wasn't right. The government ought to be providing justice, not leaving people to defend themselves. It was long past time people like him took their country back; took it away from the smooth talkers who couldn't fix even a broken toaster, let alone their own cars, but who thought they could run everybody else's life for them.

He thought, we had a revolution once, to take this country away from an oppressive king. Maybe it was time for another revolution.

He recalled what Jeff, at the shooting range, had said. That first revolution had started over King George's attempt to take away the colonists' guns. King George didn't trust the colonists with guns. Well, the people down in Washington, and up in Capitol City, didn't trust ordinary people like him, like Judith, like Jeff, like George, like the Browns, with guns either.

It doesn't matter what they think, he told himself. There's more of *us* than there are of *them*. We're going to take this country back from the crooks and the slick politicians and the bleeding-heart judges and the smooth-talking TV reporters and the sneering college professors. We'll do it with the ballot-box if we can, and with the cartridge-box if we have to.

But *they* controlled the cops and the Army. What could *we* do about that? That might not matter, he told himself. Most of the cops and the grunts are *us*, not *them*. *They* sneered at cops. *They* thought they were too good to join the Army. When the country got in trouble, *they* dodged the draft. When push came to shove, the cops and the Army would be with *us*, not with *them*.

Tomorrow, he told himself, he'd start looking for other people who thought the same way he did. People like George, like Jeff, like the Browns. We've got to get organized, he told himself. If we start working together, we can get the government back to defending us against crooks. We can make the Justice Cooperative unnecessary.

Satisfied with his decision, he took another look at Judith. He reached out to touch her cheek, then stopped himself.

Don't risk waking her, he told himself. No point in spoiling what might be the first good sleep she's had since our apartment was broken into.

JOSEPH MARTINO

He turned to look at the nightstand. The tritium sights on his gun glowed reassuringly in the blackness of the room. Then he rolled over and went to sleep.

Printed in the United States
17432LVS00001B/274-297

9 781932 762006